Eat London

Eat London

All about food

Peter Prescott &
Terence Conran

Photography by Lisa Linder

 conran OCTOPUS

Where a view is expressed by a particular
author, this is denoted by (PP) for Peter
Prescott and (TC) for Terence Conran.

Contents

Those of us who work in the restaurant business in London have long thought that our city has the best collection of restaurants, bars and cafés of anywhere in the world. However, being modestly British we don't really like to say it too often or too loudly.

So it was with enormous pleasure that early in 2005 *Gourmet* magazine, America's leading foodie mag, devoted an issue to London's restaurants and indeed claimed that they were the best places to eat in the world. The cover of the magazine was brilliant: four young chefs walking over a rather famous zebra crossing in Abbey Road. That said it all. Ever since the war, Britain has had a reputation for awful food and it's true it was pretty terrible, and obviously President Chirac still believes this to be the case. Many people gave as their reason for not visiting Britain the fact that the food is so dire, and as you travel around the UK there are still pockets of direness, (British Tourist Authority please note) but they are disappearing fast. Why has this dramatic change happened? In London it is helped by the multi-ethnic nature of our society, so you can eat food from practically every corner of the world. The movement for change started with a small group of entrepreneurial people – doctors, authors, actors and publishers – in the 1950s who had travelled abroad and read Elizabeth David's books and enjoyed the social buzz of the restaurant world. They also believed they could make some money, and some did, which encouraged les autres. Most of them were total amateurs with no experience and no idea how to run a restaurant professionally, but enthusiasm and energy kept them going – usually. The professionals from France and particularly Italy began to move into London when they saw that there was beginning to be a market for good restaurants, and this influx of professionalism speeded up the change and taught many aspiring English people how to become restaurateurs. Thank you, Roux Brothers.

London restaurateurs benefit from a very virile collection of restaurant and food critics which keeps them on their toes. Fay Maschler of the *Evening Standard* is always dependable, A.A. Gill is always hilariously acerbic and a crowd of others are constantly reviewing what London has to offer. Of course, the relaxing of employment barriers in EU countries helped enormously, as many Spaniards, Italians and even French found life in London and its restaurants more rewarding than in their own countries and with the enlargement of the EU, this is certainly still the case.

So why has London become such a restaurant mecca? There are lots of reasons. First Londoners have discovered the pleasures of eating out. Let's go out for a meal rather than going home and cooking and then having to do the washing up. They have also discovered the amazing diversity of good food on offer. They like the social mix and buzz of a good restaurant.

Secondly, we notice that many people now prefer to entertain their friends and business colleagues or associates in restaurants rather than at home, it's quite often easier and more fun.

Thirdly, so many people now work from home that meetings in restaurants have become the equivolent of going to the office.

Fourthly, the quality of food and cooking, wine and cocktails and most particularly service has improved in recent years out of all

Foreword
Terence Conran

recognition and the ambience of most restaurants is also pleasant, comfortable and well lit.

There really is practically nothing that is not available in London and also at practically every price level from very economical to outrageously expensive. On the whole you get what you pay for.

Fifthly, the restaurant business has become an exciting activity for young entrepreneurs, and so today you will find plenty of bright young people who dream about opening a restaurant – a very different situation from 20 years ago when the catering business was not surprisingly seen as a dead-end career. Chefs and managers have a great opportunity and good rewards in today's food world. If you make a success in London the world wants a little bit of you. This used to be what France always claimed but now it is London. Caution, London, stay modest.

And another word of caution to people reading this who think, terrific, I cook rather well, I'll go off and start a restaurant – don't even consider it until you have worked for a time in a professional restaurant and discovered what a hard, tough life it is. Exhausting too. You will be amazed at the amount of detail that is involved in everything from all the bureaucracy imposed by government, health & safety, employment law, VAT returns to the control of all the myriad expenses – rents, tax, heat, light, power, water, phone etc and obviously the control of food, wine, alcohol and most importantly wages. Sadly theft by staff and customers is a constant problem that has to be monitored, as are the servicing and repair of kitchen equipment and air-con. I could go on for ages, but at the end of the day, managing a restaurant can be one of the most exciting and rewarding things you ever do in life, though if you think you are going to make a lot of money think again. When your restaurant is up and running smoothly, packed with a happy buzzing crowd of punters having a good time, enjoying their food and wine and the atmosphere, suddenly all the problems vanish and you are convinced it is the most rewarding job in the world. That, I think, is the reason that so many bright people have opened wonderful restaurants and cafés and bars in London. It has become an entrepreneurial epidemic, with each new one trying to do better than the last and very often succeeding.

One of my sadnesses about the contemporary London food scene is the disappearance of most of London's traditional and classic restaurants, such as The Savoy Grill, Claridge's and most particularly, the wonderfully elegant Connaught with Michel Bourdin's delicious, classic, beautifully cooked food. All of them rather old-fashioned and part of hotels but they had something that is missing in today's market. They have all without exception been Ramsayfied and though I'm sure they are busier and more profitable, we have lost something important. I just hope that it can be rediscovered and reborn.

Peter Prescott has worked with me for a number of years, managing our restaurant business. He knows the London scene very well and has done most of the legwork and writing in this book. Our views of what makes a good restaurant and a bad one are virtually identical, so if you enjoy this book, he deserves the praise. If you don't, it's definitely his fault.

Eat London

Ultimately an impossible task, we have endeavoured to present the best places to eat and buy food in London. Our aim is simply to highlight the breadth of dining options and articulate the vast diversity in this illimitable food capital. Dividing London in to 18 geographic areas, the competition for inclusion is more intense in certain quarters, yet each place has deserved merits, although the selection is slightly biased towards our tastes. Whether visiting or living in London, we hope that the extra background information on somewhere new or your local eatery will prove interesting and you will enjoy cooking some of the recipes provided by these celebrated chefs.

Left **The terrace at Le Pont de la Tour (see page 297) remains one of the most desirable dining locations in London.**
Above right **Steve Hatt fishmonger (see page 196) – the best in London.**

Introduction
Peter Prescott

I've been enthusiastically eating out in London for over 15 years. This isn't a huge amount of time, but when I say enthusiastically, it has been at times an average of 10 out of 14 meals per week at a restaurant or café. Having worked in the hotel and restaurant business since 1986, my dining out is often connected to work. Despite being around chefs, kitchens and dining rooms during my business life, if I hear about a new restaurant launch, a chef who is cooking particularly excellent dishes or a restaurant that has been refurbished, I will rush to visit. At the same time, I also try to stay loyal to my favourites and support past colleagues. The London restaurant scene is constantly evolving and improving. It is exciting and, I think, the best in the world.

We have a limited number of pages in this book; therefore, sadly, numerous excellent restaurants and food stores have been excluded. Furthermore, I want to stress that all of the comments are subjective and personal. More than any other trade or industry, the restaurant business is about personalities, unique experiences and, in some situations, good luck. What is superlative for me might be abhorrent for others. Certainly, I harbour a bias towards humble, simple dishes, no-frills cooking, strong flavours and gutsy regional foods. I firmly believe in attractive presentation on the plate, but this shouldn't result in contrived or manipulated ingredients. If a dish is over-dressed or garnished, for me it signals that the chef is trying too hard to compensate for a shortcoming. Equally, I try to seek out places that employ the very best pure ingredients, seasonal treats and chefs who have garnered great knowledge, employ studious technique and respect the customers' desires.

Quirkiness, wonderful personalities, service, ambience, design, location and the customer profile have all been considered when selecting certain establishment for inclusion. Consistency, history and a sense of tradition have also influenced my opinions. In some situations, the narrative is purposely restricted so that you can explore the restaurants and form your own judgement. Sometimes, it is better not to know too much before your visit and hopefully you will discover assets and characteristics that I have failed to recognize. I'm sure there will also be occasions when you fervently disagree with me or when things go wrong even though I have said a certain restaurant is renowned for its consistency. That's the food business for you.

I hope that *Eat London* motivates you to travel to new areas of our great city, experience different foods and visit restaurants that have been established for a long time. Hopefully the map and directory will prove helpful, but please do check before venturing across London. While many new restaurants open each week, the failure and closure rate is also very high.

Now that the book is complete, I'm looking forward to regular visits to my favourites places: Blueprint Café, Racine, St. John – both, Sushi-Say, Rivington Grill (in Shoreditch), River Café, Bistrotheque and the Anchor & Hope. As a result of the research for this book, I am also hoping to visit Arbutus, Bar Shu and Story Deli on a more frequent basis. More leisurely visits to London's food markets and fine food stores are also high on my to-do list. Cooking at home, when I get a chance, is my next big love.

Please support your favourite restaurant, but also, in measured fashion, explore the new.

Right **My favourite dish; roast grouse served with its liver and heart, add a little bread sauce and crumbs, game chips and a few choice greens and you've got the perfect English meal. The wine is Cheval Blanc from my collection of 1970 claret.**

Baker Street
Fitzrovia
Marylebone

Fitzrovia and Marylebone probably have the highest concentration of blue plaques in London – earthenware-glazed discs affixed to the outside of all manner of buildings to mark the former residence of eminent individuals – and an equally high number of top-quality restaurants and food stores. The area has rapidly developed over the last ten years and this is probably due to the many high-profile restaurants and the foodie reputation of two main streets: Marylebone High Street and Charlotte Street.

With the exception of the elegant Hertford House and the Wallace Collection on Manchester Square, the area has few other tourist attractions. Located at the dividing line between both areas, the BT Tower, formerly the Post Office Tower, is a bizarre and slightly moribund sight. In the 1960s it was the tallest building in London and the first purpose-built tower to transmit high-frequency radio waves. At the same time, it housed a restaurant on the top floor that rotated completely in 22 minutes. How fabulous that must have been, and what a challenge for the restaurateur to create food to compete with the views! (TC) My children always wanted to celebrate their birthdays there when we lived in Fitzroy Square.

Today, Charlotte Street and its arterial roads sate the appetite of most well-travelled creatives, whereas Marylebone High Street has a village theme with one of chicest retail destinations in London. Starting at the Conran Shop, progress along Marylebone High Street taking in Scandinavian furniture stores, the best cheese shop in London, patisseries and antiquarian booksellers, before turning left into Marylebone Lane and progressing to St. Christopher's Place to sample continental-style pavement dining.

PINK SEA BREAM
these fish are lovely
braised with fennel
tomato and roasted

MONKFISH TAILS
...k in the oven with
...ed garlic and fennel.

FISH
WORKS

FISH
WORKS

RED GURNARD
a great fish that poaches
exceptionally well, try
saffron, garlic, chilli
and parsley

FISH
WORKS

Busaba Eathai 8–13 Bird Street, W1U 1BU
020 7518 8080

Young, trendy staff serve food that possibly isn't strictly authentic Thai, but it's certainly moreish and ideal for a quick one-course large bowl of noodles, stir-fry or a great curry. This is the third London Busaba by Alan Yau and, unlike other brands, hopefully more will follow.

The power drinks and juices, such as carrot, apple and celery with dandelion and nettle extract, must be good for you.

The design is mainly dark teak and large square communal tables, with central low lamps and bench seats. It has a no-bookings policy and queues normally apply at the other outlets, but it's easier to get a seat here. ◉

Carluccio's Caffè St Christopher's Place, W1U 1AY
020 7935 5927 www.carluccios.com

Il Negozio buzzes with shoppers from early morning and the outside seats are full all day at this flagship location. Antonio and Priscilla Carluccio assiduously source ingredients from across Italy and have a great range of own-brand products in stylish packaging. Whether you are searching for special pasta, polenta or biscotti, the selection is inspirational. The décor is casual and bright with simple stainless-steel shelves and black and white chequered tile floors. Essentially, it's a modern version of your favourite old Italian deli with a very enjoyable caffè on the side. As with everything that 'funghophile' Antonio touches, you can be assured of a great selection of fresh and dried mushrooms and they have a fungi market in September. ◉

Above and right
Larder staples from Carluccio's plus freshly baked bread, cakes and tarts.

Giancarlo & Katie Caldesi

"For something completely different from our own Italian cooking we like to escape to the exotic surroundings of Chor Bizarre with Depinder's wonderful authentic Indian flavours

Owners, La Cucina Caldesi Restaurant, Caffè and Cookery School

La Cucina Caldesi 118 Marylebone Lane, W1U 2QF
020 7935 1144 www.caldesi.com

In the 1980s it seemed that every successful chef aspired to establish his or her own cookery school, but very few examples remain. Rick Stein in Padstow and Raymond Blanc at Le Manoir Aux Quat' Saisons in Oxfordshire still operate excellent schools; London has La Cucina Caldesi. As an offshoot of the estimable Caldesi restaurant at 15–17 Marylebone Lane and the more simple Caffè Caldesi, the La Cucina is stylishly appointed with a technically brilliant kitchen studio suitable for a range of masterclasses and tutored cookery classes.

Giancarlo and Katie Caldesi share recipes handed down from generation to generation, in keeping with the Tuscan family tradition. How to prepare a typical Tuscan three-course meal and make a pizza are just two examples. They even have cookery classes for six- to ten-year-olds. The programme of events includes talks from food writers, mixologists, patisserie experts, celebrity chef demonstrations and Italian wine classes.

Above left **Sam (left) and Eddie Hart (right) outside Fino.**

Eat and Two Veg 50 Marylebone High Street, W1U 5HN
020 7258 8595 www.eatandtwoveg.com

A modern rarity, this is a vegetarian diner occupying a prominent high-street location, open for breakfast, lunch and dinner. ◉

Fino 33 Charlotte Street, entrance on Rathbone Street, W1T 1RR
020 7813 8010 www.finorestaurant.com

Two Hispanophile brothers, Sam and Eddie Hart, have created a restaurant offering probably the best Spanish food in London. The inspiration is clearly tapas or pintxos, but the end result is something much better. The three-star Michelin-quality head chef takes all the usual ingredients – Padrón peppers, chorizo, morcilla, tortilla, bacalao – and then fashions a dish of superb quality. The hams from Iberico to Joselito are always served at the exact temperature and condition.

When you sit at the bar overlooking the kitchen you can watch a busy team working la plancha, the perfect cooking method for the seafood delights of chiperones, scallops and clams. The arroz negro is best-in-class and milk-fed lamb, pork belly and marinated quail are delicious carnivorous hits.

Fino has significantly contributed to the re-emergence of sherry on the London scene and their selection is outstanding. The wine list is, save for one or two Portuguese bottles, completely Spanish and all are good or better. We had particularly charming service and an excellent martini when we ate dinner there recently. ◉

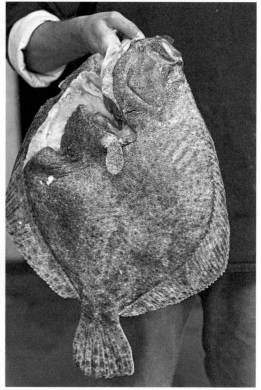

Above right **Whole turbot** Above **English brown crab and salmon.** Left **Simple recipe cards and suggested cooking methods alongside the Fishworks fresh catch.**

Fishworks 89 Marylebone High Street, W1U 4QW
020 7935 9796 www.fishworks.co.uk

The display of alluring wet fish virtually leaps out on to the pavement from the counter inside the large open window of this modern fishmonger with an adjoining café-cum-restaurant. Launched in 1995 in the West Country by Mitchell Tonks, this rapidly expanding chain is operated by young, skilled staff who know their fish. Sea bass, halibut, scallops, mussels, oysters, kippers and the customary catch from the waters around the British Isles are all in mint condition, and they also sell prepared piscatorial delights such as fishcakes or herring salad. While the blackboard offers a summary of the day-boat haul, the wall-mounted plasma screens detail the latest news from the fishermen and fishworks suppliers.

Whole fish and shellfish are on ice at the front of the premises and a delightful dining area is located at the rear. They keep it simple in the restaurants and allow the fish-only menu to speak for itself. We like the option to select whole fish from the shop and ask the chef to recommend a cooking method and then prepare it for you.

If you are interested in cooking great fish dishes at home then I also suggest that you visit the superb Fishworks website. There is a regular blog about what the Fishworks team are up to and they offer great advice on fishing seasons, how to store fish, shopping tips and many interesting recipes and information on a range of cooking methods and the best equipment. ●

La Fromagerie 2–4 Moxon Street, W1U 4EW

020 7935 0341 www.lafromagerie.co.uk

As you enter the shop your olfactory sense is accosted by the pungent smell of the innumerable cheeses stocked at Patricia Michelson's homage to perfectly conditioned fromage. Inside the actual cheese room (also the name of Patricia's remarkable and passionately written book about discovering and cooking with the world's best cheeses) the affineur ensures the ripeness and perfect storage of a mainly continental collection, including interesting Spanish Manchego and gooey Dolcellatte Italian offerings and a few British and Irish un-pasteurized cheeses. The extremely knowledgeable staff offer a tasting of every product before you buy. They even ask when your cheese will be consumed so that they can advise on the storage conditions and whether it will be ready or not.

Patricia is an ardent fan of the Slow Food movement and regularly hosts interesting events at La Fromagerie. We suggest that you visit the website regularly for news of tutored tastings and various other events held in partnership with some of London's top food heroes.

The shop has a superb selection of wild leaves and vegetables, plus great high-mountain Miel de Pyrenees, muesli, roasted and cured meats, chocolates and oils, plus much more. The stock changes regularly so you need to visit every month or so just to keep abreast of what's seasonal.

You can also dine in the store and enjoy great pastries, salads, traiteur-style dishes and exceptionally delicious cakes. ❍

Galvin 66 Baker Street, W1

020 7935 4007 www.galvinbistrotdeluxe.co.uk

Sibling success is found at Galvin. Chris Galvin has over 30 years' experience in top kitchens, latterly gaining a Michelin star at Orrery and launching The Wolseley as head chef. Jeff Galvin has cooked at The Savoy, with Marco Pierre White and Nico Ladennis. They now cook simple bistro food which has without exception been lauded by the critics. Overall you can eat and drink the bourgeois way for very good value.

Joelle Marti-Baron, Director of Wine at The Great Eastern Hotel speaks highly of Galvin: 'What I love about Galvin's Bistrot de Luxe is the chef – well, I should speak plural here: Chris & Jeff. They have been able to create a place that serves delicious food at a reasonable price without being pretentious. Similar to what they are, very talented chefs with no ego (very rare in the industry!). The wine list is lively and reliable and the food changes every week, giving you the possibility to return there endlessly, with the guarantee of enjoying yourself.' ❍

Fromagerie

Pasta with Truffled Cheese

by Patricia Michelson

500 g (1 lb) fine tagliatelle, either fresh or dried
a little extra-virgin olive oil
125 g (4 oz) fromage blanc or fromage frais, low or full fat
a few sage leaves, finely chopped
freshly ground black pepper
250 g (8 oz) Fomaggio di Tartufo, a hard cow's and goat's milk cheese, or Caprini Tartufo, a fresh goat's milk cheese with shavings of truffle on top

Place the pasta into a large pan of lightly salted boiling water. Cook the pasta until it is al dente, remove from the heat and drain it well. Pour a little olive oil into the pan, add the cooked tagliatelle and toss it in the olive oil to coat it lightly.

Stir in the fromage blanc or fromage frais, the sage leaves and some black pepper. Place the pan over a low heat for a few moments to reheat the pasta. Pile the pasta on to a dish or plate, then grate or crumble over the cheese. Using two large forks, gently lift the pasta so that the cheese can mingle loosely but not get lost in the pasta.

Serve immediately with a salad of mixed leaves, dressed with a little truffle oil and walnut vinegar (or a good-quality wine vinegar that will not overpower the other ingredients).

(Recipe featured in *The Cheese Room*, published by Michael Joseph, 2001. Reproduced by permission of Penguin Books Ltd.)

Mourad 'Momo' Mazouz

La Fromagerie has the most superb selection of cheese in London! I always love to have a large selection of cheese at home. I also love Villandry, plus Lidgates the butchers in Holland Park, and Micha Nicobros – a local greengrocer to where I live on Clarendon Road where I can choose my own fresh fruit and veg. I always find he has high quality produce.

Restaurateur, Momo and Sketch

Right **Just one corner of the amazing cheese room at La Fromagerie.**

The Ginger Pig 8–10 Moxon Street, W1U 4EW

020 7935 7788

This is how the archetypal local butcher's shop should look, smell and sound! This meat-lover's paradise, located at the epicentre of foodie Marylebone, has only been trading for a couple of years, but it feels like it has been around for decades. Timothy Wilson now presides over one of the best retail experiences in London, with diagrams on the walls indicating the various cuts of meat, a huge walk-in cold room with countless carcasses awaiting the knife of consummate professionals in bloodstained white coats and the smell of game pies baking in the oven.

Longhorn cattle, Swaledale and Black Face sheep, plus at least two rare-breed pigs, come from Timothy's organic Grange Farm on the North York Moors. Free-range geese, chickens and turkeys are sourced from the 500-acre Belvoir Estate in Rutland and game is from the most reputable shoots. The extensive selection of sausages, bacon, hams, terrines and pies is not inexpensive, but the value is in the taste.

Bill Baker

Above **One of the skilled butchers at The Ginger Pig and his quarry.**

"I love The Ginger Pig because the meat is respected, properly butchered and tastes exactly as it should. You can ask to look at several home-reared sirloins before choosing the piece hung just as long as you prefer. Personally I go for the ones which are almost black on the outside – well-hung English beef with fresh horseradish still ranks alongside the world's greatest dishes. **Wine merchant and consultant**

Above and left
Subterranean decadence, masses of teak and seriously considered mood lighting at Hakkasan.

Hakkasan 8 Hanway Place, Hanway Street, W1T 1HD
020 7927 7000

Seminal Hong Kong meets Chinese cuisine in glamorous surroundings. World-renowned designer Christian Liaigre, in partnership with Alan Yau, has wrought a nightclub feel with comfortable dining quarters.

The rumour among many of the chefs is that Alan Yau insisted on engaging Hong Kong's legendary Mr Sun as the dim sum chef for the opening of both Hakkasan and Yauatcha. Mr Sun, in his late sixties, if not older, has now reportedly returned home, but the dim sum remains excellent and the main menu offers amazingly creative and inspiring dishes. Nothing similar exists in London. Even Michelin have honoured the place with a star.

If you can't get a dining table, try the Ling Ling bar for a wide menu of great cocktails. The interior is sleek and stylish, so sit back and admire the design details, especially the lighting scheme. ○

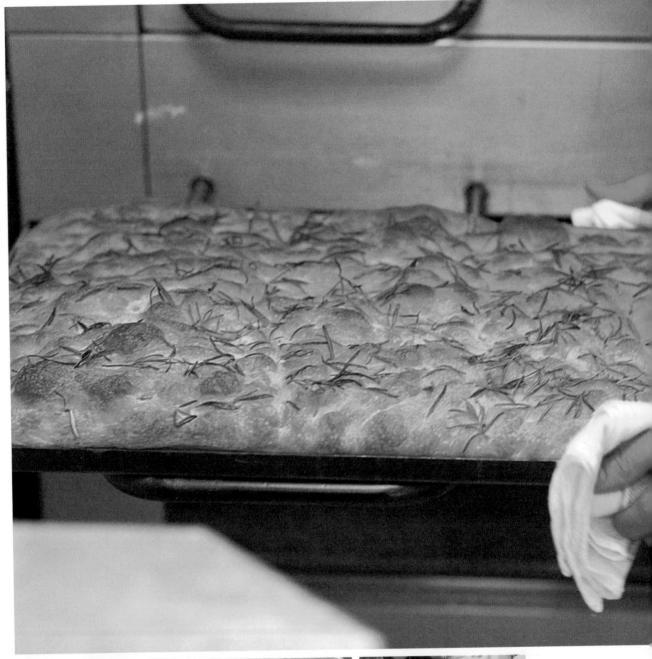

Great meals at Locanda Locatelli start with great freshly baked Italian-recipe breads.

Giorgio Locatelli

"
The word 'organic' isn't shrugged off as being middle-class neurosis any more and is being accepted as a better option. This shift in the attitude towards food reflects that now, in every part of London (not just the West End), there is a huge variety of good restaurants springing up. London has come a long way since the 80s.

Owner, Locanda Locatelli

Locanda Locatelli 8 Seymour Street, W1H 7JZ
020 7935 9088 www.locandalocatelli.com

After Giorgio Locatelli's achievement at Zafferano it was destined that his own little *inn* (locanda) would be a success. The diaries seemed to be full from the moment the paint was drying on the David Collins-designed modern and elegant room. Apparently, it is Madonna's favourite. Along with The River Café in Hammersmith, it is definitely in our top two Italian eateries.

As you'd expect, you start with a generous basket of beautiful bread, from a deliciously moist focaccia to wafer-thin pane. In addition, the tables are laid with two-foot-long grissini. Go with an appetite; it would be a shame to have anything less than four courses. The menu is vast. Antipasti deliver artichokes, mozzarella, seasonal insalata, scallops and on my last visit a thinly sliced calves head 'lampascioni' with rocket, parsley and capers. Then you struggle to select a pasta dish from a perfect selection of about a dozen, followed by an exceptional choice of main courses, with zucchini fritte as the essential contorni. Finally, it's got to be the pick-me-up tiramisu.

In some respects, it would be enough to receive food of this standard, but the front of house, overseen by Plaxy Locatelli, is close to perfect. The specials are recommended with such passion and while all of the team are ultimate professionals, you just get the feeling that they live and dine together as a happy family. Intuition and anticipation of your every need happen subconsciously. ●

Locanda Locatelli

Spaghetti 'Latini' alla Vongole

(Spaghetti 'Latini' with Clams)
by Giorgio Locatelli

Serves 4

70 ml (3 fl oz) extra-virgin olive oil
3 garlic cloves, peeled and finely chopped
1 chilli, finely chopped
1 kg (2 lb) veraci clams (palourdes or carpetshell)
½ wineglass of dry white wine
400 g (13 oz) spaghetti 'Latini'
1 handful parsley, finely chopped

Place a large pan of lightly salted water over a high heat and bring it to the boil. Meanwhile, heat half of the olive oil in a large sauté pan over a medium heat. The aim is to cook the garlic (so that it is digestible) but not burn it (or it will be bitter), so it is a good idea to tilt the pan a little. This way, the oil flows to one spot. Place the garlic and chilli into the oil so they can cook in this depth and will be less likely to burn. Cook gently for a few minutes until they start to colour.

Place the pan back down fully onto the stove and add the clams. Cook them for about 30 seconds and then add the white wine. Cover the pan with a lid to allow the clams to steam open. After about one minute or up to 90 seconds, remove the lid and discard any clams that haven't opened.

Leave around one-quarter of the clams in their shells, but scrape out the rest, discarding the shells. Turn off the heat.

Once the large pan of salted water has come to the boil, place the pasta into it and let it boil for about a minute less than the time given on the packet (usually 5–6 minutes), until al dente. Drain the pasta, reserving the cooking water.

Add the pasta to the clams along with the remaining oil and toss thoroughly for about a minute to let the pasta absorb the flavours and allow the starch to thicken the sauce. If you need to loosen it slightly, add a little cooking water from the pasta. You will see that the sauce starts to cling to the pasta, so that when you serve it the pasta it will stay coated. Sprinkle with chopped parsley and serve straight away.

Giorgio in the kitchens of Locanda Locatelli making Spaghetti 'Latini' alla Vongole.

Marylebone Farmers' Market Cramer Street Car Park, off Marylebone High Street. Sunday 10 am–2 pm

Marylebone High Street already has its full complement of food stores, but when the market comes to town on Sunday the vast choice will sate any foodie's deepest desires. On its day, the Marylebone market is London's largest *pure* farmers' market: Borough Market is significantly larger, but it doesn't follow the same strict rules set down by the London Farmers' Market Association. You might want to browse the www.lfm.org.uk website for further details and information about where to find the other London markets.

(PP) It's always enjoyable to visit these markets and talk with the farmers, growers, fishermen and producers themselves. Over time, I have learnt to focus my purchasing on the meat, game, fruit, vegetables and salad leaves. The cheese is eclipsed by the selection from nearby La Fromagerie or Neal's Yard Dairy and the cakes are better from other specialist shops.

One of the better stalls is Ranger Organics, which provides award-winning beef from The Hardwick Estate near Reading. You can also order your beef via telephone in advance and collect on market day; otherwise, arrive early to be sure of the best cuts, such as bavette or sirloin. ◗

Orrery and Orrery Epicerie 55 Marylebone High Street, W1U 5RB
020 7616 8000 www.conran.com

Orrery delivers on every level, but it's the Jacques Vermier 'Maitre Fromager de France' cheese trolley that is most exciting. If you are serious about cheese, and we are very, this is the place to dine. The service is French slick and the restaurant boasts a large band of regulars. Over recent years the direction has progressed ever closer to the dominance of the menu gourmand and degustation-style serious dining, but they also have a short and attractively priced Sunday evening menu. The wine list is naturally exhaustive and the bijou bar that adjoins it has a much-lauded collection of rums from Martinique. Named after the mechanical device that illustrates the relative positions of the planets in the solar system (it also happens to share the name of the second Conran restaurant in 1954), the space is long and narrow and sits atop The Conran Shop as part of a converted stable building. Large windows overlook the carefully tended grounds of the churchyard opposite and a row of banquette seating provides the opposite flank. The summer terrace upstairs offers a unique dining location that not too many people know about.

(PP) Terence has demonstrated prodigious fecundity over his years as a restaurateur, but Orrery is the only operation to have gained a Michelin star. For me, Bibendum should also achieve the same honour – or better – but maybe the building's past history as a headquarters for Michelin is preventing objectivity.

The Epicerie, located on the corner of the building at ground-floor level, stocks a fine selection of olive oils, truffles, coffee, Viennoiserie, Madeleine or fleur de sel from The Camargue. The Sud and Ouest-influenced traiteur dishes such as cassoulet, pot au feu and confit de canard, plus the renowned saucissons, terrines and rillettes, are definitely worth adding to any larder. ◗

Above **Mickael Weiss in the kitchen at Orrery.**
Left **The kitchen brigade share a simple meal between busy service periods at Orrery.**

Ranger Organics Salt Beef

Serves 4

salt beef from Ranger Organics (use a minimum 1 kg (2 lbs) or 250 g (8 oz) per person)
selection of herbs
black peppercorns
2 sticks of celery, roughly chopped
2 carrots, roughly chopped
2 onions, studded with cloves

Cover the salted beef with cold water and let it soak for about an hour, changing the water at least once.

Drain the salted beef and place it in a large saucepan over a medium heat. Pour in enough water to cover the beef and add the herbs, peppercorns and celery but no salt. Slowly bring to the water to the boil and let it simmer for at least an hour.

Now add carrots, onions and any other vegetables and cook for another couple of hours or more depending on weight.

When it is cooked, lift the meat from the sauce and place it on a chopping board. Carve the beef into thick slices and serve it with mustard and gherkins. Serve the vegetables using some of the cooking liquid as gravy. This dish is delicious with parsley dumplings. If there is any leftover beef, put it back in the cooking liquid and allow it to get cold. Then remove it, wrap it in greaseproof paper and refrigerate it. This dish is equally delicious hot or cold and makes excellent New York hash browns, too.

Above **The cheese trolley at Orrery has 30 different cheeses all kept in perfect condition.**
Left **There are also over 1,000 wine bins and a top-flight sommelier team.**
Right **The pavement-level epicerie is ideal for morning coffee and pastries.**

Le Pain Quotidien 72–75 Marylebone High Street, W1U 5JW
020 7486 6154 www.lepainquotidien.com

To quote the words of Alain Coumont founder of Le Pain Quotidien,
'the idea behind "Le Pain Quotidien" is simply to make a good daily bread:
a hand-made bread with a good crust and a firm slice, the kind of bread
that makes great tartines; bread not only to nourish the body but the
spirit as well; a bread best shared around a table to be savoured among
friends.' High ambitions indeed.

 This branch of the international chain occupies a favourable corner
position at the top end of Marylebone High Street, a perfect location
for many of the local residents to call in for their *daily bread*. Or possibly
take time out from the exigencies of London life to dine at the communal
table and enjoy the pastries, tarts, brownies, cakes and meringues.

 All of the breads are hand-made, baked in stone ovens and made
by using just three ingredients: water, stone-ground flour and salt.
It sounds simple, but the care and skill (not to mention the starter
or 'mother')required to bake such bread are enormous. And they do
make great tartines. ●

Passione 10 Charlotte Street, W1T 2LT
020 7636 2833 www.passione.co.uk

Gennaro Contaldo cooks Amalfitana regional Italian food.

 This is what Jamie Oliver says about the restaurant: 'I love going
to my mate Gennaro's restaurant, Passione. I think it's the best Italian
restaurant in London. Gennaro makes the most delicious ribbon pasta
and amazing risotto.' ●

The Providores 109 Marylebone High Street, W1U 4RX
020 7935 6175 www.theprovidores.co.uk

Roast Norwegian cod on pan-fried Kipfler potatoes, tamarind, olives
and barba di frate with brown shrimp nage and Christian's pickled Grand
Union walnuts. Or roast Gressingham duck breast in smoked-tea smashed
swede with black vinegar lentils, wild garlic leaves, pickled shiitake and
verjus-braised hedgehog mushrooms… just two of the main-course
dishes from the huge menu at The Providores which, we think, say more
than we can write about the overall direction of the restaurant. Fusion chefs
have been much maligned over recent years, but New Zealander Peter Gordon
seems to have been the exception. Instead, his menus are highly praised.

 The ground-floor Tapa Room, named after a wood-fibre ceremonial
cloth used throughout the Pacific for celebratory feasts, offers probably the
most innovative breakfast brunch menu in the whole of London. Examples
include French toast stuffed with banana and pecans with grilled smoked
streaky bacon and vanilla verjus syrup or kumara, caramelized red onion,
kawakawa and feta tortilla with Turkish yoghurt, piquillo peppers and
rocket. (PP) If, like me, fusion food isn't at the top of your list, I would
still highly recommend the Tapa Room. Plus, you've got to admire the
procurement and knowledge of ingredients and combinations of flavours
demonstrated by this kitchen. ●

Peter Gordon

I have two favourite London food
shops: the first would have to be
Food World on Kilburn High Road
which has the most fabulous range
of Indian and Middle Eastern
spices, grains, vegetables and fruit.
I head there as soon as I get a whiff
of the arrival of the Alphonso
mangoes – there's always something
new to discover. My second would
be Brindisa at Borough Market,
which is great for easily accessible
Spanish produce, which I use a lot
of, and the Sunday Farmers' Market
in Marylebone has to be one of the
best of its kind in London.

Head Chef, The Providores

Right **The
Providores chef
Cristian Hossack's
pan-fried halibut
on a kawakawa
potato cake with
morel, shiitake and
edamame ragout
and samphire.**

Wild and English Asparagus with Buffalo Mozzarella, Yellow Bean and Cherry Tomato Salsa

This truly is a fusion dish – but in reality it couldn't be simpler. Ingredients from around the world, served in their prime – delicious.

Serves 4 as a starter

16 cherry tomatoes, halved
2 tablespoons yellow bean sauce
(available from Chinese food stores)
¹/₂ piece of stem ginger, chopped
50 ml (2 fl oz) extra-virgin olive oil
40 ml (1¹/₂ fl oz) aged red Greek wine vinegar
¹/₂ spring onion, finely sliced
a small handful of coriander leaves
400 g (13 oz) English asparagus, trimmed
300 g (10 oz) wild asparagus
4 mozzarella di buffala

Mix the first five ingredients together in a bowl to make a salsa. Leave them to macerate for an hour. Then mix in the spring onion and coriander and leave for another 30 minutes.

When the salsa has nearly finished macerating, bring a large pot of water to the boil and lightly salt it to cook the English asparagus. (Or you could use a steamer.) Cook the English asparagus until the lower part of the stem is tender – a thick stem will take about 3 minutes. Remove the asparagus from the pot and drain them. Bring the water back to the boil and add the wild asparagus. Cook them for 1 minute and then drain them. Divide both types of asparagus among four plates.

Cut a cross into the top of each of the pieces of mozzarella to open them up slightly. Place one mozzarella on each plate on top of the asparagus. Stir the salsa one last time and spoon this over the mozzarella. Eat immediately.

changa
Turkish Eggs

The Providores have worked with changa restaurant in Istanbul since 1999. This is a dish we have eaten many times in Turkey and it is one of our most popular dishes at breakfast time in the restaurant. In Turkey the yoghurt has raw garlic beaten into it but we've found that's a bit too much for the English breakfast palate.

Serves 4

300 g (10¹/₂ oz) thick yoghurt
¹/₂ teaspoon fine sea salt
1 clove garlic, peeled and finely chopped (optional)
80 ml (3 fl oz) extra virgin olive oil
80 ml (3 fl oz) white vinegar
8 medium or large eggs
50 g (2 oz) butter
1 teaspoon kirmizi biber (dried Turkish chilli flakes)
2 tablespoons roughly chopped parsley
whole-wheat sourdough toast

Beat the yogurt with the salt, garlic and ¹/₂ the oil and divide ²/₃ of it amongst four bowls.

Bring a deep pot (about 3 litres/6 pints in capacity) of water to the boil. Reduce the temperature so the water just simmers and add the vinegar. Crack the eggs in one by one and poach them until the whites are set but the yolks are still runny. This should take about 5–7 minutes.

Meanwhile heat the butter in a small pan until it turns pale nut-brown. Add the chilli flakes and let them sizzle. Then remove them from the heat, add the remaining olive oil and set aside.

Carefully lift the eggs out of the pot with a slotted spoon and place two in each bowl, on top of the yoghurt. Spoon the remaining yoghurt on top of the eggs. Give the chilli butter a good stir and spoon this on top.

Scatter with the parsley and serve the toast on a separate plate.

Wild Strawberry Sorbet with Gooseberry Espresso Compote, Vanilla Cream, Hazelnut Praline and a 'torta de aceite' Biscuit

This dessert has a few steps to it but once the component parts are made, they will keep for three days in the fridge or freezer, then it's quick to assemble. If you don't have a sorbet machine, buy a good-quality strawberry or raspberry sorbet and place a few wild strawberries on the plate in place of the regular ones.

Serves 8

For the Wild Strawberry Sorbet

40 ml (1½ fl oz) glucose syrup

80 g (3¼ oz) caster sugar

1 tablespoon lemon juice

250 g (8 oz) wild strawberries, hulled

Put the glucose, caster sugar and 100 ml (3½ fl oz) of water in a small saucepan and bring to the boil. After 5 minutes, take the pot off of the heat, add the lemon juice and then leave it to cool completely.

Place the wild strawberries in a blender or food processor and pour the cooled sugar syrup over them. Blitz the mixture well. Pass it through a fine sieve, and then churn it in a sorbet machine according to the manufacturer's instructions until it is ready. Remove the mixture from the sorbet machine and place it in a suitable container in the freezer.

For the Gooseberry Espresso Compote

200 g (7 oz) gooseberries (use either green or red ones)

150 g (5 oz) caster sugar

1 single shot of espresso

Put everything in a saucepan, place over a medium heat and slowly bring the mixture to the boil. Turn the heat down and allow it to simmer and cook until half of the gooseberries have popped their skins.

Take the pan off the heat and leave it to cool. Then pour the gooseberry mixture into a container, seal it with a lid (or cover it with cling film) and place it in the fridge to cool.

For the Hazelnut Praline

150 g (5 oz) caster sugar

50 g (2 oz) roasted skinned hazelnuts, chopped

Line a baking tray with silicon paper and set it aside.

Place the sugar in a small nonstick pan and cook it over a moderate heat, stirring often but gently, until it begins to melt. When the sugar turns dark golden, stir in the hazelnuts. Then pour the mixture on to the lined baking tray and leave it to cool.

Break the pieces up into bite-sized chunks. Place them in a food processor and blitz them to coarse crumbs. Store the crumbs in an airtight container, sealed with a lid or covered with cling film.

For the Vanilla Cream

200 ml (7 fl oz) double cream

2 tablespoons vanilla sugar

Make this just before you serve the dessert. Whip the cream and sugar together in a chilled bowl to form soft peaks. Keep it in the fridge.

8 torta de aceite

These are delicious crunchy Spanish biscuits made with olive oil. We buy ours from Brindisa, one of The Providores' favourite food suppliers.

a large handful of strawberries, to serve

To serve

We serve this dessert in glass tumblers resting on a bamboo leaf, which we buy from our Japanese supplier Tazaki Foods. To assemble this dessert, gently stir the gooseberry compote and divide it among eight glasses. Then spoon the vanilla cream on top. Take a scoop of the sorbet and place this in the centre of the cream and sprinkle with a teaspoon of the praline. Place a biscuit on the plate and set the strawberries on top.

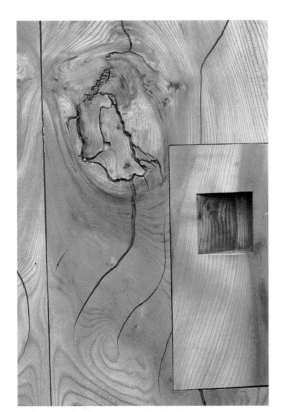

32   **Roka** 37 Charlotte Street, W1T 1RR

020 7580 6464   www.rokarestaurant.com

Launched after its now-renowned sibling Zuma in Raphael Street, Knightsbridge, Roka is perceived as a less serious offering, but for us it is much better. Zuma is fantastic in its own way, but it is loud and a celebrity hotspot; we prefer the ambience and interior at Roka. Japan's esteemed Super Potato and Noriyoshi Muramatsu collaborated on the architecture and design. Light floods through the window walls during the day making perfect conditions in which to admire the food. An abundance of natural materials, especially timber, combined with pickling jars on shelves, completes the interior design aspects. The principal feature is most certainly the central robata grill, which is a type of Japanese barbecue.

This open kitchen allows guests to observe the chef preparing lamb cutlets with Korean spices, tiger prawns with ginger, yuzu and mirin or scallop skewers with wasabi and shiso. The menu includes sashimi, nigiri and much more. The desserts are particularly good and the presentation is inspired.

Named after Japan's version of vodka, the Shochu Bar in the basement is sexy and cool. Unlike sake, which is brewed, shochu is distilled. This creates an alcohol content of about 25% and working-class Japanese men traditionally drink it. Yet this cocktail list has elevated the drink to new heights. Expertly devised and perfectly executed, a drink downstairs before or after your meal upstairs is a must. ◉

Peter Gordon

"

When it comes to eating out, I love the tea room and dim sum at Yauatcha, the rice and wasabi tobiko pot at Roka and the Kiwi Burger at GBK restaurants.

Head Chef, The Providores

Above left
Timber dominates the design at Roka. The dining counter adjacent to kitchen is cut from one large trunk.
Above right
Chefs work from the central open kitchen and prepare dishes on the robata grill – a type of Japanese barbecue.

Selfridges Food Hall Selfridges, 400 Oxford St, W1A 2LR
08708 377 377 www.selfridges.com

Selfridges is now a modern department store food hall with everything from sushi to San Daniele ham. It also has a Daylesford Organics concession, as well as an interesting range of restaurants and cafés. The sandwich counter serves the most expensive sandwich in the world at £85. Created by head chef Scott MacDonald, it offers a truly decadent gourmet experience. It may sound a lot for a packed lunch, but when you consider that each sandwich contains rare Wagyu beef, the finest fresh duck foie gras, black truffle mayonnaise, Brie de Meaux, rocket, red Piquillo pepper and mustard confit with English plum tomatoes in a sourdough bread, for food-lovers it represents remarkable value. However, some might say this rather gimmicky end product is less than its parts – possibly disgusting! ○

Spoon @ Sanderson Hotel 50 Berners Street, W1T 3NG
020 7300 1444 www.spoon-restaurant.com

This is an interesting, but expensive concept by one of the world's most successful chefs. Alain Ducasse currently holds more Michelin stars than any other chef on the planet. His unique 'mix and match' menu allows diners to customize their own meal, pairing proteins with a choice of sauces, condiments and other accompaniments. It's actually quite difficult to understand and I dread to think about the possible confusion in the kitchen. The adjoining Long Bar attracts a flashy cocktail-swigging crowd. ○

Above
The world's most expensive sandwich at Selfridges.

34

Villandry 170 Great Portland Street, W1W 5QB
020 7631 3131   www.villandry.co.uk

Villandry has every possible gourmet comestible and is everything from
a restaurant and bar to a bakery and cheese counter, plus take-away fare and
even an outside catering resource and bespoke hamper service. The wine
and drinks selection is also top class, although the service is rather relaxed.
The restaurant is light and airy, with simple food, strong flavours and fine
ingredients. You can easily while away the hours over weekend brunch. ●

Ian Wood

"Villandry is a great place to
stock-up the larder, collect some
charcuterie, select a couple of ripe
cheeses and take home a few bakery
products. Having everything in one
shop makes it very convenient.
My favourite London restaurant
is J. Sheekey (see page 130). I
particularly like the small alcove
dining room and the menu is lovely,
with an abundance of fresh British
fish. I recently enjoyed the most
amazing crab bisque.

Head Chef, Almeida

Above **Scenes from
Villandry, where
they sell everything
from flowers and
cakes to olive oils.**

Breast of Barbary Duck with Fondant Potatoes, Bordelaise Sauce and Fresh Morels

Serves 2

For the Fondant Potatoes

3 baking potatoes cut into 3-cm (1¹/₂-in) slices
sprig of fresh thyme
2 fresh bay leaves
2 large garlic cloves, peeled
250 ml (8 fl oz) melted butter
salt and freshly ground pepper

Layer the slices of potato into a roomy saucepan with the fresh thyme, bay leaves and garlic. Season the potatoes with the salt and pepper. Cover with the melted butter, and cook on a medium heat for approximately 12–15 minutes or until the base is golden brown. Turn off the heat and leave for 10 minutes, them remove from the heat, drain off the butter and keep warm.

For the Duck

Duck breasts are sometimes referred to in French as magrets. The best are plump and firm with a good layer of fat and a dark meat colour (similar to claret) with a strong flavour.

2 large Barbary duck breasts

Trim down some of the fat from around the duck breasts and season them with salt and pepper. Fry them in a pan over a medium heat for 2–3 minutes, skin-side down, until they are golden brown. Turn the breasts over cook skin for a further 8–10 minutes.

Remove from the heat and leave to rest for 4 minutes before slicing them for serving. Cover lightly in foil while they are resting to keep warm.

For the Bordelaise Sauce

a ¹/₂ bottle of good French red wine
50 g (2 oz) chopped shallots
sprig of fresh thyme
2 fresh bay leaves
300 ml (¹/₂ pint) of veal stock
A small handful of morels (Morels are a delicious type of mushroom, prized for their tobacco rich scent and oaky, woody flavour. They are among the most exciting springtime fungi. Both fresh and dried morels are readily available seasonally. A splash of Madeira will enliven and lift the flavour – delicious!)
1–2 tablespoons of Madeira
25 g (1 oz) fresh butter
salt and pepper

Put the red wine, shallots, thyme and bay leaves in a saucepan over a medium heat and bring it slowly to the boil. Allow the mixture to bubble away until the liquid has reduced down to a concentration of approximately 2–3 tablespoons. Pour in the veal stock and then turn down the heat to a low setting. Allow the mixture to simmer for 15–20 minutes.

Pass the liquid through a fine sieve into a new pan, and add the morels and Madeira. Bring the sauce back up to the boil, and then whisk in the butter. Keep the sauce warm over a very low heat until you are ready to serve the duck.

Arrange the slices of duck on two plates, spoon over the sauce and serve the fondant potato on the side.

Barnes
Chiswick
Richmond
Teddington
Twickenham

Just eight miles from central London, a journey best made on a train from Waterloo Station, Richmond is a beautifully green and leafy suburb. Life in this part of London is far more sedate and village-like, with the river meandering through the region and most of the urbanization congregating close to the bridges at Kew, Chiswick, Richmond and Barnes.

The aeroplanes en route to Heathrow punctuate the air space and Twickenham rugby stadium can be seen peeking over the distant tree line, but otherwise the view from Richmond Hill is the same today as it was hundreds of years ago. Ham and Petersham beyond Richmond are particularly attractive and fabulously wealthy villages. In 1625, Charles I walled the open heaths of Richmond Park to create a great hunting estate. The original perimeter remains today, forming Europe's largest urban enclosed park, with wild red and fallow deer roaming the park for all to see, but not hunt.

Cycling in Richmond Park is a popular activity, with many people progressing on to the river and the many small restaurants and cafés that can be found along this stretch of the Thames. For those interested in the history of food as far back as Tudor times, then a visit to Hampton Court Palace is recommended. For the last five years the palace's food historians and archaeologists have been researching recipes and food that was once served to Henry VIII and his courtiers. You can visit the vast kitchens and they occasionally host cookery classes. The Royal Botanical Gardens at Kew is another great attraction in the area.

T. Adamou & Sons 124–126 Chiswick High Road, W4 1PU
020 8994 0752

You can be assured of assertive, friendly and knowledgeable service at this Cypriot-family run grocer's. The emphasis is on Mediterranean foods, with a fine selection of feta cheese, vine leaves, tinned items, dried foods and olive oils. The pavement fresh fruit and vegetable display is a welcome relief from the more mundane neighbouring retailers. ●

La Brasserie McClements 2 Whitton Road, TW1 1BJ
020 8744 9598

John McClements is undoubtedly the people's restaurateur of west London. All three Francophile restaurants in the area have a strong local following and also benefit from other folk who struggle to find respectable French bistrot and brasserie food in their own neighbourhood. The quality of cooking is exceptionally high especially for an out of the centre restaurant. I find the menu a joy to read and eat, think rillette of rabbit and crab with truffle oil, parmentier of oxtail, mousseline of lobster, slow cooked pigs head with piquante sauce and pommes purée, calves sweetbreads, steak tartare, Anjou squab pigeon, tarte Tatin and passion fruit soufflé.

They also have the wonderful poulet en vessie on the menu (although it is advisable to call ahead and request), created by Fernand Point, the legendary chef at La Pyramide in Vienne. A whole chicken is placed inside a pig's bladder together with Champagne, morels and sometimes truffles. We would willingly travel across London to enjoy this special dish. ●

Right **Poulet en vessie as it comes out of the oven and about to be served. Cooking and piercing the pig's bladder of this very rare dish involves serious skill and can be dangerous if not handled carefully.**

Above
The Carluccio's deli counter.
Middle
Simple dishes like spaghetti and clams are why Carluccio's is successful.
Left
Atmospheric dining at The Depot.

Carluccio's 342–344 Chiswick High Road, W4
020 8995 8073 www.carluccios.com

The popular chain of Italian caffè and delicatessens has arrived on the high street opposite picturesque Turnham Green and enjoys a convivial all-day atmosphere. Inside, a huge black and white mural of an Italian feast dominates one of the walls. **O**

Covent Garden Fishmongers 37 Turnham Green Terrace, W4 1RG
020 8995 9273 www.coventgardenfishmongers.co.uk

This is the leading independent fishmonger in the area. They can source any kind of fish or seafood and will prepare and delivery locally. **O**

The Depot Tideway Yard, Mortlake High Street, Barnes, SW14 8SN
020 8878 9462 www.depotbrasserie.co.uk

Overall, the experience isn't worth writing home about, but when you live locally you don't always want special, just honest food and sensibly priced wine. Notwithstanding, if you find yourself in the area, I would still recommend a visit. The Depot has been around for over 20 years and that counts for something; the locals vote with their feet and the bar remains buoyant. The food might not reach the high standards achieved at nearby Riva or Sonny's, but the view along the Thames far outstrips its local competitors. Plus, as you are behind glass, it's available all year round.

A recent refurbishment and the installation of experienced chef Garry Knowles have lifted the standards. Menus are 'eclectic Mediterranean', or, dare I say-it, 'modern European'. From duck egg Florentine to moules mariniere to seared yellow fin tuna with soy and ginger dressing or a simple plate of charcuterie from the first-course selection. Main courses include char-grilled cote de boeuf, roast wood pigeon and pan-fried sea trout with crayfish. The desserts are all ideal for a simple midweek supper – think crème brûlée, Eton mess, baked alaska or a plate of cheese. **O**

Ma Cuisine Le Petit Bistrot 6 Whitton Road, Twickenham ,TW1 1BJ
020 8607 9849

Like its neighbouring soeur La Brasserie McClements – they also share a kitchen, but not the same dishes, we are particularly fond of the menu here. **O**

Mackens Bros 44 Turnham Green Terrace, Chiswick, W4 1QP
020 8994 2646

If you buy your fish from Covent Garden Fishmongers, the meat course must be procured after a lengthy discussion with butcher Rodney Macken. **O**

Mortimer and Bennett 33 Turnham Green Terrace, Chiswick, W4 1RG
020 8995 4145 www.mortimerandbennett.co.uk

This is a leading delicatessen and fine-food store with products from across the globe, including Lebanese honey, Turkish delight, Austrian honey, chocolate from Madagascar, plus Provençal tapenades and Italian salamis. They also have a useful range of store-cupboard essentials from gelatine to flour and polenta. The online hampers make good gifts for gourmets. **O**

Skye Gyngell

"

I love La Fromagerie because Patricia Michelson's continuous commitment to quality is such an inspiration and encouragement. I also enjoy Marylebone Farmers Market on a Sunday – a great opportunity to see what is seasonal and meet the growers, farmers and producers direct.

Chef, Petersham Nurseries

Petersham Nurseries Café and Teahouse, Off Petersham Road, Richmond, TW10 7AG 020 8605 3627 www.petershamnurseries.com

Take the day off for this one. Jump on the train at Waterloo Station and within 20 minutes you arrive at Richmond Station. Then walk to the arcadia that is Richmond Hill, progress down the hill towards the meandering Thames and cross Petersham meadow in full glare of the grazing cattle. Already it sounds perfect.

When you enter the Petersham Nurseries it continues to get better. Everything, and I mean everything, has been done with an enormous portion of style and taste. This is like no other garden centre – you shouldn't even use the term in any association with Petersham. (PP) Botanical experiences are not normally high on my list of things to do, but I certainly enjoyed the plants and flowers in the grounds and under the glasshouses. Alongside the horticultural qualities, you can also pick up a copy of *Saveur* magazine, some Balinese furniture, scented candles or Italian plant pots.

Assuming it's not inclement, the café is without doubt the best out of the centre al fresco experience in London, if not the entire country. Like the River Café and Blueprint Café, no irony is lost in the word café and they probably all share a similar food ethos. Yes, the environment is relatively informal, but it attracts serious well-heeled local patronage, plus a few foodies on a culinary pilgrimage.

The hand-written daily-changing menu is short, with five first and main courses to choose from, with the desserts listed on a small blackboard, which is brought to the table. Start with a rose bellini, then progress to the likes of pan-fried squid with white polenta, rocket and chilli or a salad of Umbrian lentils, beetroot and capra fresca. Main courses could include slow-cooked lamb, a saffron rabbit stew with cucumbers or corn-fed chicken with anchovy butter and green tomatoes. From what looks like a converted shed, Skye Gyngell selects the finest ingredients and crafts great tasting food that satisfies the senses.

You will need to book in advance and the café only opens from Wednesday to Sunday. ◉

Barnes / Chiswick / Richmond / Teddington / Twickenham

41

Opposite
Outside dining tables alongside the plants and flowers at Petersham Nurseries.
Above **River 'Old-Father' Thames.**
Right **Cattle on Petersham meadow.**
Below right
The view from Richmond Hill.

Strawberry Granita

By Skye Gyngell

Serves 4

For the Sugar Syrup

200 g (1 cup) caster sugar

475 ml (16 fl oz) water

3 punnets of English strawberries

juice of 1 lemon

Put the sugar and the water into a saucepan, and place it over a medium heat. Bring it to the boil, turn down the heat and then cook it for a couple of minutes to ensure that the sugar has dissolved. Remove the saucepan from the heat and allow it to cool completely.

Hull the strawberries, place them in a Magimix or other food processor and blend with the lemon juice until pureed and set aside.

When the syrup is completely cool, combine it with the strawberries. Pour the mixture into a freezerproof container, cover and leave it to chill. After 1 hour, remove it from the freezer and stir it up with a fork, dragging the mixture in from the sides. A granita's texture is not the same as a sorbet; it is meant to be icy and crunchy! Reseal the container, return it to the freezer and leave it to chill until it has set.

To serve, remove it from the freezer and scoop the granita into glasses.

Recipe featured in *A Year in My Kitchen* published by Quadrille, 2006

Above and right
After lunch stroll through the gardens and nurseries and buy a horticultural memento of lunch at Petersham Café.

Above right **Modest glassware, simple tableware and white napery combine with excellent Italian food at Riva.**

Riva 169 Church Road, Barnes, SW13 9HR
020 8748 0434

A small, probably fewer than 50 seats, romantic dining room with purposeful Italian food that attracts celebrities and big-wigs who have all heard about this discrete restaurant's excellent reputation. Andrea Riva, the owner, seems to effortlessly host the room, offering a few well-versed recommendations. While the room and table settings appear to be overtly simple, the food is world-class. ●

Sam's Brasserie Barley Mow Centre, Barley Mow Passage,
Chiswick, W4 4PH 020 8987 0555 www.samsbrasserie.co.uk

A true modern neighbourhood all-day brasserie, it is hard to fault this professionally run and comfortable Chiswick eatery. It seems that they have thought about everything and addressed each and every point with sincerity and generosity. Whether you are seeking a simple late-morning or early-afternoon croissant with a freshly squeezed juice or smoothie, or a serious foodie experience, Sam's Brasserie provides the perfect setting.

Located on a quaintly named narrow passage off the Chiswick High Road, the comfortable bar is the ideal destination for lazy Sundays with a Bloody Mary or kedgeree and poached-egg brunch. The central raised table is littered with newspapers, the music is suitably upbeat without being overpowering and the young staff are trained to be both welcoming and technically proficient. On a sunny day they open the large doors and windows to allow a lovely breeze to pass through the space. Having served as Rick Stein's general manager, Sam Harrison has stepped out on his own with this relaxed and informal venture – although Rick is an investor. As the omnipresent proprietor, Sam patrols the tables with a smile, confidence and pedigree that are rare in these parts.

Rufus Wickham, the chef, cooks from the heart and with much passion for the job. He has an enviable career record, having served in the kitchens of Pierre Koffman, Rowley Leigh, Philip Howard and several others. His menu is perfectly balanced and starts with simple brunch dishes such as American hotcakes with maple syrup or French toast, crispy bacon and caramelized apples, or organic yogurt and muesli.

As you progress through the menu you start to experience seasonal delights, perennial favourites and technically demanding dishes served to perfection. Rufus buys the best produce and knows how much or little to adjust the raw ingredients before they reach the plate.

The prices are reasonable, the wine list touches all of the key areas, they welcome children with open arms and have an interesting programme of events from jazz evenings to wine tastings. Oh, I do wish my home was next door. ⦿

Above **The main dining area features a window through to the kitchen.** Left **The bar at Sam's where they have wi-fi connectivity for the business-minded.**

Steamed Mussels and Clams, with Chorizo and Chickpeas

Serves 2

1 kg (2 lb) mussels
1 kg (2 lb) palourde clams
500 g (1 lb) good-quality cooking chorizo, peeled and cut into small nuggets
5 shallots, minced
2 garlic cloves, minced
1/2 bunch parsley, chopped
500 g (1 lb) cooked chickpeas
125 g (4 oz) butter
salt and freshly ground black pepper
200 ml (7 fl oz) dry white wine

Wash the mussels and clams under cold running water, and debeard the mussels. If you can't get palourde clams, cockles will do but they can be very gritty.

Put all the ingredients except the wine into a bowl. Heat up a large, heavy saucepan with a lid until it is very hot. Toss all of the contents of the bowl into the pan, quickly pour in wine, and jam on the lid. Shake the pot a few times during the cooking process. This will take a couple of minutes, (you can tell the mussels and clams are ready when they begin to open).

To serve, pour the mixture into bowls and serve with crusty bread.

Right **The brasserie menu is full of simple dishes and strong flavours, like Sam's terrine with onion marmalade.**

Left and right **The always interesting wall art at Sonny's.**

Sonny's 92–94 Church Road, Barnes, SW13 0DG
020 8748 0393

Sonny's has been a Barnes staple for more than 20 years, yet it still feels fresh, modern and relevant. The good range of dishes offered on the menu in the pleasant dining room, which has interesting artworks on the walls, consists of essential modern European dishes, from a first course plate of charcuterie to main courses of veal chop, venison or guinea fowl. This restaurant is ideal for late midweek suppers and Sunday lunch is also very popular. ○

La Trompette 5–7 Devonshire Road, Chiswick, W4 2EU
020 8747 1836 www.latrompette.co.uk

Owned by Nigel Platts-Martin, the master of high-quality neighbourhood restaurants, and Bruce Poole, the Chez Bruce maestro, it was certain that La Trompette was destined to be the leading high-quality restaurant in Chiswick. If Sam's Brasserie is my everyday all-purpose refectory then La Trompette is my once-per-month, celebration or bonus day special treat. In reality, however, the prices are not too over the top – with the possible exception of the coffee and cheese.

The menu is serious south and south-west France with plenty of prime cuts of the best meats and fish (think red mullet, halibut and sea bass), plus the gourmet treats of foie gras and confits, though the menu also includes a warm paysanne salad and steak and chips, plus crème brûlée. Cherry clafoutis, supposedly the staff-canteen dessert of France, is served with slightly more elegance and a pistachio ice cream. My favourite from the current menu is the daube of veal Provençale, with olive oil mash and sautéed baby artichokes.

James Bennington, the chef, was previously the sous chef at Chez Bruce and he clearly learnt about quality at the number-one restaurant in London. At La Trompette the presentation on the plate is loose and stylish with only a slight West End over-the-top accent. ○

Ray Neve

Despite having been the chef there in the early 90s, my favourite London restaurant has got to be 'Mosimann's'. You can always be assured of a warm welcome from Andrew, the manager, a fantastic ambience with impeccable service and food. The place is timeless and holds so many happy memories!

Chef and proprietor, The Wharf

Le Vacherin 76–77 South Parade, Chiswick, W4 5LF
020 8742 2121 www.levacherin.co.uk

A great local restaurant brought to you by experienced chef patron Malcolm John, this French bistrot has a hint of Parisian under-designed style. As the name suggests, the menu has a strong cheese inclination, especially during the Vacherin season of October to December. The Bastille Day menu is also worthy of a visit. ⊙

The Wharf 22 Manor Road, Teddington Lock, TW11 8BG
020 8977 6333

After a career leading the kitchens at the Dorchester Hotel, Mosimann's, The Bankers Club in Kuala Lumpur and Conrad Hotels, Ray Neve, the proprietor and chef at this converted riverside boathouse, has started his independent career with a local favourite. The ground floor serves an eclectic European menu with several Asian specials. Unlike other chefs who have tried to fuse these culinary styles, Ray doesn't confuse the two. You can either expect cod brandade, moules marinière, duck confit, ham hock terrine with crusty bread, *or* Thai-style beef, Chinese spiced pork belly and Morrocan lamb with couscous and charmoula. The menu also includes a few brunch specials like a Caesar salad or a meaty hamburger.

Upstairs the bar and event space has fine views overlooking the river Thames and Teddington Lock. It is the perfect venue for a riverside wedding or celebration. ⊙

Above right
French-style dining at Le Vacherin.

Battersea
Brixton
Clapham
Putney
Wandsworth

In London, the great 'north or south?' debate is all about the best place to live. If your first London home is located in north London, you rarely migrate to south London and vice versa. North London has better transportation with a total of 246 tube stations north of the river and only 30 south. The south has more cultural attractions and event destinations such as the Wimbledon Tennis Championship. The *Evening Standard*, London's midweek daily evening newspaper, or *Time Out* magazine will, from time to time, issue a more detailed comparison with fun advantages and shortcomings for each. For us, given the size of each area, the south and south-west are grossly underserved with decent restaurants. It isn't a question of quantity but quality. Both areas have hundreds, probably thousands, of poor restaurants and high street food-and-drink concepts. Conspicuous by their shortage, however, is the volume of high-quality food and drink destinations in both areas. The Northcote Road area has started to garner respect for its food retailers to help rectify the balance, and Chez Bruce is a lone example of a top-end neighbourhood restaurant.

The population of Battersea, Clapham, Wandsworth and Putney is often characterized by people wanting to live in Chelsea or Fulham. Jovially, Battersea is sometimes known as south Chelsea. Young families that cannot yet afford property on the north side of the river (not really considered as north London) arrive on the south side of the Thames and rapidly fall for the area's charms, especially around Clapham Common, before gradually losing the desire to move.

Balham Kitchen and Bar 15–19 Bedford Hill, SW12 9EX

020 8675 6900 www.balhamkitchen.com

Soho House comes to south-west London with a non-members all-day European brasserie, an impressive pewter cocktail bar and a large helping of metropolitan style. ○

Brady's 513 Old York Road, SW18 1TF

020 8877 9599

This small café and take-away fish and chip shop serves both grilled (tuna, lemon sole, skate) and battered (cod, haddock, plaice) fish with great chips and mushy peas. You can also get potted shrimps or half a pint of prawns, plus treacle tart and apple crumble for pudding. Brady's is only open evenings, Monday to Saturday. ○

Chez Bruce 2 Bellevue Road, SW17 7EG

020 8672 0114 www.chezbruce.co.uk

This is by far the best restaurant in the whole of south London and was recently voted the best restaurant in London, eclipsing Gordon Ramsay and The Ivy.

This address has form; before changing to Chez Bruce it was the infamous and celebrated Harvey's, the restaurant that acted as a platform for the great Marco Pierre White and his book *White Heat*. The book revealed a revolutionary kitchen and groundbreaking photography by Bob Carlos Clarke who for the first time made chefs sexy. Bruce Poole, an alumnus of the Bibendum heyday, has, together with Nigel Platts-Martin, owned the restaurant since 1995; therefore you can expect a copious wine list. Although it is principally a neighbourhood restaurant, it's virtually impossible to just call in; reservations must be made some time in advance and tables at sensible dinner times are usually unattainable. The food is classical French with a few Spanish and Italian excursions. You can go from foie gras and chicken liver parfait with toasted brioche to rabbit lasagne or gazpacho Andaluz with salted almonds, frozen olive oil and basil. The main courses always include Châteaubriand with hand-cut chips and béarnaise, but also get more complicated in the form of grilled halibut with roast scallops, braised gem lettuce, pea purée and Bayonne ham. Similarly, the desserts can go from crème brûlée to a dainty trio of small apple desserts. The cheese board is pretty good.

Inside, the ground-floor dining room introduces an informal and casual element. The slender chairs, simple tableware and close proximity of other tables help soften the overall experience. This is another restaurant with interesting wall art that has been well chosen. ○

Above right **The menu at Brady's.**

Gourmet Tour

Dinner in South London
When shopping for dinner in south and south-west London, call on the following:

Champagne and wine
- Either Philgas and Swiggot, 21 Northcote Road, Battersea SW11 1NG, 020 7924 4494 or The Grape Shop, 135 Northcote Road, SW11 6PX, 020 7924 3638.

Fresh flowers
- Pay an early morning visit to New Covent Garden Market for inspiration and fresh flowers for the table. Vauxhall, SW8 5NX, 020 7720 2211 www.cgma.gov.uk.

Equipment and gadgets
- To ensure you have the kitchen equipment to impress your guests, take a trip to La Cuisinière, 81–83 Northcote Road, SW11 6PJ, 020 7223 4487 www.la-cuisiniere.co.uk. Enthusiastic amateur chefs can find every possible kitchen gadget or utensil with an extensive range of pans from the nonstick variety to Le Creuset and knives from Laguiole to Global.

Bread
- Bread from Lighthouse Bakery (see page 56).

Pasta and antipasti
- Fresh pasta, salumi and olives from I Sapori di Stefano Cavallini (see page 54).

Fish and Meat
- Fish from Moxons, Westbury Parade, Shop E, Nightingale Lane, Clapham, SW4 9DH, 020 8675 2468 and meat from Moen and Sons, 24 The Pavement, Clapham Common, SW4 0JA, 020 7622 1624, or A. Dove and Sons, 71 Northcote Road, SW11 6PJ, 020 7223 5191.

Fresh fruit and vegetables
- Fresh vegetables and fruit can be purchased from the Northcote Road street market or Kelly's Organic at 46 Northcote Road, SW11 1NZ, 020 7207 3967.

Cheese
- Hamish Johnston, 48 Northcote Road, SW11 1PA, 020 7738 0741 www.hamishjohnston.com.

Cakes and pastries
- Macaron, 22 The Pavement, Clapham SW4 0HY, 020 7498 2636 for cakes and pastries.

Top and middle
New Covent Garden market at Nine Elms.
Below **An extensive sausage and bacon selection at Moen and Sons.**

The Greyhound 136 Battersea High Street, SW11 3JR
020 7978 7021 www.thegreyhoundatbattersea.co.uk

This is no ordinary gastropub conversion. Mark van der Goot, an ex-head sommelier at The Greenhouse Restaurant in Mayfair, and his wife have converted the old Greyhound in one of the less attractive areas of Battersea and created a dining and drinking destination worth travelling for. A small à la carte menu is operated at lunch and a prix fixe in the evening. The food comes from a chef who has spent time in the experimental kitchens of El Bulli and, more sensibly, Locanda Locatelli, creating his own style of food, which is making his name.

Flabbergasted – that must the response of most first-time visitors to The Greyhound as they are served with a copy of the almost 1,000-bin wine list. Despite this seriousness and the owner's past involvement with one of the best wine restaurants in the country, the opening page features an interesting introduction: *At the Greyhound it is our philosophy to make wine accessible and fun, 'at the end of the day it's only grape juice'.* ●

The Hive Honey Shop 93 Northcote Road, SW11 6PL
020 7924 6233 www.thehivehoneyshop.co.uk

Although tiny inside, this place is special, particularly at a time when the bee population is declining and conservation groups are alerting the public to the perils of collapsing bee numbers. A glass-fronted hive with 20,000 bees is in the store and the owner creates his own honey from several apiaries around London. But you can also find beekeeping equipment, protective clothing, beeswax, honeycombs, royal jelly and much more. ●

Above **Inside the narrow dining room at The Greyhound. Wine is everywhere you turn at this inspirational gastropub.**

Squid Ink Risotto with Sautéed Squid

by Marco Torri

Serves 6

olive oil
2 spoonfuls finely chopped white onion
480 g (15 oz) Carnaroli risotto rice
½ glass good dry white wine
18 sachets squid ink (available in most good fishmongers)
1½ l (2½ pints) good-quality fish stock, heated
6 medium-sized squid, thinly sliced
1 tablespoon finely chopped flat leaf parsley
180 g (6 oz) unsalted butter
8 spoonfuls grated Parmesan cheese
juice of ½ a lemon
salt and freshly ground pepper

Place a saucepan over a medium heat and add some olive oil. And the onions and let them sweat until they are translucent. Add the rice and continue stirring until the rice goes slightly opaque in colour.

Pour in the white wine and stir until such time as the wine is entirely evaporated. While continuously stirring, slowly add all of the squid ink, then start adding hot fish stock one ladle at a time and keep stirring until it is entirely absorbed by the rice. Season, then repeat this process five times. Then add the rest of the stock. This process should take around 17 minutes. After this time check the rice; it should be firm to the bite (al dente).

Take the risotto off the heat and let it rest for 1 minute. Now heat a frying pan over a medium heat and add a little olive oil. Add the squid and sauté it for no more than 30 seconds. Stir in the chopped parsley, remove the pan from the heat and leave it to one side.

To finish the risotto, stir in the butter, the Parmesan cheese and the fresh lemon juice. Spoon the risotto on to a flat plate to ensure it doesn't continue to cook. Garnish the risotto with the sautéed squid and serve.

53

I Sapori di Stefano Cavallini 146 Northcote Road, SW11 6RD
020 7228 2017

Before it was Nahm at the The Halkin Hotel in Belgravia, the space housed an equally successful eponymous restaurant by Stefano Cavallini, which was renowned as the most sophisticated Italian restaurant in London. Since 2000 the residents of south-west London have benefited from Stefano's flavours (sapori), skills and experience.

Fresh pasta is made on the site daily. Lasagne, insalata, pizza, crostini and other Italian essentials come directly from the kitchen. Many of the dishes adopt Stefano's 'La Cucina Essenziale' style that eschews heavy sauces, fats and cream and focuses on vegetable broth, olive oil and ingredients more suited to a lighter balanced diet. If it's synonymous with Italian cooking it can be found at I Sapori, from salumi and cheese to gelati and amaretto, plus wines, grappa and coffee. They even stock Italian eggs.

They also operate a thriving party-catering business that must be a godsend for the busy households close to Wandsworth Common. ○

Stefano Cavallini

"Hakkasan is one of my favourite London restaurants. Alan Yau is a true visionary, always searching for the best ingredients and creating amazing restaurants.

Owner, I Sapori di Stefano Cavallini

Above left
San Daniele ham.
Above right
Handmade fresh spinach and ricotta ravioli.
Opposite **Leek and courgette quiche.**

Lighthouse Bakery 64 Northcote Road, SW11 6QL
020 7228 4537 www.lighthousebakery.co.uk

Every neighbourhood needs an excellent bakery where local residents
can collect artisanal breads and pastries. The Lighthouse is a beacon of
quality in the area affectionately known as Nappy Valley. They bake
English, European and American breads and, given the high population
of children and young families in the area, you won't be surprised to
know that they sell a large number of gingerbread men and cookies. ◉

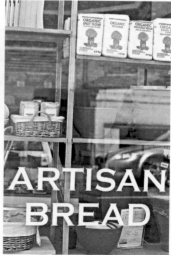

Above **All bread at
Lighthouse Bakery
is hand-moulded
to a traditional
method.**

Rebecca Mascarenhas

"

I have admired The River Café's evolution over the years from a staff canteen to the slick operation it is today. Simple food, excellent wines and friendly service. What more could you want?

Owner, The Pheonix

Top left
A beguiling outside dining terrace can be found under the parasols and behind the bamboo wall.
Above and right
Inside The Phoenix.

The Phoenix 162 Lower Richmond Road, SW15 1LY
020 8780 3131

Putney has an extensive range of branded restaurants and a few independent operations, but frankly we would ignore all of them and head to The Phoenix. This is a long-established true neighbourhood restaurant serving mainly Italian-orientated high-quality ingredients with a well-researched menu which includes an eighteenth-century wild mushroom and truffle lasagne recipe called Vincigrassi Maceratesi. The food overall offers good value for money, and is overseen by seasoned restaurateurs. The menu changes regularly and Sunday lunch is very popular. The setting is also pleasant. The outside seating, with its wall of bamboo shielding diners from the busy road, and the outside space heaters and atmospheric lighting all create a very agreeable space. This is the sister restaurant to Sonny's in Barnes and, as with all of Rebecca Mascarenhas's restaurants, the modern art is tastefully selected. •

Upstairs Bar and Restaurant 89b Acre Lane, entrance on
Branksome Road, SW2 5TN 020 7733 8855

It might be small, with only 25 covers in the dining room, but it is well
worth a visit. Three restaurant-business professionals have established
this small bar and restaurant on the upper floors of what must have been
a typical three-storey terrace house. With restricted financial resources
and help from friends, they have shaped one of the more stylish concepts
in the area. The limited resources have led to them making the tables
themselves, with the help of a local metalwork shop and a timber merchant.
The working fireplaces have been retained and the light fittings have been
precisely selected to illuminate the space with more than a hint of panache.

The menu is confidently small, with just three first-course, three
main-course and three dessert options, plus cheese and a few daily specials,
for example, beef tartare, grilled sardines and Provençal vegetables,
Charentais melon and spiced port, steamed lemon sole, white chocolate
and raspberry trifle and iced cherry parfait. ●

Vrinat
Romain

" I love The Square (see page 260);
they manage to perfectly balance
the atmosphere and food to create
an excellent restaurant, not too
formal and also not overly casual.
Excellent ingredients combine to
create dishes that are both rustic
and smart at the same time.

Co-director, Upstairs Bar
and Restaurant

Above **The bar at
Upstairs Bar and
Restaurant.**

Chocolate and Orange Marquis

by Daniel Budden

Serves 6

225 g (7½ oz) dark chocolate, not less than 70% cocoa solids
125 g (4 oz) unsalted butter
2 eggs, yolks and whites separated
285 g (9½ oz) icing sugar
zest of 1 orange
splash of Grand Marnier
pinch of white sugar

Slowly melt the chocolate and butter together in a plastic bowl over hot water, making sure that the water does not touch the base of the bowl.

In a separate bowl, whisk together the egg yolks and icing sugar until light and fluffy.

Add the orange zest and Grand Marnier to the melted chocolate and butter mix. Then combine this with icing sugar mixture.

In another bowl, add a pinch of sugar to the egg whites and whisk until soft peaks form then slowly fold into the chocolate mix.

Line the inside of a suitable container or small terrine dish with cling film then pour in the mix. Place in a refrigerator to set for at least 12 hours, ideally 24 hours.

To turn out the whole mix place the container/terrine in hot (not boiling) water for about 15 seconds and then turn upside down and use the cling film to help gently remove the marquis.

Serve slices with fresh raspberries, candied orange segments, a compote of kumquats, a shortbread biscuit or ice-cream – whatever you enjoy.

Above **Chocolate and orange marquis with raspberries.** Right **Asparagus and girolle risotto.**

Bayswater
Camden
Kings Cross
Maida Vale
Paddington
Regent's Park

This section deals with the ugly area of London. While the engineering success of Isambard Kingdom Brunel's Paddington Station and the gothic edifice created by George Gilbert Scott above St. Pancras Station are architectural marvels, the zone between these two points is weak in terms of the built environment. The office population is increasing thanks to various modern buildings along the Euston and Marylebone Roads, but it urgently needs an architectural marvel to draw favourable attention to the area. Proposals leaked to newspapers have indicated the council's speculative intention to convert the main thoroughfare, past Madame Tussaud's and the Baker Street intersection, into a grand boulevard akin to the Champs-Élysées, but although they have garnered attention, action has failed to follow. Please Mr Mayor, insist on a more creative solution and quicker action.

Notwithstanding, significant development is already underway at St. Pancras and Kings Cross. Manhattan Loft Corporation is converting the former Midland Hotel into a new hotel and apartment complex and the station is gearing up for the Eurostar's change of terminus.

Paddington is also undergoing a huge redevelopment. What were once the railway sidings and goods yards outside the station are now Paddington Central and Paddington Basin mixed-use residential, retail and office complexes. All have the great ambition to achieve the same success as Canary Wharf.

Early signs of new and exciting restaurant development in this area has started to appear; the future will surely hold more promise.

Chris Wood

My advice for dining out in London: go real. Seek out authentic ingredients cooked by expert chefs. Go for the restaurants that know exactly what they're about – real Chinese, real Italian, real French. Listen to other diners, check out real customer reviews and you'll find yourself at a restaurant with good service and a real chef cooking real ingredients who focuses on what they're really the best at. Check out real dim sum at the Royal China, real cooking at the Blueprint Café, real pasta at Locatelli and a real French bistro at Galvin. And a culinary tour of London's restaurant scene wouldn't be complete without a meal at Gordon Ramsay and Tom Aikens. The next rule is not to get too hung up on seasonality, provenance or macho 'carcass-eating'… leave that to the 'foodies'. London food rocks. Enjoy it!

Managing Director,
www.toptable.co.uk

Left **The essential blue and white façade for an Athenian grocer.**

Athenian Grocery 16a Moscow Road, Bayswater, W2 4BT

020 7229 6280

A typical Greek Cypriot corner shop that's been established for more than 40 years, full of tinned foods, feta cheese, olives, pickled chillies, wines and spirits. ○

Four Seasons 84 Queensway, W2 3RL

020 7229 4320

Go for the Cantonese roast duck in this Chinese restaurant, definitely *not* the service or a friendly welcome. ○

Garden Café Inner Circle Regent's Park, NW1 8LD

020 7935 5729

Listed on the left-hand side of the menu at the Garden Café is a summary of summer seasonal ingredients, most of which have been incorporated within the menu. Henry Harris of Racine is a consultant and the senior management team is committed to excellence on a

Left **Preparing Cantonese duck in the window at Four Seasons.**

budget. Being at the mercy of the British weather must present its own challenges and have a serious impact on the profit or loss over the summer months, not to mention the operating practices. On the day we visited to photograph the café it was an early June day, yet the conditions were monsoon-like. Fortunately they have a few indoor tables and chairs. On another occasion, it was almost 30 degrees centigrade and pleasantly busy with families, cyclists stopping for a refuel and small groups enjoying a light lunch in the sun. We saw two dowagers alighting from a chauffeur-driven Rolls-Royce to repair to the café and enjoy tea and strawberries.

You can choose from the full-service café area or the self-service counter and tables. Both offer great value for money. The surrounding flora are perfectly tended and seem more flowery than other Royal Parks in London. Designed in 1811 by John Nash, the park covers a staggering 410 acres and regularly hosts major events, including the summer opera evenings, when the Garden Café makes a perfect start to a cultural evening. ○

This page **Sixties retro and The Number Seven Chair by Arne Jacobsen – an ideal café chair – at the Garden Café.**

Rhubarb Crumble

Serves 4

For the Filling
a knob of unsalted butter
3-4 sticks of rhubarb, coarsely chopped
2 tablespoons soft brown sugar
1 tablespoon white wine

For the Topping
3 tablespoons plain flour
1½ tablespoons butter
3 tablespoons caster sugar
2 tablespoons porridge oats
2–3 tablespoons soft brown sugar, to sprinkle

1 small jug of warm custard, to serve

Preheat the oven to 220°C (425°F) Gas Mark 7. Gently melt the butter in a large saucepan and sauté the rhubarb over a medium heat for 5–6 minutes, to soften. Add the sugar and white wine and heat gently for a further 2 minutes.

To make the crumble topping, place the flour and butter into a bowl and work them together with your fingertips until the mixture resembles breadcrumbs. Fold in the sugar and porridge oats. Remove the rhubarb mixture from the heat and spoon into a small ovenproof dish. Sprinkle with the soft brown sugar and then scatter the crumble topping over the top.

Bake in the oven for 8-10 minutes, or until topping is golden brown. Remove from the oven, allow to rest for 2 minutes and serve with warm custard.

Gilgamesh
The Stables Market, Chalk Farm Road, NW1 8AH
020 7482 5757 www.gilgameshbar.com

Camden has witnessed great excesses, but never a restaurant on this scale and ambition. Recently opened with Pan-Asian specialist Ian Pengelley at the wok, this lavish, opulent mega-project has reportedly cost £12million to set up. Named after the legendary Babylonian king of Uruk, it has a choice of dining options from sushi at the bar to the Oriental Teahouse. The main restaurant menu offers pan-Asian salads, noodle dishes, dim sum, hot and sour dishes and much more. It is worth a visit if only to see the décor and the retractable roof on a summer's day. It would be a great place for a lively party at weekends. ●

Haché
24 Inverness Street, NW1 7HJ
020 7485 9100 www.hacheburgers.com

Haché is the brainchild of Susie and Berry Casey, with help from daughter Verity, who set up the restaurant, and son Christopher, who handles the PR. It's a proper restaurant that just happens to serve burgers. They managed to win the coveted Time Out Best Burger Bar award for 2005.

The Caseys serve the highest-quality ingredients with deliberately competitive prices without copying any established formula. The meat comes from Scottish Lowlands farm and is haché, and chicken and tuna are also served as steaks or with a salad. They offer a choice of about 15 burgers, including three vegetarian options. They also have good simple desserts, champagne, wine, beers, smoothies and much more. ●

Berry Casey

" My favourite 'eatery' is not actually a restaurant; it's a deli opposite where I live in Primrose Hill. Melrose and Morgan have a similar strategy as we have at Haché: use only the very best basic ingredients and life is much simpler.

Owner, Haché

Above **Hughes André Johnson, one of the Haché chefs.**
Right **The Haché steak Catalan burger.**

Organic produce has very much arrived and formed part of the nation's psyche when buying food and eating out. Some have said organic food is overpriced and others have questioned its green credentials when you consider that the ingredients may have flown halfway around the globe before they arrive on our plate. Among the chef fraternity the new buzzwords are 'locally produced' and 'sustainability'. How long will it be before supermarkets recognize the importance of these directions? If Oliver Rowe has much to do with it – not very long. His television programme *The Urban Chef* was based on the food procurement concept here.

The cooking is northern European, but the key difference is that Oliver aims to source all of his produce from within the London Orbital M25. So you can expect to see honey from Tower Hill served with Norbury blue cheese, seared Sevenoaks ox tongue, grilled Amersham pork, braised leg of Stansted duck and fish caught in the Thames. There are no air miles involved with any of these items and it is certainly a tough challenge when designing the daily menu.

Thomas Heatherwick, the Michelangelo of architecture and design, who has a studio virtually next door to this converted pub, designed the restaurant beautifully. The room is relatively small, with a tiny open kitchen that abuts the tables. Everything is painted an intriguing shade of green. Overhead the unusual light fittings are based on square frames with what look like chain mail 'swooshes' coming down from the ceiling. ◉

Right **The interior of Konstam at The Prince Albert is a major departure from the gastropub refurbishment paradigm.**

Right and below **Interesting postcards and eclectic printed images form the wall art at the tiny Konstam Café.**

Konstam Café 109 King's Cross Road, WC1X 9LR
020 7833 2615 www.konstam.co.uk

King's Cross has never been a smart area of London and has generally been accepted as having a seedy reputation. Things are changing; we don't ever think that gentrification will take hold, but the area will certainly benefit from the new station and the arrival of the Eurostar platforms. In the meantime, the area is rapidly gaining an edgy and arty reputation with the renowned Larry 'Go-Go' Gagosian opening a huge gallery nearby and the rapid appearance of loft living developments. In addition, the Victorian gothic St. Pancras Hotel is soon to open, together with an upmarket apartment complex. Already, the small and stylish Konstam Café has started to benefit from the influx. We've also heard a rumour that major restaurant groups are looking to open new eateries in the area. ◗

Mandarin Kitchen 14–16 Queensway, W2 3RX

020 7727 9012

Queensway is very much a tourist area and benefits from a good number of Oriental restaurants. This particular restaurant specializes in lobster prepared in six different styles. Mandarin Kitchen also serves other premium seafood, such as sea bass, turbot, red snapper and Dover sole, with the menu offering a different cooking method and accompanying sauces for each. ◐

Maroush 21 Edgware Road, W2 2EG

020 7723 0773 www.maroush.com

All over London you will find many Lebanese restaurants, including a few modern interpretations with over-the-top designs. However, the best place to really soak up the Lebanese atmosphere has got to be Edgware Road. The Maroush group operate a few businesses along the 'strip', starting with the original Maroush restaurant at 21 Edgware Road, Ranoush Juice at number 43 and the deli selling everything from fresh fish to sweets or coffee beans and other speciality items at numbers 45–49. ◐

Melrose and Morgan 42 Gloucester Avenue, NW1 8JD

020 7722 0011 www.melroseandmorgan.co.uk

This is a small and modern grocery store in harmony with the Primrose Hill set. The picnic foods are very tasty, and when selecting ingredients, the owners appear to focus on flavour, seasonality and traceability. They also cook for local dinner parties. Closed on Mondays. ◐

Above **Steamed fish at Mandarin Kitchen.**
Right above **Waiters at Mandarin Kitchen fold napkins in advance of the crowds later in the day.**
Right below **Revolving lazy Susan table centres on the dining tables at Mandarin Kitchen.**

Above top
Beautiful packaging from Raoul's.
Right, second from top and second from bottom **Delicious deli items and prepared foods.** Middle **A Parmigiano-Reggiano wheel being portioned.**

Raoul's Café 13 Clifton Road, W9 1SZ
020 7289 7313 www.raoulsgourmet.com
Raoul's café opens early and serves simple but good sandwiches, breakfast pastries, brunch or light lunches and great smoothies. The surrounding Little Venice and Maida Vale are affluent areas and a distinguished and loyal clientele all seem to be choosing Raoul's as a reliable and discreet location. ○

Raoul's Deli 8–10 Clifton Road, W9 1SS
020 7289 6649 www.raoulsgourmet.com
This is a great local deli opposite the café, with traiteur-style prepared foods. They offer different breads, including poilâne, charcuterie, organic fruit and vegetables and innumerable cheeses and continental ingredients. A selection of goodies from the Raoul's menu are on sale to takeaway, or sit and enjoy a coffee and a piece of cheesecake on the outside pavement seating. ○

Royal China 13 Queensway, W2 4QJ

020 7221 2535 www.royalchinagroup.co.uk

This is the original restaurant from the highly rated and probably the most reputable Chinese restaurant group in London. The two distinct black and gold dining rooms seat about 200 people, yet you can still expect queues for the strictly authentic dim sum at the weekend. Each of the London-based Royal China restaurants share the same à la carte menu, but they also have an extensive chef's menu unique to each of the restaurants. The dim sum chef only works 8 am to 5 pm, so don't go after this time if you want the real thing. However, the main menu is also very good. ◉

Trojka 101 Regent's Park Road, NW1 8UR

020 7483 3765 www.trojka.co.uk

Simple Eastern European food, with a buzzy evening scene and live musicians on Friday and Saturday. The extensive menu includes Russian, Ukrainian, Polish and Jewish dishes. ◉

Jason Li

I love Hunan, 51 Pimlico Road, it's an excellent Chinese restaurant, but don't ask for a menu as you will be treated like a tourist. Allow the owner to prepare a special menu for you and then trust what he brings.
Manager, Yakitoria

Opposite
A nigiri, sashimi and maki roll platter at Yakitoria.
Above **Salmon sashimi with keta caviar.**

Yakitoria 25 Sheldon Square, W2 6EY
020 3214 3000 www.yakitoria.co.uk

Paddington has for many years been a culinary desert, but this looks likely to change over the coming years. Yakitoria is one of the first serious restaurants to arrive at the new Sheldon Square development that has grown out of what were previously railway sidings at the rear of Paddington Station. This modern Japanese restaurant occupies a prime location along the Grand Union Canal. Unlike other new mixed office, retail and residential developments across London, the Paddington Central and Basin developments have been fully occupied since the buildings were completed. The scheme also benefits from interesting public sculpture, large open public spaces in the form of an amphitheatre and an innovative roll-up bridge across the canal by architect and designer Thomas Heatherwick. Little Venice and prosperous Maida Vale are just a short walk along the cleaned up and, at some points, quaint Grand Union Canal.

Inside Yakitoria the design direction is industrial chic. High ceilings, large windows and exposed ceiling-mounted ductwork accompany black and grey hues. The brightness is provided in the form of wasabi-green panels and similarly coloured ergonomically designed chairs. Shocking cerise-pink panels and light boxes sound extreme, but actually complement other aspects and give the feeling of a modern twenty-first-century space.

The basement bar is something completely different. It's a sexy destination bar with intimate corners, heavily upholstered furniture and leather armchairs. The lighting and music help create an ideal after-work urbane drinking spot. The sake list is one of the best in London with plentiful choice in each of the five key categories; junmai, daiginjo, ginjo, honjozo and nigori. The prize bottle has got to be the unimaginatively named Datsay YN23 – the annual production of this is limited to just 500 bottles.

Yakitoria's menu features modern new-wave style Japanese dishes and a few of the traditional specialities. Customers face the sushi bar, which is joined by a Kushi-Yaki station – a Japanese open grill where individual skewers of meat, fish and vegetables are cooked to the customer's specification and served with Japanese herbs and green-tea salts. The menu is not unlike a French brasserie in that it offers extensive choice at a wide range of prices. For example, there is ohitashi, the slowly dashi-poached spinach, which is served with bonito flakes or kaisen sunomono, which is octopus pickled in sweet vinegar. The kaiso salad includes seven different seaweeds served with a peanut sauce.

The sushi bar departs from the norm in offering aburi sushi, where the fish is exposed to a blowtorch before being dressed with a unique sweet dressing and garnish. They also offer a choice of rice for the classic nigiri-style sushi. Hot fried rolls, tempura seafood and soft-shell crab are the antidote to the healthy foods found elsewhere on the menu.

Of all the dishes on the menu at Yakitoria the most indulgent is the whole lobster for two. The restaurant keeps live two-pound lobsters, and when the dish is ordered the chef skilfully prepares a three-course lobster meal. This starts with a salad, then the rare lobster sashimi and finishes with a thin soup. ◐

Opposite **Aburi sushi – nigiri style fish and foie gras on rice then blow-torched.** Above **Kushi-Yaki (individual skewers of meat, fish and vegetables) served on a toban-yaki.** Right **Live 2lb lobsters.**

Lobster Sashimi, Soup and Salad

Serves 2

1 kg (2 lb) live Cornish lobster
100 g (3½ oz) total weight of green, red and white tosaga seaweed and wakame
baby spinach, for garnish
chives, chopped, for garnish
½ lemon
2–4 teaspoons shiso sauce (available from most Japanese food stores)
½ carrot
½ medium daikon white radish
½ cucumber
3 teaspoons wasabi
200 ml (7 fl oz) soy sauce
4 shiso leaves
500 ml (17 fl oz) shiro miso (miso soup diluted with bonito-flake flavoured dashi)
3–4 teaspoons sansho pepper seasoning (available from most Japanese food stores)
30 g (1 oz) shiitake mushrooms, chopped
3 spring onions, sliced
30 g (1 oz) enoki mushrooms

Note: The sashimi will be completely raw, it is important for food safety, and the taste, that the lobster is still live before the preparation starts. Equally, you should try to use lobsters that have recently been caught and not spent long periods in filter tanks.

Salad

The salad uses only the lightly cooked meat from the claws of the lobster. Put a large pot of generously salted water over a high heat and bring to the boil. Once the water has come to the boil, and whilst the lobster is still alive, remove the claws at the base. Place them in the boiling water for 5–7 minutes until cooked. Then remove them and place them in iced water for a moment or two only. Lift them out of the water and, using a knife and kitchen scissors, remove the shell without damaging the internal flesh. Place the green, red and white tosaga seaweeds, together with the wakame and the baby spinach, on a plate and garnish with chopped chives. Set the lobster, which should still be slightly warm, on the same plate and add a few very thin slices of lemon. To serve, pour some of the shiso sauce into a small dish for dipping the lobster into, or add a few slices of lemon.

Sashimi

Take the live lobster and carefully remove the head from the body. Take the body of the lobster and cut away the small and large legs, and then remove the thin, almost translucent, cartilage that lines the underbelly. Once the internal flesh is completely exposed, take a spoon and carefully remove it in one piece. Do not discard the shell. Rinse the meat under cold running water and pat dry on kitchen paper. Set aside in the refrigerator.

Put a pot of water over a high heat and bring to the boil. Place the lobster shell in the boiling water. Once the colour changes remove the shell and place under cold running water to chill it. Once it has chilled, line it with the grated daikon to make a presentation platter for some of the sashimi. Dress the serving plate with a fine julienne of carrot, daikon and cucumber and serve with wasabi and a small pot of soy sauce.

Remove the lobster flesh from the refrigerator and slice the flesh in to thin pieces using a sashimi knife. Place a slice of lobster meat on to the shell, then a slice of lemon, followed by a shiso leaf. Repeat until all the lobster meat is used up.

Soup

When the lobster head is removed from the main body the brain is immediately identifiable and should be removed and discarded. Then crack and break the remaining legs, claw shell, head and all remaining parts of the lobster. Cover and place in the refrigerator.

Place the shiro miso into a saucepan over a high heat and bring it to the boil. Once it is boiling, drop in the lobster shell pieces and allow them to simmer for 15–20 minutes. (Ordinary miso will be too strong and possibly dominate the flavour of the soup. However, you can use miso that has been diluted with dashi.)

Whilst the soup is simmering, add the sansho pepper seasoning. Three or four shakes from the filter-top container, similar to how you would add salt and pepper to a normal soup, will do the trick. Skim off any brown scum that forms. Unlike conventional soups, you should repeat the seasoning process every 2–3 minutes. The process of seasoning and skimming should take place at least four times. Now add the shiitake mushrooms and spring onions and simmer.

While the soup is simmering, place a flameproof ceramic serving dish with a lid in a warm oven. When the soup is ready, pour it into the hot ceramic serving dish. Then add the enoki mushrooms, replace the lid and put the dish over a medium heat for 1 minute for a final simmer. Take the ceramic dish to the table and remove the lid in front of your guests.

Belgravia Knightsbridge Pimlico

With Her Majesty the Queen as the area's most famous resident, you can only imagine that the hotels and restaurants in the area are entirely five star standard. Embassies, high commissions, consulates and official residences of those connected with the Court of St. James's are also prominent. The Duke of Westminster owns much of the land and His Grace's company, Grosvenor, protects the heritage of the area involving everything from the colour of paint adorning the building façades to controlling who and who cannot take a lease. With the arrival in London of the billionaires, Russian oligarchs and plutocrats, the residents have started to change. The headquarters of charities and industrial institutions are leaving the area and builders, engaged to craft marble masterpieces with sumptuous interior designs, quickly occupy the vacant premises on behalf of their super-rich clients.

The largest of the squares are Belgrave and Eaton, which were built by the revolutionary architect and builder Thomas Cubitt (1788–1855). Cubitt was commissioned in 1824 to build most of the late Georgian and Regency buildings in the area and it was he who reformed the building trades. A very good pub and dining room at 44 Elizabeth Street is named in his honour.

The area is also known for its luxury shopping, with Sloane Street the home to many of the world's top fashion labels and jewellery shops. While the expensive restaurants are in bountiful supply, it is the more modest Racine with its value-for-money, simple French bistro menu and consistently excellent service, that is favoured by the important people.

As an interesting aside, Knightsbridge has the most (six) consecutive consonants of any word in the English language!

Derek Quelch

"I love Galvin Bistrot de Luxe on Baker Street because they consistently serve good food at sensible prices. It's always a pleasant atmosphere and an enjoyable evening out.

Head Chef, The Goring Hotel

Amaya Halkin Arcade, Motcomb Street, SW1X 8JT
020 7823 1166 www.realindianfood.com

The reputation of Indian food and restaurants has seen a near vertical trajectory over recent years, and with the opening in 2004 of Amaya it is set to reach new heights. Unlike other modern high-profile Indian restaurants, the focus at Amaya is on grilled ingredients, not curries or spiced ingredients served in heavy sauces. The open kitchen focuses on three core Indian cooking methods: tandoor – cooking food in a really hot clay oven; sigiri – cooking over a coal flame; and tawa – cooking or griddling food on a hot, thick, iron plate.The food is designed to be eaten with your hands, if you feel comfortable doing so, and shared. The menu includes plenty of fish and shellfish, as well as game in season.

The Goring Hotel and Dining Room Beeston Place, Grosvenor Gardens, SW1 OJW 020 7396 9000 www.goringhotel.co.uk

Four generations of the Goring family have overseen the most British hotel in the capital. With Her Majesty The Queen as your next-door neighbour it would be traitorous to be anything but quintessentially British. The hotel is immaculately managed with every detail addressed with gentlemanly aplomb. This extends to the recently refurbished dining room where Her Majesty's cousin, David Linley, was engaged as the designer. The dining room is now light and airy, with heavy comfortable armchairs, large tables and acres of space between the tables, yet still retains a pleasant atmosphere. Swarovski Crystal chandeliers add a hint of effeminate style. This is a restaurant for grownups, celebrations and important luncheons.

Derek Quelch, who has previously garnered experience at the Savoy and Claridge's, oversees the kitchens. His menus are sizeable, but not overwhelming, with virtually all of the ingredients procured from the most impeccable sources in the British Isles. Despite the overall direction being British, a few nods in recognition of the French culinary lineage appear.

Between September and November, you can be assured of a fine selection of the best game birds available all with traditional garniture.

Above **The interior details and dining area at Amaya.**

Traditional Roast Grouse

Serves 4

For the Grouse

4 plump grouse (with hearts and livers inside)
4 rashers of green streaky bacon
kitchen string
olive oil
salt and freshly ground black pepper
50 g (2 oz) unsalted butter
4 small bunches of watercress (optional)

For the Sauce

50 ml (2 fl oz) red wine
100 ml (3 1/2 fl oz) grouse jus

For the Liver Parfait

100 g (3 1/2 oz) soft unsalted butter
4 heart-shaped pieces of bread, for croutons
30 g (1 1/4 oz) sliced shallots
1 small sprig of thyme
25 ml (1 fl oz) Madeira
oil
hearts and livers from the 4 grouse,
cleaned and any veins removed
30 g (1 1/4 oz) chicken livers, cleaned
and any veins removed
30 g (1 1/4 oz) duck foie gras, cleaned
and any veins removed
salt and freshly ground black pepper

For the Bread Sauce

2 knobs of unsalted butter
1/2 onion, roughly chopped
1/2 bay leaf
200 ml (7 fl oz) milk
100–150 g (3 1/2–5 oz) white breadcrumbs
salt and freshly ground black pepper
small knob of unsalted butter to finish

Fried Breadcrumbs

100 g (3 1/2 oz) unsalted butter
150 g (5 oz) fresh dried breadcrumbs
salt and freshly ground black pepper
25 g (1 oz) chopped parsley
10 g (1/2 oz) chopped rosemary
10 g (1/2 oz) chopped thyme

Remove the insides from the grouse. Set the hearts and livers into a bowl, cover them with cling film and place them in the refrigerator. Discard the rest of the insides. Remove any hairs that remain on the birds and then remove the feet at the first joint and discard them. Cut the rashers of streaky bacon in half across the bacon. (If they are a bit thick you may need to just lightly bat them out in between two pieces of cling film.) Place two pieces of bacon along the breast of each grouse and tie them in place with string.

Preheat the oven to 170°C (340°F) Gas Mark 4. Heat a roomy thick-bottomed pan with a little oil. Season the grouse inside and out with salt and pepper and place the grouse into the pan. Add the butter to the pan and place it into the oven for approximately 5–7 minutes. Baste the bird regularly with the cooking butter to prevent the birds from drying out.

Take the pan out of the oven and turn the bird onto the other side and repeat the process. Then turn the birds onto their backs and place back into the oven for 3–4 minutes. Take the birds out of the oven and cut the strings off of it. Remove the bacon from the birds but put it back in to the pan to go crispy.

Baste the breasts with the cooking butter and place the pan back in the oven for 3–8 minutes, depending on how rare you prefer your meat.

When they have finished cooking, remove the birds and bacon from the pan and place them on a wire rack to rest in a warm place. If the cooking butter is not too dark, pass it through a sieve and keep it on the side.

Now place the pan over a medium heat, add the red wine and deglaze the pan. Reduce the wine to a sauce consistency. Add the grouse to this jus and allow it to cook in it gently for 10 minutes.

Lift the birds out of the jus and keep warm. Pass the liquid through a sieve. Adjust the seasoning to taste and set the jus aside to keep warm.

Liver Parfait

This can be made in advance.

In 25 g (1 oz) of the butter, cook the heart-shaped croutons until they are golden brown. Remove them from the pan and allow them to cool.

Melt another 25 g (1 oz) of the butter in a pan over a medium heat. Add the shallots and thyme and let them sweat until they are cooked through. Add the Madeira and reduce to a sauce consistency.

Place the oil in another frying pan over a high heat until it is hot. Season the livers, hearts and foie gras and then quickly fry the livers and hearts. Do not cook them right through but keep them very pink. Remove them from the pan and set them aside. In the same pan quickly fry the foie gras. Place the shallots, livers, hearts and foie gras into a blender while they are still hot and purée them. Pass the purée through a sieve and allow it to cool. Once it has cooled, mix the purée with the remaining 50 g (2 oz) of soft butter. Put the parfait to one side until needed.

Bread sauce

This can be made in advance

Place the knob of butter in to a small saucepan over a medium heat. Add the onion and bay leaf and let them sweat until translucent. Add the milk and warm it through until you can taste the onion in it. Pass the milk through a sieve and discard the onions.

Re-boil the milk and gradually add enough breadcrumbs until the sauce thickens as it cooks. If it becomes too thick, add a little more milk. Season it with salt and freshly ground black pepper then remove from the heat. Place a knob of butter on to the top to stop the sauce forming a skin.

Fried Breadcrumbs

This can be prepared in advance.

In a thick-bottomed pan, heat the butter over a medium heat until it becomes frothy. Add the breadcrumbs, salt and pepper and fry them, stirring continuously, until they are golden brown. (You can add more butter if necessary.) Pour off any excess butter and allow the breadcrumbs to cool. Combine the herbs and mix them in to the breadcrumbs.

To serve

Reheat the grouse and cooking butter. Place each grouse on a plate with a piece of bacon on the breast. Drizzle a little of the cooking butter over the breast. Place some liver parfait on each of the heart-shaped croutons and serve one next to each grouse. Reheat the bread sauce with a little milk and place it in a sauceboat. Reheat the grouse jus and place it in another sauceboat. Place the breadcrumbs into a serving dish. You can stuff some watercress into the cavity of each grouse if you wish. This dish is nice served with some sautéed potatoes and braised red cabbage.

77

Right **Goring
Hotel Head Chef
Derek Quelch,
carving meat in
the dining room.**

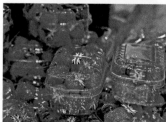

Harrods 87–135 Brompton Road, SW1X 7XL

020 7730 1234 www.harrods.com

Over recent years the Food Halls seem to have lost some of their grandeur and opulence, but you cannot deny the scale and range available here. Every possible food is on offer at the endless counters, from meat, fish and Oriental foods to cheese, coffee and caviar. Harrods have 28 restaurants from the flagship Georgian Restaurant and Mo's American diner to sushi bars, a pizzeria, an oyster bar and tapas restaurants, to mention just a few. (PP) In the 1980s, when I first arrived in London, I would visit Harrods as often as possible to learn more about food and marvel at the displays. The Food Halls are still sumptuous and offer great choice and the hampers will be forever popular at Christmas.

Across the Brompton Road Harrods have opened an upmarket convenience store called Harrods102. The opening hours are longer and later, the music is louder and younger and the range is more focused on the time-pressed occupants of the nearby luxury apartments. ◉

Above left
The legendary Harrods food hall. Right **More modern surroundings at Harrods 102.**

Harvey Nichols Vth Floor 109–125 Knightsbridge, SW1X 7RJ
020 7235 5250 www.harveynichols.com

Harvey Nicks, as it is often referred to, is renowned for its ground-floor window displays and for once being Princess Diana's favourite shopping destination. It is also considered to be a more fashionable and younger person's version of Harrods, just a short walk along Brompton Road. When the Vth Floor first opened, it transformed the public's view, not only of dining in a store, but of food retail areas within large department stores. Expectations were raised; new modern interiors were merged with the deli, butchers, fishmongers, bakery and cheese counter and all became wrapped in a busy café, along with an excellent restaurant. An entire floor was devoted to food and drink. The packaging, especially the own-label products, was modern and different from most other food halls' or department-store 'catering'. Before this point, restaurants in stores usually involved an appalling hot buffet, soggy foods and tray service.

Today, the format is still similar and a Yo! Sushi conveyor-belt sushi operation has been installed. The café, with its glass ceiling and rooftop terrace, is still an enviable place for a light lunch or afternoon break.

The adjoining restaurant interior was until recently a very civilized setting with comfortable armchairs and a semi-open kitchen. However, the design was given a radical overhaul and the new incarnation has got to be one of the most absurd restaurant interiors in London. The walls and ceiling are covered in light fittings that change colour according to the time of day, the weather and other factors. It is quite off-putting and must have cost an absolute fortune. (PP) I haven't met anybody who likes it. However, I don't know too many Ab Fab girls! ((TC) I do, and they don't like it either!) We recently heard rumours that they no longer use the light system.

Despite the bizarre interior, the food is still high in quality and the wine policy allows diners to take advantage of the adjoining wine shop. We suggest you request a window table so that you can focus on the great view towards the impressive architecture of the Mandarin Oriental Hotel across the road and, to the amusement of some, the adjacent bar full of 'ladies of the night'. ◉

Far right **The Champagne trolley in the restaurant at Harvey Nichols Vth Floor.**
Left **Harvey Nichols food halls and the extensive range of grocery items with stylish packaging.**

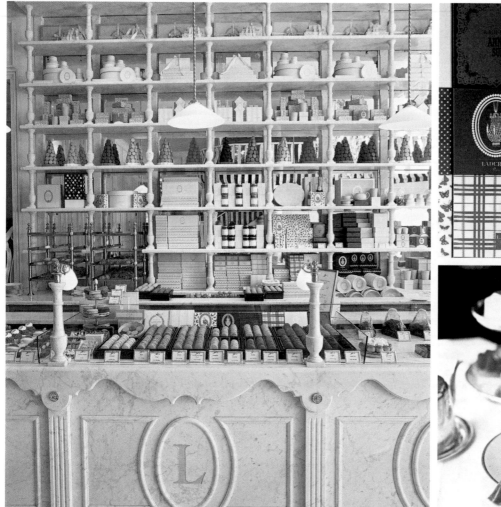

Ladurée at Harrods 87–135 Brompton Road, SW1X 7XL
020 3155 0111 www.laduree.fr

Much hype surrounded the arrival in London of this Parisian institution. They serve an extensive range of French pastries from éclairs to Saint Honoré cakes to mille-feuilles, but it is the macaroons that gain most attention. These small pastry shells – made from eggs, sugar and almonds, plus a special Ladurée ingredient, then glued together with ganache-like fillings of various flavours – are particularly good. Ideal in the afternoon with a cup of tea or after dinner as an alternative to a full dessert in the form of large petits fours, they are delicious and never fail to melt in the mouth. The very chic packaging makes them a perfect gift. ○

Above **An impressive display of patisserie, chocolates and macaroons.**
Right top **The perfect gift package for your patisserie.**
Right **Afternoon tea at Ladurée.**

Gary Rhodes

" My favourite corner shop – that would have to be Harrods. This wonderful establishment holds the finest food halls in London, feeding you with great flavours which always result in a heavier carrier bag!
Chef and Restaurateur

Left **Inside
Mr Chow.**
Right middle
**A David Hockney
designed matchbox
at Mr Chow.**

Mr Chow 151 Knightsbridge, SW1X 7PA

020 7589 7347 www.mrchow.com

When it opened in 1968, the design details and art became renowned. It
was possibly the first seriously designer restaurant. The food is authentic
Beijing, but some say more modern Chinese restaurants now eclipse it.
We still think Mr Chow is worth a visit. It is just one of those places that
you must experience, despite the poor reputation that has started to surface.
They also have other celebrity outposts in New York and Los Angeles. ●

Salad of Lemongrass with Prawns, Chicken, Squid and Toasted Coconut

by David Thompson

Serves 1

For the Dressing

1 coriander root
a good pinch of salt
1/2 large red chilli, de-seeded
2 tablespoons lime juice
1/2 tablespoon white sugar– to taste
1/2 tablespoon fish sauce – to taste

50 g (2 oz) chicken breast
several small prawns (about 30 g/1 oz each), shelled and deveined
6 small pieces squid, cleaned and scored
2–3 pieces (about 2 tablespoons finely sliced lemongrass, cleaned
1 large red shallot, sliced medium fine
1 heaped teaspoon toasted small Thai peanuts
1 heaped teaspoon toasted shredded coconut
a few picked coriander leaves and mint leaves
a few torn betel leaves (optional)
3–4 dried small red chillies, deseeded and deep fried

Make the dressing by pounding the coriander root in a pestle and mortar with the salt and chillies until they become a fine paste. Add the other dressing ingredients. It should not be too strong, otherwise it will overwhelm the ingredients – but nor should it be too weak: it should taste salty, sour and then equally hot and sweet.

Place a pot of salted water to boil. Add the chicken, turn down the heat, and simmer for several minutes until completely cooked. Remove and allow to cool before shredding.

Return the water to the boil and blanch the prawns and squid for a moment until they begin to change colour. Drain.

Combine the chicken, prawns and squid with the remaining ingredients, dress well then serve.

Nahm The Halkin Hotel, Halkin Street, SW1X 7DJ
020 7333 1234 www.halkin.co.uk

Situated beyond the marble hall of this discreet and sophisticated Milanese-style hotel is Nahm Restaurant by David Thompson. It's a relatively small area and a very cool space, but the cooking is certainly fiery. David Thompson has modernized and mastered the flavours of royal Thai cooking to create a Michelin-starred restaurant of some note. Forget the phad Thai noodle dishes that have appeared elsewhere in London; Nahm operates on a far superior level. First courses could include hot and sour soup with wild seabass or a salad of grilled squid and Middle White pork with chilli jam, and the main courses offer Chiang Mai pork curry with shredded ginger, pickled garlic and shallots or stir-fried venison with chilli paste, onions and cumin. ◐

Pétrus The Berkeley Hotel, Wilton Place, SW1X 7RL
020 7235 1200 www.the-berkeley.co.uk

The Berkeley was one of the first five-star hotels to outsource its restaurants, starting with Vong, then Pierre Koffman with La Tante Claire. It now houses Pétrus by Marcus Wareing and Boxwood Café.

Marcus Wareing, the chef patron at Pétrus, is Gordon Ramsay's high-profile protégé and his food is clamouring to find its own identity. The dishes at Pétrus are favoured by wealthy individuals and City bankers who like theatrical elements and numerous ingredients on their plate. If you want to eat carpaccio of gerkin, this is the place to do so! The love-it-or-hate-it rich interior is by David Collins, once the restaurant designer du jour. ◐

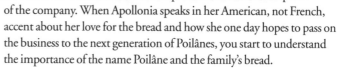

Poilâne 46 Elizabeth Street, SW1W 9PA
020 7808 4910 www.poilane.fr

Pierre, the first generation of Poilâne bakers, opened, in 1932, a small bakery in St Germain des Prés in Paris. Today 22-year-old Apollonia oversees the international multi-million pound business. It was always Appollonia's intention to work in the family firm and at an early age she underwent a lengthy apprenticeship alongside her father, Lionel. Following his untimely death, Apollonia was propelled to the role of CEO while also studying business in Boston.

Every day Apollonia calls or visits the head production manager to check on the quality of the bread, how the local climate has affected the loaves, the quality of the flour and much more. Regular trips to Europe and a demanding schedule also mean that she can maintain regular contact with the staff. This is certainly not an honorary position; she is more of an involved and caring colleague who is passionate about both the craftsmanship and the commercial aspects

Left **Buying croissants and bread at Poilâne.** Right **The trademark Poilâne sourdough loaf.**

of the company. When Apollonia speaks in her American, not French, accent about her love for the bread and how she one day hopes to pass on the business to the next generation of Poilânes, you start to understand the importance of the name Poilâne and the family's bread.

Apparently, 3% of all the bread consumed in Paris today is Poilâne, with the loaves exported daily to Milan, Brussels, Berlin, Tokyo and to over 3,000 private clients in America. The bakery in Elizabeth Street has a loyal and distinguished type of customer for the now legendary sourdough. Unlike many other bakers, they keep their product range limited. Yet this limited selection is one of the reasons that Poilâne is special. You can buy a small selection of other breads and *Punitons* (punishments) butter shortbread sables, but it is the large four-pound sourdough with the trademark 'P' in flour on the top of the loaf that is most certainly the real reason for such distinguished patronage.

When talking with Apollonia recently, she expressed her joy that the business now has a foothold in London. She told me how she enjoys the multi-cultural and diverse London restaurant scene more than that in any other city, although she is sad about the congestion charge!

You can buy Poilâne bread at many fine delicatessens across London and countless restaurants include the sourdough in its breadbasket, but visiting the shop is definitely a worthwhile experience. If you ask, they will also provide a quick tour of the bakery and office where you can see a bread chandelier made by Salvador Dalí, following his great friendship with Lionel. ⊙

Calves' Brains with Brown Butter and Capers

by Henry Harris © copyright 2006
Serves 2 as a starter

It is often much easier to find lambs' brains than calves' brains in a good halal butcher. If you use lambs' brains allow one set per person. Don't bother trying to remove the membrane. It is a futile task as they are so delicate.

1 set of very fresh calves' brains
splash of red wine vinegar
salt and freshly ground black pepper
2 tablespoons plain flour
3 tablespoons clarified butter or vegetable oil
100 g (3½ oz) unsalted butter
1 teaspoon capers
30 ml (1 fl oz) red wine vinegar
1 tablespoon freshly chopped parsley.

Take the fresh calves' brains and soak them in cold salted water for 1 hour. Separate the two main lobes from the top of the spinal column piece. In a bowl of fresh water gently work at each lobe to lift off the membrane that nestles among the folds of the lobes. This is slow and fiddly work for the first-timer!

Rinse the brains, place them in a saucepan of cold water and add a splash of vinegar and a seasoning of salt. Bring to the boil and simmer gently for 10 minutes. Remove from the heat and leave to cool in the poaching liquid.

Remove each piece from the liquid and cut it in half. Season the flour with salt and pepper and lightly dust the brains with this seasoned mixture.

Heat the clarified butter in a frying pan and carefully slip in the brains. Fry over a medium heat for about 10 minutes or until the brains have a healthy golden crust. Tip out the clarified butter and add the unsalted butter. Let it melt and foam. Let the butter cook to a good nut-brown colour, then add the capers swiftly followed by the vinegar. (Stand back as the vinegar hisses and splutters.) Then throw in the parsley. Lift the brains from the pan and arrange them on two plates. Spoon the butter mixture over the top and serve immediately.

Right **Cooking the calves' brains.** Top right **The finished dish.**

Racine 239 Brompton Road, SW3 2EP
020 7584 4477

Racine is at the pinnacle of French provincial cooking and service in London.

Henry Harris is the chef and Eric Garnier the front-of-house maestro. Together they have created and maintain one of the most enjoyable restaurants in London. Both have an excellent CV, with Henry having worked as sous chef to Simon Hopkinson at Bibendum in the early days (Henry's brother is now the head chef). Then Henry held the head-chef job at Harvey Nichols Vth Floor before opening Hush. Eric was the opening and, probably, the best-ever general manager Quaglino's had (not least because it was the legendary restaurant of the early 1990s). He then became managing director of Bank restaurants before opening a string of fish restaurants. Their combined personal talents, style and experience have wrought a close-to-perfect restaurant.

Some have described the food as a mature Englishman's nostalgic view of the French brasserie. We personally don't like to judge or label in this manner, but we will just say that the food tastes great, the presentation on the plate is attractive without the aid of unnecessary adornment, the familiar menu is the perfect size and balance, the prices are reasonable despite exceptional demand and the service is friendly and efficient. Most tables also benefit from the charm effused by Eric as he patrols the room.

The dining room seats about 75 with tables close together yet never too much so, the linen is pristinely white and pressed, the staff are sharply attired in black and whites and the ambience is always convivial.

Meals start with French baguette and Echiré butter, then you can expect seasonal salade Lyonnaise, Jésus de Lyon with cornichons, lapin à la moutarde, celeriac remoulade, pâté de foie de volaille, calves' kidneys, roast skate with braised endive, petit pot au chocolat and Mont Blanc. All are dishes that we know well and love when they are executed with such merit. Tête de veau à la sauce ravigotte – a rarity in London – can also be found on the menu. It's what we call a *real* restaurant and you certainly never leave feeling at all hungry. ○

Filet au Poivre

by Henry Harris © copyright 2005

Serves 2

2 fillet steaks weighing about 230–250 g (7½–8 oz) each
3 teaspoons cracked pepper
salt
2 tablespoons clarified butter
50–75 g (2–3 oz) butter
50 ml (2 fl oz) Cognac
100 ml (3½ fl oz) veal stock

Preheat the oven to 100°C (210°F), Gas Mark ¼. Take the two fillet steaks and place them on a dish. Place the pepper on to one cut side of each steak only and press it into the meat with the heel of your hand to ensure it is well attached. Then season the steaks with salt and set them aside.

Heat the clarified butter in a frying pan over a high heat and add the steaks pepper-side down. Cook them briskly for 3–5 minutes or until that first side is crusted and brown. Then turn over the meat and cook for 1 minute. Tip out the clarified butter from the pan and slip in half of the regular butter. Turn down the heat to a medium temperature and let the butter foam and cook to a gentle hazelnut colour. Baste the meat with the butter regularly. If the butter appears in danger of turning too dark then just lower the heat. Continue this process for 3–4 minutes. Add the Cognac and cook off the alcohol. Then add the stock, bring it to the boil and add the remaining butter. Reduce the liquid to a syrupy consistency.

Remove the steaks from the pan and transfer them on to a dish to rest in the oven for 8 minutes. Move the steaks to warm plates and add the juices that seeped out of the meat and into the pan. Adjust the seasoning, spoon the sauce over the steaks and serve immediately.

Right **Eric Garnier and Henry Harris.**

Alexis Gauthier

"

Sillfield Farm shop in Borough Market is probably the best place in London for sausages, pigs belly, plus their rolled bacon which is cured and glazed with maple syrup – it is quite exceptional.

Head Chef, Roussillon

Right Junior gastronomes at Roussillon.
Above A throw back to nouvelle cuisine-style presentation – not our idea of attractive presentation, but many people favour this style.

Rippon Cheese Stores 26 Upper Tachbrook Street, Pimlico, SW1V 1SW (020 7931 0628) www.ripponcheese.com
Although less atmospheric than other cheese shops in London, Rippon Cheese Stores has excellent breadth of range that serves both commercial customers and the public. While the retail space may be simply fitted out with basic shelving, Philip Rippon, Compagnon du Guide des Fromagers, has over 500 cheeses. Goat's, cow's and sheep's cheeses from all over Europe are stocked. They sell about 40 per cent British, 40 per cent French and the remainder comes from Spain, Greece and Italy, along with a few breakfast-type cheeses from Scandinavia. ⦿

Roussillon 16 St Barnabas Street, SW1W 8PE
020 7730 5550 www.roussillon.co.uk
Chef patron Alexis Gauthier has a hugely impressive CV with stints at the Hotel Negresco in Nice and the Restaurant Louis XV Alain Ducasse inside the Hôtel de Paris in Monte Carlo, probably the most glamorous restaurant in the world. His menus at Roussillon are classic French but use the best English ingredients which always results in a winning combination. The menu is conveniently split into three key headings; The Garden; The Sea and River; and The Land. If you visit in May during the Chelsea Flower Show, Alexis creates a special menu incorporating petals and floral essences. Roussillon has also recently introduced a seven-course menu for mini gastronomes under the age of 11. ⦿

Zafferano 15 Lowndes Street, SW1X 9EY

020 7235 5800 www.zafferanorestaurant.com

We have mentioned in other sections of this book that the River Café and Locanda Locatelli are our two top Italian restaurants in London. Zafferano is definitely number three. For others, it is certainly number one.

A combination of professional – but never overbearing – service from a mainly Italian team, and the mentality of a small unassuming restaurant imparts a content ambience. The room has recently been extended to incorporate a small bar and extra tables, yet it has retained elements that strike a humble chord. This is especially evident in the private dining room in the basement which also serves as the restaurant's cellars.

Andy Needham, who has an enviable CV, cooks with fine ingredients, such as burrata cheese (the more sophisticated version of mozzarella), truffles when in season, cured pigs' cheeks, and excellent veal, lobster and fish. The menu is based on a fixed-price system with a few supplements for the more luxurious ingredients. ●

Zuma 5 Raphael Street, SW7 1DL

020 7584 1010 www.zumarestaurant.co.uk

(PP) Personally, I'm not overly fond of Zuma, but I can't deny it is fabulously popular and since it opened in 2002 'everybody' has raved about the food. Rainer Becker, the chef and restaurateur, has created a contemporary version of a Japanese izakaya (an informal bar with simple food). Many of the dishes are designed to share among friends and it's a great location for a small party. The sushi, sashimi and rolls are inventively prepared and from the robata grill the fish and especially the pork and beef are particularly good. The tasting menu is a full-on gustatory experience, but like most of the menu items, it carries a heavy price tag, especially if you go for the black cod or Wagyu beef.

The bar is wildly loud and always busy as the cocktail staff create inspirational drinks, many employing sake and Japanese spirits. ●

Right
Zafferano's crab and asparagus salad.

Tuna Carpaccio with Orange, Fennel and Mint

Serves 4

200 g (7 oz) tuna loin
3 heads fennel
20 fresh mint leaves, cut in to strips
3 bunches rocket leaves
salt and freshly ground black pepper
20 ml (1 fl oz) sweet vinegar
40 ml (2 fl oz) light olive oil, plus extra for brushing
3 juicing oranges, cut into segments
juice of 1 lemon

Cut the tuna loin into eight thin slices. Place each slice inside a freezer bag and seal. Using a meat bat, gently flatten the tuna to give an even, thin disc. Place the tuna in the refrigerator.

Using a mandolin, thinly slice the fennel bulbs from top to bottom, keeping the root attached to hold each slice intact. Place the sliced fennel in to a bowl of iced water. (This will make the fennel curl and crisp up.)

Toss the mint leaves and the rocket together in a large bowl. Remove the fennel from the iced water, drain and dry it thoroughly, and add it to the bowl. Add the seasoning and then dress the salad with the vinegar and olive oil. Add the orange segments, keeping 12 back for the garnish.

Divide the salad on to four plates. Cut open the freezer bags. Season and brush the tuna with oil and the lemon juice. Then carefully place two slices on top of each plate, and garnish each with three orange segments.

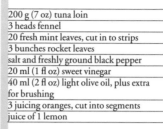

Crudo di Mare

(Marinated Seafood)
Serves 4

For the Dressing
juice of 2 lemons
1 bunch chives, finely chopped
50 ml (2 fl oz) light olive oil

For the Seafood
150 g (5 oz) tuna loin
salt and freshly ground pepper
50 g (2 oz) cucumber, diced
olive oil
lemon juice
8 fresh langoustine
8 Manzancolle (red sweet) prawns
4 large scallops
baby salad leaves, to garnish

Mix together the lemon juice, chives and olive oil and set it aside while you prepare the fish.

Place a frying pan over a medium heat. Add the belly of tuna and fry for 3–4 seconds each side. Season it and set it aside to allow it to cool, then place it in the refrigerator to chill. Cut the rest of the tuna into small cubes. Add the diced cucumber, season the tuna and dress it with the olive oil and lemon juice. Place it in the refrigerator to chill.

Place a saucepan of water over a high heat and bring to the boil. Plunge the langoustine into the boiling water for 10 seconds. Remove from the water, then remove the heads and claws, and peel away the outer shell. Season the langoustine tail and chill.

Under cold running water, remove the heads, tails and outer shell of the prawns. Season the remaining flesh and chill.

Remove the shell from the scallops, and discard the roe and skirt. Slice the scallop into thin discs, season them and chill.

When all the seafood is ready, divide it neatly on to four plates, and garnish each with some baby salad leaves. Pour the dressing over and serve. For the best results, keep all the fish as chilled as possible before serving.

Bethnal Green
Dalston
Hoxton
London Fields
Shoreditch
Wapping
Whitechapel

This is our favourite area in all of London. The East End is creative, vibrant, edgy and the home of original talents. The stagnant view of the East End being exclusively based on jellied eels, pie and mash, and possibly the Blind Beggar pub, with its link to the infamous Krays, is so passé. Currently the East End is the most exciting corner of London and the future looks vivid. The Olympics in 2012 will transform the Lea Valley, along with much of Hackney, bringing fantastic opportunities, improved transport links and prosperity.

While some areas remain run down, modern and innovative residential and loft developments have started to arrive. The architect David Adjaye is responsible for several such projects and has recently completed the redevelopment of the Whitechapel Library, forming the Idea Store, a modern-day learning and research centre.

The easterly end of Old Street and the area's arterial roads have been buzzing for some time with endless bars, clubs and new restaurants. When the White Cube Gallery opened on Hoxton Square, it brought relative order to the scene and became the official platform for the YBAs. (TC) Between 1949 and 1952 I shared a workshop in Roman Road with Eduardo Paolozzi. We were so broke that we lived on bacon sandwiches!

The area in the triangle created by the junction of Shoreditch High Street and Bethnal Green Road, incorporating the Arnold Circus estate is one of the more appealing areas, with its small galleries, young fashion labels and exciting retail concepts. Advertising agencies are now infiltrating the area and this has led to the arrival of the best new bars and restaurants.

Bistrotheque 23–27 Wadeson Street, E2 9DR

020 8983 7900 www.bistrotheque.com

(PP) Bistrotheque is currently in my top five London restaurants. I just feel so comfortable and relaxed when eating in the upstairs dining room.

It's not exactly easy to find the restaurant; as you progress down the dark cobblestone street, the discreet entrance has no obvious sign. The downstairs bar is suave and usually full of Bethnal Green's coolest denizens. The owners have a previous life in the fashion world and that has certainly influenced the whole operation, you just know that all of the staff are models during the day. On Wednesday evenings they usually have a risqué camp cabaret or drag-artist performances in the private area off the downstairs bar.

As you ascend the concrete staircase you may wonder if you haven't taken a wrong turn and entered a fire exit or staff area, but continue walking and you will arrive at the kitchen. We like the fact that you walk through the kitchen to get to your your table! The dining room is set in the eaves of this old East End sweatshop with polished white tiled walls, nautical pendant lamps and steel-frame windows with mottled glass.

The menu is full of brasserie classics – everything you want to eat. On one of my early visits the menu had shades of New York's Balthazar, but it seems to have now found its own identity, confidently delivering French favourites such as Bayonne ham and cornichons, steak tartare, croque monsieur, omelette aux fines herbes, alongside Barnsley chop, new potatoes and spring onion salad or fish and chips, plus other British classics. You can dine inexpensively, especially from the two-course prix-fixe menu, or enjoy lobster and chips with garlic butter. Puddings are as you expect, and include crème brûlée, lemon tart, chocolate pot or excellent British cheese.

Top left **Glamorous light fittings in the second dining room at Bistrotheque.**
Above right
A Bistrotheque chef enjoying moules marinière.
Left **Tasty, simple and unassuming food is served at Bistrotheque.**

The most expensive wine on the list costs about £30 and you've got to appreciate that statement from the owners. The dedicated staff care about every little detail and they seem to know what you want before you want it. ○

Above right
Goat's cheese, fennel, radish and peach salad.
Right **Lemon tart.**
Left **The main dining room and less glamorous light fittings –** more to our taste.

Broadway Market E8

www.broadwaymarket.co.uk Saturdays 9 am–5 pm

Broadway Market is probably one of the youngest examples of the new style of weekly street-food markets. Every Saturday a narrow road between the oft-forgotten greenery of London Fields and Goldsmith's Row comes to life. Broadway is not a farmers' market, but more welcoming to all styles of food. The Ghanaian fast food is great, and there is even the odd fashion or small-objets stall. Nestled between a few small galleries, a florist and a couple of book shops, theses artisanal food retailers offer an ideal excuse to avoid the ghastly supermarket fare and shop in the community. The crowd is more modish and orientated towards students at the moment, but expect this to change over the coming years. Its location and lack of major transport links will thankfully mean that this food market will mainly be for locals.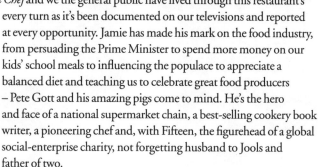

Cat and Mutton 76 Broadway Market, London Fields, E8 4QJ

020 7254 5599

A single room that combines dining and drinking, this gastropub has an open kitchen alongside the bar, and is especially busy on Saturdays with market stallholders and customers.

Fifteen Westland Place, N1 7LP

0871 330 1515 www.fifteenrestaurant.com

At just over 30 years of age Jamie Oliver is already a national treasure. He's achieved so much since his early days as TV's *Naked Chef* and we the general public have lived through this restaurant's

Right and opposite **Graffiti and mosaic wall art in the basement restaurant at Fifteen.** Left **A large hole in the wall allows diners to watch the chefs at work in the main kitchen.**

every turn as it's been documented on our televisions and reported at every opportunity. Jamie has made his mark on the food industry, from persuading the Prime Minister to spend more money on our kids' school meals to influencing the populace to appreciate a balanced diet and teaching us to celebrate great food producers – Pete Gott and his amazing pigs come to mind. He's the hero and face of a national supermarket chain, a best-selling cookery book writer, a pioneering chef and, with Fifteen, the figurehead of a global social-enterprise charity, not forgetting husband to Jools and father of two.

The subject of another television series, Fifteen the restaurant was set up to inspire disadvantaged young people, and to provide training and employment for the undereducated and low-skilled. The business is owned by the Fifteen Foundation, a registered charity, and has subsequently spawned outposts in Cornwall, Amsterdam and Australia, with more to follow.

Like Jamie, the food at Fifteen has its own unique identity, based on traditional Italian Mediterranean cooking. The rustic and relaxed ground-floor trattoria is open for breakfast, lunch and dinner, and there is a more formal retro-style restaurant in the basement with an open kitchen. Both enjoy Jamie's own menu-writing vernacular, with such delights as, 'the ultimate breakfast sarnie', 'the lightest potato gnocchi "alla Sorrentina"', 'Jamie's pukkola muesli' or 'mixed funky leaf salad'.

Fifteen

Marinated Leg of Lamb with Smashed Cannellini Beans and a Rosemary Anchovy Dressing

Serves 6

For the Lamb Marinade

zest of 1 lemon, cut with a speed peeler
2 teaspoons black peppercorns, crushed
3 cloves of garlic, peeled and crushed
a sprig of fresh rosemary, leaves picked
a drizzle of extra virgin olive oil

1 leg of lamb, boned and butterflied
(ask you butcher to do this for you)

For the Beans

3 x 410 g tins cannellini beans, drained
1 bulb of garlic, cut in half
1 bouquet garni (see tip)
1 plum tomato, chopped
50 g butter
2 teaspoons freshly picked thyme leaves
sea salt and freshly ground black pepper
white wine vinegar
extra virgin olive oil

For the Dressing

3 sprigs of fresh rosemary, leaves picked
and roughly chopped
5 anchovy fillets in oil, drained
juice of 1/2 a lemon
1 clove of garlic
extra virgin olive oil
sea salt

The day before

Mix all the lamb marinade ingredients together and rub all over the leg of lamb. Put the lamb in a roasting tray, cover with tinfoil and leave for at least 24 hours in the fridge.

The day of cooking

Preheat the oven to 180°C (350°F) Gas Mark 4. Pop the tray with the lamb (and the foil still on) in the preheated oven and roast for 1 to 1 1/2 hours, until it's just to your liking.

Meanwhile, place the cannellini beans, garlic, bouquet garni and chopped tomato in a large pot and cover with water. Bring to the boil, then cover and simmer for 10 minutes.

Once the beans are ready, drain them, discarding the garlic and bouquet garni, and reserving some of the cooking water. Put a third of the beans in a bowl with the butter and a bit of the cooking water, and lightly mash with a fork. In a separate bowl, mix the mashed beans with the whole beans, the thyme, some salt and pepper, vinegar to taste and a drizzle of olive oil.

To make the dressing, crush the rosemary with a little salt in a pestle and mortar until it forms a paste. Add the garlic and anchovies and continue to pound until smooth. Mix in the lemon juice and about three times as much extra virgin olive oil until you reach the right consistency.

When the lamb is ready, take it out of the oven, Preheat a griddle pan until hot and griddle the lamb for about 5 minutes on each side until nicely charred. Leave the lamb to rest for 10 minutes and then carve. Serve on top of the cannellini beans and drizzle with the rosemary anchovy dressing.

Tip: if you can't find a bouquet garni, make your own by tying together the following bits in a little bundle: a bay leaf, a few sprigs of fresh thyme, a few sprigs of parsley, a 3 inch stick of celery and a 3 inch piece of thin leek.
© Fifteen Restaurant 2007

Mini Chocolate Puddings with Orange and Vin Santo Crème Fraîche

Makes 12

140 g unsalted butter, plus a little extra for buttering the cups
150 g best-quality chocolate (70% cocoa solids)
4 tablespoons cocoa powder, sifted
sea salt
4 large free-range or organic eggs, separated
200 g caster sugar
100 ml crème fraîche
zest of 1/2 orange
a splash of vin santo
6 sesame seed biscuits, smashed

Preheat the oven to 180°C (350°F) Gas Mark 4. Butter 12 small espresso cups.

Place the butter, chocolate, cocoa powder and a pinch of salt in a bowl over a pan of simmering water and allow the butter and chocolate to slowly melt, stirring occasionally until everything's well mixed together.

In a separate bowl, beat the egg yolks and sugar together until light and pale. In a third bowl, whisk the egg whites with a pinch of salt until stiff.

Stir the chocolate mixture into the egg and sugar mixture, mixing well before folding in the egg whites. Spoon the mixture into the cups, filling them to the top, and place in a deep roasting tray of hot water – the water should be two-thirds up the sides of the cups. Bake in the preheated oven for 20–25 minutes.

Mix together the crème fraîche, orange zest and vin santo. Take the puddings out of the oven and serve them with a little dollop of flavoured crème fraîche and a sprinkling of smashed sesame seed biscuits.
© Fifteen Restaurant 2007

Great gastropub
food at The Fox
from top to bottom
**Poached Sutton Hoo
chicken, spring
greens and anchoïde;
Salt beef sandwich
on rye; Chicken
livers, bacon and
poussé; Cheddar
Ploughmans.**

The Flea Pit   49 Columbia Road, E2 7RG

020 7033 9986   www.thefleapit.com

An ideal refuelling point after or before the Sunday flower market, this laid-back café serves organic vegetarian dishes, cakes and juices, plus ethical coffee and tea. It also has free broadband and an active programme of events, which include screenings, poetry and script readings. ◉

The Fox Dining Room   28 Paul Street, EC2A 4LB

020 7729 5708

Just about ten years ago The Eagle in Farringdon and The Cow in Notting Hill started something unique by giving birth to the gastropub. At the time, the food-loving entrepreneurs behind these businesses generally converted properties previously owned by the big breweries into pleasant places to meet and enjoy simple food at reasonable prices. The paradigm invariably involved a ground-floor bar with reclaimed sturdy furniture, stripped-back floorboards and larger windows and better lighting. The beer selection now had a continental flavour and the wine list was chock-full of New World Chardonnays and big fruit-bomb Cabernet Sauvignons. Upstairs, a small dining room would appear, a place where young chefs fed up with the star-chasing culture so evident in the big restaurant and hotel kitchens could secure a small foothold in the food business. The gastropub afforded these creative individuals opportunity and autonomy. In the wrong hands, menus went adversely tangential and confused, especially following the popularity of fusion cooking. However, in the main, local residents were pleased to greet their new reshaped midweek drinking-and-dining destination. Menus were labelled as Modern British and generally served food that had previously been pioneered by the likes of Kensington Place and The Brackenbury in Chiswick.

The pervasiveness of the gastropub continues and the East End of London seems to have a generous share. Paul Street boasts two beautiful examples.

The Fox is atmospheric and not too shiny or new – essential to maintain that true pub feel.

Upstairs the comfortably sized dining room, with a small outside terrace, has a short menu, but the quality of the ingredients is excellent and the cooking technique is beyond reproach.

Michael Belben is involved with the Fox and he also had a hand in The Eagle. It might have been some time since the Eagle first opened, but this gastropub is as good as the original. ◉

Great Eastern Dining Room 54–56 Great Eastern Street, EC2A 3QR
020 7613 4545 www.greateasterndining.co.uk

Sibling to the amazingly popular E&O in Notting Hill, Cicada in Clerkenwell and Eight Over Eight in Chelsea, the Great Eastern Dining Room serves pan-Asian favourites to the cool Shoreditch crowd in a small and cramped but generally very busy dining room. Mushroon cheung fun, chicken gyoza and crispy pork belly sit alongside the sushi and sashimi sections. The main courses include a smart phad Thai or fillet steak on a toban grill.

This is a great location for a first date, because if it goes well you can progress to the late bar and dance floor in the basement. ◓

Green and Red Bar and Cantina 51 Bethnal Green Road, E1 6LA
020 7749 9670 www.greenandred.co.uk

Green and Red celebrates the distilled product of the agave plant and its culture. The tequilla list is impressive and extremely well researched at this the London Evening Standard 2006 Bar of the Year. In addition to the tequila emphasis, they also serve Mexican Jalisco-style cantina and taqueria food, with dishes ranging from rancheros with refried beans and corn tortilla to the delights of chorizo and salsa. The house-made tacos with pork belly, chipotle and avocado salsa with a Mama's Mary or a Morning Margarita is spicy stuff. Churros con chocolate might be more appropriate for some. ◓

Jones Dairy 23 Ezra Street, E2 7RH
020 7739 5372 www.jonesdairy.co.uk

Only open for three half-days a week from Friday to Sunday, the best day to visit Jones Dairy is most definitely Sunday when you can also experience the thronging cobbled streets of the East End and Columbia Road flower market in full bloom. Look out for the small antique market, a few independent furniture retailers, a handful of quirky clothing shops and a splattering of art galleries nearby that also add to the pleasure.

Jones Dairy consists of three small elements: the front shop, a small caff at the rear and an occasional oyster shucker down the adjacent alley – just what you need on a Sunday morning. A glass of stout at the contiguous Royal Oak pub could follow.

The shop window expresses the extensive range of handmade breads, including cholla, rustic rye, walnut cob, organic spelt, black rye, pain au levain and much, much more. Inside you'll find the best unpasteurized British cheeses, cakes, artisanal preserves, honey, chutneys and condiments. It is only a tiny room, but the attention to detail is impressive and the old-fashioned scales are redolent of an age when food retailing of this ilk was on every street corner.

Hot strong tea and coffee served in heavy white mugs, together with breakfast buns, toast, freshly squeezed English apple juice and a few choice sarnies are served in the caff. If you go on a winter's morning you can huddle against the coal-fired heater and its impressive steel chimney and warm your hands on it. ◓

Will Ricker

The constant receipt of great service in London restaurants is often overshadowed by other headliners – design, choice and quality. But for me it's the hero of our burgeoning industry.

Owner, E&O, Great Eastern Dining Room, Cicada, Eight Over Eight

Above **Zucchini carpaccio with rocket and Parmesan salad at The Great Eastern Dining Room.**

Right **Inside Korean Ch'a, taking tea is very much a ritual.**
Above **Teapots, cups and various ceramics for sale at Korean Ch'a.**
Left **The lunch buffet at Korean Ch'a.**

Above **Korean gyoza.**
Left **freshly squeezed juices.**

Korean Ch'a 146 Bethnal Green Road, E2 6DG
020 7613 1691

Ch'a is the Korean word for tea and this tiny tearoom and retail outlet stress the importance of the associated rituals. The menu card offers much more than just a list of dishes. You can learn about the history of tea, how to brew and serve your tea, plus the ch'i (vital energy) that the ch'a contains. They even go as far as suggesting that ch'a is nature's greatest gift to mankind and should be considered a health benefit. Since its introduction to Korea over 700 years ago, the Koreans have believed that tea has medicinal properties and it forms an integral role in their culture. As a result they have developed innumerable teas, using wide-ranging ingredients, and this small shop offers almost 20 of the best varieties. (PP) The Yuja ch'a is particularly restorative when you are feeling a little under the weather. Energizing and antioxidant juices and beta-carotene blasts are also available, together with a small selection of hot dishes such as tofu and soya Korean hot pot, or bulgogi – spicy marinated barbecue pork, beef or chicken. ●

The Princess 76 Paul Street, EC2A 4NE
020 7729 9270

Previously a drinking den run by East End legend One-Eyed Ron, The Princess is now more of a destination restaurant in simple surroundings. Zim Sutton, who is also the chef, and Andrew Veevers, have personally designed the entire space and now oversee a respectable accomplished operation. The simple menu in the downstairs bar (think springbok sausages or barbecue lamb) and the more refined upmarket cooking in the dining room both reflect the Australian origins of these two creative individuals.

A spiral staircase leads to a dining room upstairs, with teak chairs, generously appointed tables, leather benches, and brightly coloured floral wallpaper. The walls also include large 1920s-style oil paintings of female figures by artist Amy Alderson.

The succinct wine list is unusually, yet usefully, listed by style rather than region or grape variety. ○

Zim Sutton

We had the daunting task of opening our first pub, The Easton, just around the corner from The Eagle (see page 192) in 2002. I still sneak down for their house speciality, Bife Ana, at least once a week. It's a rich and juicy marinated steak sandwhich, and although I'll pretend to see what else is on offer (I even coo 'ooh the fish looks good', to my girlfriend), I always end up ordering it. Owner, The Princess and The Easton

Above **The upstairs dining room at The Princess.**

Freekah Salad with Preserved Lemon, Parsley and Mint

Serves 6

400 g (13 oz) freekah or bulgar wheat
1.25 litres (2 pints) of cold water
sea salt
olive oil
2 quarters of preserved lemon
2 generous handfuls of flat leaf parsley, chopped
2 generous handfuls of mint, chopped
juice of 2 lemons
freshly ground black pepper

Put the freekah (or bulgar), cold water, salt and 1 tablespoon of olive oil into a saucepan and gently bring it to the boil, stirring occasionally. Cover the pan with a tight fitting lid, and then reduce the temperature. Simmer it for 10–15 minutes if you are cooking cracked grain or 25–30 minutes for whole grain. The water should have been absorbed by the time the freekah is cooked, and the grains should be tender. Remove it from the heat and allow it to cool.

Remove and discard the pulp from the lemons, and wash and cut them into tiny dice. Toss the cooled freekah with the preserved lemon, chopped herbs and lemon juice. Add a little olive oil, season it to taste and serve.

Barbecued Quail in a Lemon, Basil and Fig Bath

Serves 6

6 quails, boned

For the Bath
2 lemons
2 cloves of garlic, crushed
125 ml (4 fl oz) olive oil
60 g (2½ oz) basil leaves
salt and freshly ground black pepper
6 figs, halved

Light the barbecue. While it is heating up, make the bath. Remove the zest from the lemons using a peeler, then juice one of the lemons and place the zest and juice in a shallow bowl. Add the garlic. Mix in the olive oil and stir to combine. Add the basil. Season the mixture to taste with salt and pepper. (It should need a couple of teaspoons of salt to take the edge off of the lemon's tartness.) Set the bath aside.

Barbecue the quail for 10 minutes or until they are cooked through, then rest them in the bath, turning them once or twice for 5–10 minutes. Place a quail on each serving plate and pour the dressing and zest over the top. Serve two fig halves with each quail.

Above **A local in the downstairs bar at The Princess enjoys pork, chorizo and butter bean soup.**

New Tayyabs 83–89 Fieldgate Street, E1 1JU
020 7247 6400 www.tayyabs.co.uk

Roll up your sleeves and enjoy Tayyab for what it is – an extremely busy 100 per cent halal Pakistani Punjabi fresh produce restaurant. London now has more than its fair share of modern and 'posh' restaurants serving all manner of foods from the subcontinent, but when you want the old style, this is the place to come. Drummond Street in the West End and Brick Lane, only a short walk from Fieldgate Street, have long been associated with similar experiences, however, over recent years they seem to have lost their allure. New Tayyabs has remained truly authentic, probably due to its back-street location and neighbouring Mosque, which is one of the largest in London.

Unless you are going as a group, don't bother making a reservation. You still need to join the queue behind the ropes and stanchions. Any restaurant that operates a queuing system has got to be worth at least one visit. When you do get a seat you immediately feel that you've stepped on to a conveyor belt, but sit comfortably and enjoy your poppadams and dips.

Unlike other places, the menu is not an arduous read. Instead, it's a moderate-sized laminated card with rather unflattering photographs. Most of the first courses are generally tikka-marinated chicken, mutton, lamb chops – chew them to the bone – or paneer, all presented on hot sizzling skillets, plus the ubiquitous samosa, pakora and shami kebab. Similar to the wok used in Asian kitchens, most of the main courses are prepared stir-fried in a karahi and brought to the table in steel balti-style dishes. The karahi dhal gosht (lamb), sometimes spelt ghost or ghoust, is probably the best meat main course and it goes without saying that the menu includes a good selection of vegetarian main courses.

Don't forget to BYO (bring your own) Tiger beer or wine, otherwise you'll only be drinking London water or a daily-changing lassi. They don't charge corkage, but you need to take your own corkscrew or bottle opener.

When you ask for the bill and the staff immediately start to relay your table, you certainly get the sense that you're one of five or six other people to occupy the same seat that night, such is the popularity of this place. With this negative, it might seem surprising that New Tayyabs is considered one of the best restaurants in its category, but it is the food and value for money that matter the most. ◉

Top right **Anna Pellicci at the hot water still.**
Right **An old-fashioned till still being put to good use at Pellicci.**

Nevio Pellicci Snr

Welcoming the local resident students and their parents visiting London for the day makes me happy. We must be doing a good job if that happens!

Owner, E Pellicci

This page **Inside the tiny Pellicci cafe.**

E Pellicci Bethnal Green Road, E2 0AG

020 7739 4873

We love Pellicci's because it's a family business and a London tradition with a strong Italian accent.

Nevio Pellicci, the 81-year-old patriarch, was born upstairs in this very establishment while his father was running the café downstairs. Photographs of Nevio's parents still hold pride of place on the walls of the restaurant. After all these years, Maria, Mrs Pellicci, still only speaks limited English, but she's the fastest hand-chipper in London. Arriving promptly every morning at 5 am, Maria is the culinary inspiration, creating and approving every new dish on the menu. It might be simple café food, but it's still high concept and carefully followed with every dish. The all-day breakfast is the most popular, but Mrs Pellicci prefers to suggest the cannelloni, spaghetti bolognese or the pollo peperonata. Everything is freshly made on the premises.

The Pellicci's children Nevio Jnr, Anna and Bruna, together with nephew Toni (real name Salvadori), cover most of the shifts these days, but you can still chat to Nevio Snr as you wait in the queue for a table on a Saturday.

My question to Nevio Snr was: 'What makes you most happy about the café business?' His answer: 'Welcoming the local resident students and their parents visiting London for the day. We must be doing a good job if that happens!' ◗

104

The Real Greek and Mezedopolio 14–15 Hoxton Market, N1 6HG
020 7739 8212 www.therealgreek.co.uk

In September 1999 Theodore Kyriakou opened The Real Greek and
in 2000 he won *Time Out's* prestigious best newcomer award. The
restaurant offers a true Hellenic experience with regional specialities.
You can enjoy stuffed vine leaves, tzatziki, dolmades, taramasalata and
Greek salad, plus many other cliché ingredients, but the menu also
offers far more with a large helping of style and substance. Moreover,
Theodore creates authentic Greek dishes with a sprinkling of the best
ingredients available in the UK and sumptuous Greek specialities.

Next door the Mezedopolio serves excellent meze in a more
relaxed setting.

Several other Real Greek Souvlakis have started to appear across
London, but our advice is to visit the original for the true experience. ⊙

Ridley Road Market Dalston, E8

Monday to Wednesday 9 am–3 pm, Thursday 9 am–noon,
Friday and Saturday 9 am–5 pm

Hackney is a melting pot of ethnicity and the best example must be the
market. Over the years Jewish immigrants, then Asian, Greek, Turkish
and West Indian communities have dominated the stalls. The Reggae
music certainly indicates the latter. The market now allows all to rub
shoulders in this loud and raw vibe. If you are preparing an exotic feast
or a Turkish delight, this is the only place to buy the comestibles. ⊙

Above **The bar at
the Real Greek.**

Above left **English asparagus and hollandaise – the perfect way to serve asparagus.** Top right **Roast Lancashire suckling pig with greens and apple sauce.** Left middle **Inside the adjoining small deli at Rivington Grill.** Left **Wine and books on shelves behind the bar.**

Rivington Grill, Bar and Deli 28–30 Rivington Street, EC2A 3DZ
020 7729 7053 www.rivingtongrill.co.uk

A few years back when the Rivington first opened, there was a muted rumour that über-chef Mark Hix, he of The Ivy and Caprice, was 'involved'. First, the gossip suggested that he was overseeing the menu, then it advanced to him being a shareholder and ultimately his hand was revealed and matters appeared above the parapet. The Rivington is now a fully paid-up member of Caprice Holdings and a second branch has opened in Greenwich with more in the pipework – according to reports.

Whatever the situation, the Rivington seems to have offered simply prepared and excellently procured ingredients since day one. Much the same as the stylish recipes in Mark's weekly *Independent Magazine* column and his various books, the food direction is truly the best of British. The menu shouts provenance at every corner and includes many regional classics, such as Weatherall's Black Face mutton hotpot with pickled red cabbage and Bakewell tart. There's a good selection of crustacea, from oysters to a half pint of prawns or lobster and chips if you are feeling decadent. The section of the menu called On Toast includes soft herring roes, Welsh rarebit, eggs Benedict, devilled lambs' kidneys and Morecambe Bay shrimps.

The whole operation seems to be executed with a generous helping of Shoreditch style. Simple white walls lightly adorned with modern art and a few well-chosen leather sofas demonstrate confidence in its identity.

Rivington is open early for hearty breakfasts through until late. They also offer great banquet menus for eight diners or more. ◉

Les Trois Garçons 1 Club Row, E1 6JX

020 7613 1924 www.lestroisgarcons.com

As pub conversions go, this must be the most surreal London has to offer. The inside of this formerly run-down East End drinking den has been converted into an Alice-in-Wonderland film set. Taxidermy, ostrich feathers and handbags combine with crystals and Victoriana. An expressive bulldog greets you on arrival, while a tiger prowls along the bar, observed by a bow-tie-wearing monkey. One wall is covered with all manner of stuffed game from the African savanna, including a tiara-wearing antelope and a huge giraffe head juxtaposed with a huge picture featuring hundreds of naked men.

The food and service are modern French with definite shades of the international Jean-Georges Vongerichten style. Square plates abound, together with sauces served in shot glasses and quirkily shaped bowls. You start with an amuse gueule of gazpacho with brittle breadstick followed by a plethora of luxurious ingredients from foie gras to truffles to turbot. Typical dishes could include vanilla-poached tiger prawns or heirloom tomato salad with shaved fennel and apple cider dressing. Main courses include an excellently executed and, compared with other elements of the menu, relatively simple fillet of beef with creamy gratin dauphinoise and sauce bordelaise.

The desserts combine inventiveness with a detailed craft and skill. Pain d'épice cheesecake made with goat's cheese and served with a mulled-wine reduction and almond milk or a classic tarte Tatin are two very good examples and the trios chocolats is expertly prepared.

Wines are serious; the private collection offers a wealth of old world grand cru claret and white burgundy. Providentially, the remainder of the list is relatively fairly priced.

To complete the experience, start with an aperitif at sister property Loungelover, a 20-second walk around the corner. The cocktail list is definitely one the most creative in London and the not understated eclectic room décor must be seen. ◗

Hassan Abdullah

I love eating locally and for me this means Rochelle School Canteen and St. John Bread and Wine. The food at both of these unpretentious restaurants is always seasonal, fresh and designed so that you can eat from the menu every day without getting bored.

Owner, Les Trois Garçons and Loungelover

This page and opposite **Inside the eccentrically decorated Le Trois Garçons.**

Jules Wright

London's most stylish, if idiosyncratically designed, deli is Melrose and Morgan (see page 68). It's very English, and reminds me metaphorically of childhood grocery stores over whose counters one peeked. British-produced cheese and chocolate, immaculately sourced eel and purpose-baked pies, expertly cooked sausage rolls, fairy cakes and perfectly sliced pig.

Director, Wapping Food

This page and opposite **Inside the restaurant at Wapping Food, the original power station interior has been retained and the addition of iconic furniture has formed the restaurant.**

Viet Hoa Cafe 70–72 Kingsland Road, E2 8DP
020 7729 8293

Fried catfish, drunken fish and shaking beef are some of the more unusual dishes on the menu at this authentic, inexpensive Vietnamese café. (PP) The menu is huge, so I normally stick with my regular order of banh xeo (crispy pancakes) and canh chua (hot and sour soup), followed by sweet and sour pork ribs and, if I deserve it, fried ice cream. The room is certainly nothing to write home about, but it does attract a large number of families for late Sunday lunch. This stretch of Kingsland Road features several other Vietnamese diners and takeaways. If you don't go for Viet Hoa then I suggest Song Que at 134 Kingsland Road. ●

Walluc 40 Redchurch Street, E2 7DP
020 7729 6070

Walluc is tiny and a little grubby, but it's about the only restaurant in London serving raclette and fondue – the perfect peasant-style communal food. Plus, Redchurch Street is such a creative hub. ●

Wapping Food The Wapping Project, Wapping Wall, E1W 3ST
020 7680 2080   www.thewappingproject.com

Restaurants are often born out of buildings with previous uses. London has seen restaurants in old smokehouses, banks, car garages, boating sheds and warehouses. The Wapping Project was previously a hydraulic power station. The space is huge and the industrial characteristics have mainly been retained, with Ron Arad and Eames furniture creating the restaurant area. The adjoining art gallery adds further interest before or after a meal.

Wapping Wall is such an evocative and historic area, having previously been one of the most industrialized shipping-warehouse districts in London, and probably the world. The area has now been completely transformed to high-quality residential accommodation. The cooking is as modern as the warehouse apartments around it and the entirely New World wine list is inspired. ●

109

Billingsgate
Canary Wharf
Docklands
Dulwich
Greenwich

Canary Wharf (named after its past connection with goods shipped from the Canary Islands) exists because of the Roux Brothers. That's a fact! In 1984, a lunch was arranged between the late Michael Von Clemm, then chairman of Roux Restaurants, and Reg Ward, chief executive of the London Docklands Development Corporation. Lunch was served on board the boat *Res Nova*, which happened to be moored at Shed 31, close to the (at that stage) defunct West India Docks. Comparing the derelict warehouses to Boston Harbor and how they had been developed for office use prompted Von Clemm to dream up a metamorphic scheme for this part of London. Of course, luck and good fortune also played a part.

This admirable embryonic idea over lunch, together with enthusiastic support from Margaret Thatcher (especially in the form of tax breaks to enable them to develop the area), was to lead to construction starting in 1988. The first phase was completed in 1991, but when the developers, Olympia and York, went into financial administration as a result of the 1990s property crash, the scheme faltered for a while. During the formative period, there was much vocal objection from the locals and criticism of the architecture and the ersatz landscaping. But today, thanks to many reasons, not least the Jubilee line extension, Canary Wharf is booming. The trees are nearing maturity, the restaurants are chock-a-block and there is a series of vibrant retail arcades.

Between 1802 and 1980 West India Quay was one of the world's busiest docks, employing up to 50,000 people. Today, the working and residential population has eclipsed this figure – a perfect example of redevelopment.

East Dulwich Deli 15 Lordship Lane, SE22 8HD

020 8693 2525

This is a firm favourite among locals, with friendly staff, excellent displays and first-class fresh produce. •

The Gun 27 Coldharbour Lane, E14 9NS

020 7515 5222 www.thegundocklands.com

The Gun is located at the rear of Canary Wharf as you travel from the City, set among an ever-expanding number of new residential developments. While everything around The Gun has been built over the last decade or less, the contrary pub dates back over 250 years. It takes its name from the cannon that was fired to celebrate the opening of the West India Import Docks in 1802. The establishment has also enjoyed the patronage of Lord Horatio Nelson and Lady Emma Hamilton. The new owners have completely refurbished the premises, following a fire a few years back, and have installed a serious head chef and high-quality general manager. The small dining room has a menu that reflects the experience of its management. It doesn't seem to stick to a strict food direction, instead including an eclectic array of high-quality ingredients: oysters, Pata Negra, snails in garlic butter, rump of saltmarsh lamb, grilled lobster and Wagyu beef appear. The pub menu features pint o' prawns, fish pie, bookmaker's sandwiches and bangers and mash with onion gravy. •

Hope and Greenwood 20 North Cross Road, SE22 9EU

020 8613 1777 www.hopeandgreenwood.co.uk

The company logo says 'Purveyors of Splendid Confectionery' and it isn't wrong. Established as a sweet shop since 1955, the stock is nostalgic British, with shelves displaying 175 glass jars filled with sugar sweets, imps, sherbet lemons, cola cubes, chocolate mice, liquorice and the like. It makes the ideal special treat for your five-year-old on a Saturday morning, with the simple condition that a trip to the dentist must follow. They also have a small selection of handmade chocolates in elegant gift boxes for adults. •

The Palmerston 91 Lordship Lane, SE22 8EP

020 8693 1629 www.thepalmerston.co.uk

Outside the West End, very often the best places to eat decent food at reasonable prices are the gastropubs. However, sometimes they can be hit and miss, and the experience in the kitchen questionable. That is certainly not the situation at The Palmerston, with local residents benefiting from chef Jamie Younger's experience at Bibendum. It has a very small dining area with extra seats in the pub section, but the food delivers huge flavours, good provenance, seasonality and excellent combinations of ingredients.

The breadth of the menu also reflects Jamie's experience and knowledge. Without being too large, the choice includes hot and sour Thai king prawn soup or gazpacho Andaluz alongside English asparagus, Middle White pork or a simple English breakfast radish with butter and fleur de sel. Main courses offer rib-eye steaks with mushroom 'en persillade', grilled calves' kidney, roast quail with chorizo and sea trout with sauce vierge. A good choice of desserts at sensible prices completes the menu. •

Left **Jamie Younger, head chef and co-owner of The Palmerston.**

Smoked Eel with Beetroots, Pea Shoots and Horseradish Cream

by Jamie Younger
Serves 2

For the Horseradish Cream
50 g (2 oz) freshly grated horseradish
1 tablespoon lemon juice
3 drops Tabasco sauce
1 tablespoon white wine vinegar
1 tablespoon caster sugar
150 ml (¼ pint) whipping cream
salt and freshly ground black pepper

For the Smoked Eel
4 tablespoons olive oil
1 bunch (about 8) baby beetroots, cooked in salted water with a splash of red wine vinegar
150 g (5 oz) smoked eel
2 spring onions
1 punnet pea shoots
½ lemon
freshly ground black pepper

First make the horseradish cream by blitzing the horseradish in a food blender with all the ingredients except the cream and salt and pepper. When smooth, lightly whip the cream and gently fold it through the horseradish. Season the sauce and set aside.

Heat a heavy-bottomed frying pan with the olive oil. Sauté the beetroots until they are lightly coloured. Add the smoked eel and when warm take the pan off the heat and add the spring onions, pea shoots, a squeeze of lemon juice and a twist of pepper.

Divide the eel into two shallow bowls. Add a spoonful of horseradish cream and enjoy.

Above **A starter of smoked eel with beetroots, pea shoots and horseradish cream.**
Right **A hearty portion of grilled rib of beef.**

Grilled Rib of Beef with Braised Shallots, Red Wine and Straw Potatoes

by Jamie Younger
Serves 2

12 small shallots, peeled
olive oil
150 ml (¼ pint) red wine
100 ml (3½ fl oz) beef stock
1 sprig thyme
1 bay leaf
1 teaspoon redcurrant jelly
2 Cyprus potatoes, peeled
salt
ground nut oil or vegetable oil, for deep-frying
1 rib of beef weighing 650 g (5lb 5 oz)
1 bunch watercress

Place the shallots in a pan that will fit the shallots tightly together and deep enough for liquid to cover them. Fry the shallots in a little olive oil until they have coloured. Add the red wine, stock, thyme and bay leaf and cook slowly until the shallots are soft. Remove shallots onto a plate and set aside. Then reduce the liquid to a sauce consistency, and whisk in the redcurrant jelly. Pass the mixture through a sieve and set aside.

Using the julienne cutter on a Japanese mandolin, shred the peeled potatoes. Wash them thoroughly under running water until the water becomes clear and the starch is removed. Dry the potatoes on a clean tea towel and set them aside. Prepare a deep pan with oil for deep-frying and heat to 180°C (350°F). Carefully deep-fry the potatoes in the hot oil, moving them constantly until they are crisp. When they are finished lift them from the oil, drain on kitchen paper, season with salt and set them aside to keep warm.

Preheat the oven to 190°C (375°F) Gas Mark 5. Place a griddle pan over a high heat. Set the rib of beef on the griddle pan and fry it for 5 minutes on each side. Then place the beef in the oven for 20 minutes. Meanwhile place the sauce and shallots into a saucepan together over a medium heat and warm them up.

Once it has rested, carve the beef and divide it between two plates. Pour over the sauce and serve with the straw potatoes and the watercress.

Top right and right
**The Grill and Bar
at Plateau** with
Harry Bertoia
1950s mesh chairs.
Left **One Canada
Wharf tower** – the
centre piece of
Canary Wharf.

Priscilla Carluccio

I love Pimlico Farmers' Market because they sell anything from courgette flowers to garden roses.
Carluccio's

Plateau Fourth Floor, Canada Place, Canary Wharf E14 5ER
020 7715 7100 www.conran.com

Having worked for Jean-Georges Vongerichten in London and New York, Tim Tolley now heads up the kitchen at Plateau. Together with general manager Bertrand Pierson, his colleague from Vong in London, they have fashioned a formidable team when opening Plateau in October 2003. From the beginning Plateau has been the destination of choice for the senior bankers, lawyers and newspaper people of Canary Wharf. It is certainly the top ticket in Canary Wharf during the working week and also has a thriving weekend business.

Located on the fourth and top floor of an incongruously short building, the restaurant benefits from a half-glass ceiling and an entire glass wall overlooking the lawns and sculpture of Canada Square Park. At night when you look up towards the 30-, 40- and 50-storey buildings that surround the restaurant, you immediately start to think of New York or even the fictional Gotham City. In fact, part of *Batman II* was filmed at the restaurant.

The grill and informal dining area offers mainly French classics, such as charcuterie plates, duck rillettes and confit, bavette steaks, chicken paillard and tarte Tatin. The dishes have a clean and refined touch, as with all of Tim's food. He seems to take rustic dishes and add a smart and modern edge. The grill menu also benefits from a rotisserie section with suckling pig, coquelet and salmon from Loch Duart. The same modern temperament applies in the more formal adjoining restaurant, where Dover sole, foie gras, dressed crab, wild sea bass and fillet steaks can be found. The main restaurant also has a 15-vegetable main-course dish that is appealing to anybody who cares about a nutritious diet. (PP) Tim has cooked one of the best roast grouse dishes I have ever tasted and that's probably due to his attention to the details, experienced use of ingredients and great technique.

Bertrand ensures that the entire operation oozes with style and modernity. The restaurant has an attractive and cohesive team who share a common goal.

Not to be forgotten is Michael Simms, the vastly experienced head sommelier at Plateau, who is a real character with a dry sense of humour and a love of opera and ballet. (PP) I first met Michael in the early nineties at Claridge's, when he was already one of the most experienced and recognized sommeliers in London. Back then he had already served at The Ritz and went on to The Savoy and Vong before following Bertrand and Tim.

The interior design at Plateau is iconic 1950s with Arco lamps, Eero Saarinen tulip swivel chairs and tables with beautiful marble tops and wavy shaped eau-de-Nil-coloured upholstered banquettes. The cutlery is David Mellor silver and Bertrand always ensures that chic flowers are on display. The lively bar scene, outside terraces with its own barbecue and private dining room all help reinforce Plateau as the leading eatery in Canary Wharf. The restaurant is also busy at the weekends, drawing on the affluent nearby residents. ◉

Above **Canary Wharf tube station on the Jubilee line.**

Sea Bass with Green Asparagus and Port Hollandaise

Serves 2

For the Hollandaise Sauce

3 egg yolks
fleur de sel or sea salt
juice of ½ lemon
200 g (7 oz) butter
freshly ground black pepper
100 ml Port

a bunch of asparagus
a knob of butter
sea salt and freshly ground black pepper
2 sea bass
butter or olive oil, to fry the fish in
sea salt and freshly ground black pepper

Whisk the egg yolks, sea salt and lemon juice over a bain marie until fluffy. Then slowly add the butter while continuing to whisk the egg yolks until you can form a figure of eight within the mixture. Then add pepper and port to taste. Set aside.

Peel the asparagus. Reserve peelings and stalk ends and juice them in a juicer. Place a saucepan on the stove over a medium heat and add just enough water to cover the asparagus and add a knob of butter. When the mixture is simmering add the asparagus and season them with sea salt and pepper. Let them cook for about three minutes then remove, drain and keep warm. Place the asparagus juice in a saucepan over a medium heat and reduce it by half. Remove from the heat and set aside.

Season the sea bass with salt and freshly ground pepper. At Plateau, we cook sea bass directly on to a plancha (stainless-steel plaque). If you don't have a plancha you can use a regular sauté pan. First heat the pan on a medium heat. Place the seasoned sea bass in the pan, skin-side down. Cook for 5–6 minutes and then turn them over and finish the other sides for another 5–6 minutes. Then divide the asparagus between two warm serving plates, place the fish on top and spoon over the Port hollandaise.

117

The main dining room at Plateau features marble top tables with Eero Saarinen's tulip bases and the iconic swivel chair with Arco lamps.

Sea Cow
37 Lordship Lane, East Dulwich, SE22 8EW
020 8693 3111

Battered fish and chips have been popular in the UK for a long time, be it a midweek supper, a Friday evening family treat or a workman's lunch. London isn't the mecca for chippies – the North probably deserves that reputation – but maybe the Sea Cow will make some inroads to improve London's standing. The format is simple and was apparently inspired following a trip to Sydney, Australia. As you enter the premises the fish and a small range of crustaceans are presented on crushed ice awaiting your selection. Everything is purchased from Billingsgate Market and cooked to order. Starting with cod and chips, the selection progresses to red snapper, bluefin tuna or gilthead bream. You can also order a tiger prawn salad, crab cakes or calamari with tartare sauce.

The chunky bench seats, spacious room and surprisingly interesting modern art create a civilized setting. Sea Cow also has a small wine list. ○

Left **An Ubon chef preparing yellowtail sashimi with yellow jalapeño dressing.**

Ubon by Nobu
34 Westferry Circus, Canary Wharf, E14 8RR
020 7719 7800 www.noburestaurants.com

Is Nobu Matsuhisa furious or flattered by the mass plagiarism that has followed his seminal menu? Arriving in London over ten years ago, he introduced black cod, sea-urchin tempura, new-style sashimi, tomato rock shrimp ceviche and much more. Now it seems black cod is the essential dish on any new-wave Japanese restaurant menu. While some have tried to recreate the Nobu standards, the quality of his own restaurants has certainly not suffered. By all accounts Mark Edwards, Nobu's right-hand man in Europe, responsible for all new restaurants, has been the reason for Nobu's continued number-one position.

Ubon (Nobu backwards) was his second restaurant in London and, when it opened in Canary Wharf, securing a table was no big problem, unlike the first site within the Metropolitan Hotel on Park Lane. (PP) I prefer Ubon as it is less about the scene, allowing diners to focus on the food and experience the true value of well-trained professional service staff.

As in most Japanese restaurants the menu is extensive and it takes a little time to work out your selection. Regulars know exactly what they want and revel in the creativity of squid pasta that isn't actually pasta, abalone or monkfish paté and sweet shrimp sashimi. Chu and o-toro nigiri and sashimi are esoteric offerings that are only highlighted by a slighter higher selling price. If you are really feeling like a treat, try the omakase menu. ○

William Rose Ltd Butchers
126 Lordship Lane, East Dulwich,
SE22 8HD 020 8693 9191 www.williamrosebutchers.com

The sign of a good butcher is probably the length of the queue on a Saturday morning. At William Rose the line snakes out of the shop on to Lordship Lane, and that's in spite of about a dozen staff behind the counter. This traditional butcher offers an extensive selection of free-range and organic meats and poultry, including Sutton Hoo chickens from Suffolk and a selection of French birds, all at reasonable prices. The pork pies baked by a family member are an excellent fillip on the journey back home. ○

Yellowtail Sashimi with Yellow Jalapeño Dressing

Serves 2

For the Dressing

10 g (1/2 oz) yellow jalepeño
100 ml (3 1/2 oz) Japanese rice vinegar
1 teaspoon sea salt, plus a little extra
1 clove of garlic, grated
120 ml (4 fl oz) grapeseed oil

oil, for deep-frying
6 shiso leaves
2 slices yellow tomato
2 slices green tomato
2 slices red tomato
6 slices yellowtail fillet, weighing about
15 g (1/2 oz) each
sea salt and freshly ground pepper
Ito-togarashi (shredded dried red chilli),
to garnish

You will need a kitchen blowtorch.

First make the dressing by removing the seeds from the jalepeño and cutting the flesh into fine dice. Place the vinegar, sea salt, diced jalepeño and grated garlic into a blender. Blend it whilst slowly adding the grapeseed oil. Then set the sauce to one side. Pour enough oil in a medium to large pan to reach 8–10 cm (3 1/2–4 in) deep. Place the pan over a high heat and heat the oil to a temperature of 170°C (340°F). Add the shiso leaves and fry them until they are crisp (they should still retain their green colour). Lift them from the oil with a slotted spoon, drain them well on kitchen paper and set them to one side.

Season the slices of yellowtail with salt and pepper and quickly scorch the top of the slices with a blowtorch but do not cook them through. Set them to one side. Arrange the tomato slices on to a serving dish, alternating the colours. Place a slice of yellowtail on the top of each one, and then a fried shiso leaf. Garnish the dish with a little Ito-togarashi. Pour the dressing around the dish and serve.

Crispy Chu Toro with Ponzu Sauce

Serves 2

For the Sauce

2 tablespoons soy sauce
4 tablespoons Japanese rice vinegar
1 tablespoon freshly squeezed lemon juice
1 piece of Konbu approximately 10 cm
(4 in) square

8 slices sashimi-grade chu toro
sea salt and freshly ground black pepper
plain flour for dusting
60 g (2 1/2 oz) filo pastry
oil for deep frying
4 pieces hama bo-fu (red-stem trefoil)

First make the sauce by combining all the sauce ingredients in a bowl and leaving them to sit covered with cling film in the refrigerator overnight.

The next day, season the chu toro with salt and pepper. Then dust each piece with flour and wrap them individually in the filo pastry.

Pour enough oil in a medium to large pan to reach 8–10 cm (3 1/2–4 in) deep. Place the pan over a high heat and heat the oil to a temperature of 170°C (340°F). Add the chu toro pieces in batches. Allow them to fry for 20 seconds, lift them from the oil with a slotted spoon and drain them well on kitchen paper.

Arrange them on to a plate and pour the ponzu sauce around them. Garnish the plate with the hama bo-fu and serve.

Bloomsbury
China Town
Covent Garden
Soho

With the exception of the august Royal Opera House, confusingly and esoterically also known as Covent Garden, today the current Covent Garden piazza and quadrangle is little more than a children's tourist attraction with street-performance artists, novelty shops and stalls selling tourist paraphernalia. More relevant for this book is the area's past, starting in the Middle Ages. It was a thriving kitchen garden connected with the Convent of St Peter of Westminster, making the derivation of its name obvious. It became a major source of fruit and vegetables in London and was managed by grants from the Abbot of Westminster.

In the early seventeenth century the area was redesigned by Inigo Jones, one of the great English Renaissance architects. The market became more commercial, and when its competitors were wiped out during the 1666 Great Fire of London, Covent Garden became pre-eminent and continued to be so until its demise in the 1970s. New Covent Garden Market, a paler version of the old market and principally for traders and distributors only, is now located in Nine Elms, in south-west London.

Harking back to history, Covent Garden occasionally hosts modern-day farmers' markets, food fairs and a very good French market. Unless you have tickets for the opera or ballet, it's only worthwhile visiting the piazza on these special days.

Theatreland and the excitement of Soho have long supported the restaurant business. One cannot survive without the other and it makes for a happy coexistence. The best examples of this can be found when you look to the success of The Ivy and J. Sheekey.

Henry Dimbleby

I love Arbutus because my old boss Anthony Demetre is the most innovative chef in London. He uses El Bulli-esque science to create flawlessly executed classics.

Co-founder, Leon

All Star Lanes Victoria House, Bloomsbury Place, WC1B 4DA

020 7025 2676 www.allstarlanes.co.uk

This boutique ten-pin bowling alley offers more of a fun night out than a gourmet experience although the food is enjoyable. The simple diner menu has everything you would expect: hamburgers, hot dogs, Caesar salad, clam chowder and crab cakes. All are well made and generous. It's not inexpensive and the location is slightly offbeat. However, once you arrive the well-sourced beers and stylish cocktails, overseen by Henry Besant, London's leading bar supremo, loosen up the bowling arm. ○

Arbutus 63-64 Frith Street, W1D 3JN

020 7734 4545 www.arbutusrestaurant.co.uk

According to some (or is that many?), chefs are generally characterized as stubborn, rude and obnoxious. Once their personality has been set they will never change their ways, or, more importantly for the restaurateur, their style of cooking. Well, at Arbutus the chef has had a personality transplant.(PP) When Anthony Demetre was cooking at Putney Bridge Restaurant I hated every dish that I tasted and believed it epitomized everything that I didn't like about a certain style of food. However, I recently read that his new restaurant was different. Indeed it is. I thoroughly enjoyed two recent visits to Arbutus (named after a variant of the strawberry tree), and I can't wait to go back .

A move from haute cuisine typified by Michelin-orientated 'tricksy and ditziness' to bistrot moderne is very welcome. We don't know Anthony, maybe he has always favoured this style of cooking, and we certainly don't want to offend him personally with these comments. It is just interesting to use this anecdote to analogize what is also happening across the globe. Other leading chefs with worldwide reputations have started to reject the Michelin system and deconstruct the often towering dish design, reduce the number of ingredients on the plate and generally refocus on flavour.

The menu, pricing and service at Arbutus are just so. It is seasonal, not in any way overwhelming and strategically modest. You can sense that much effort, professionalism and technique have been afforded.

Another major plus about this restaurant is the wine list. First, it is not too big with about 25 white, 25 red, a few rose and five Champagnes. Wine lists that are too big are, in our opinion, antisocial. Secondly, all of the wines have been carefully selected with an even-handed representation of styles and countries. Thirdly all of the wines are available in 250 ml carafes so that you could enjoy a Chassagne-Montrachet 1er Cru or heavy-weight Bordeaux without shelling out for the whole bottle when you really only want a couple of glasses. ○

Left **Outside Arbutus on Frith Street close to Soho Square.**

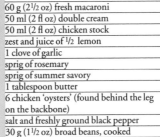

Chicken sot l'y laisse

Serves 1

60 g (2½ oz) fresh macaroni
50 ml (2 fl oz) double cream
50 ml (2 fl oz) chicken stock
zest and juice of ½ lemon
1 clove of garlic
sprig of rosemary
sprig of summer savory
1 tablespoon butter
6 chicken 'oysters' (found behind the leg on the backbone)
salt and freshly ground black pepper
30 g (1½ oz) broad beans, cooked

Fill a large saucepan with water and place it over a high heat. When it is boiling add the macaroni and cook it until it is al dente. Drain the macaroni and set it aside.

Infuse the cream, chicken stock, lemon juice and zest, garlic, rosemary and savory. Heat the mixture and then reduce it by half.

Melt the butter in a large frying pan over a medium heat. Add the chicken 'oysters' and sauté them. Season them with salt and pepper. Strain the reduced infusion and pour this in with the macaroni and broad beans. Season again to taste and serve.

Sea Bream

Serves 1

1 Maris Piper potato, peeled and diced
50 ml (2 fl oz) fish stock
extra-virgin olive oil
salt and freshly ground pepper
1 spring onion, sliced
1 plum tomato, sliced
1 head of gem lettuce, chopped
extra virgin olive oil
juice of ½ lemon
1 fillet of sea bream
a handful of fresh parsley, chopped

Place the diced potato in to a small saucepan and pour in the fish stock and one tablespoon of olive oil. Season the potato with salt and pepper and place the saucepan over a medium heat. Simmer the potato gently until cooked. Lift out the potato with a slotted spoon and set it aside on a warm place leaving the fish stock in the pan.

Add the spring onion to the fish stock and let it simmer until it is soft, and then add the plum tomato until warmed through. Add the chopped gem lettuce and let it simmer until it has softened. Pour the mixture in to a blender and liquidize it. Slowly add olive oil in a steady thin stream until the mixture has the consistency of a thick mayonnaise, then add the lemon juice. Set it aside while you cook the fish.

Preheat the oven to 150°C (300°F) Gas Mark 2 and place a serving dish in the oven to warm while you finish preparing the dish. Drizzle the fish in olive oil, place it in a baking dish and bake in the oven. After 8 minutes, take the fish out of the oven and carefully remove the skin.

Assemble the fish and potato on to the warmed plate and spoon the mayonnaise mixture on the side. Sprinkle with the chopped parsley and serve.

Arigato Japanese Supermarket 48–50 Brewer Street, W1F 9TG
020 7287 1722

A great source for all manner of Japanese and Asian ingredients, from wasabi to special rice or vinegars. They also have a small in-store sushi bar.

Bar Shu 28 Frith Street, W1D 5LF
020 7287 6688

Immediately after you read this entry on Bar Shu we urge you to call seven or eight friends and arrange with them to meet for dinner at Bar Shu as soon as possible. We suggest a large table so that you can taste and enjoy as many of the varied dishes as possible. The descriptions are great; the following are actually taken from the menu: numbing-and-hot dried beef; smacked cucumbers in hot-and-garlicky sauce; fire-exploding kidney flowers; pock-marked Old Woman's bean curd; 'bear's paw' bean curd in a spicy sauce; chicken soup with silver ear fungus and medicinal milk vetch root.

This restaurant specializes in food from the Chinese province of Sichuan, and Fuchsia Dunlop, the highly rated author of *Sichuan Cookery* has acted as their consultant. In nearby Chinatown you can find a glut of Cantonese dining options, but with the exception of only a few, these have become homogeneous in a sea of MSG. (PP) Bar Shu is a chilli-fuelled alternative that is, for me, more of a cultural experience. The menu includes traditional Chengdu street snacks with noodles and dumplings, plus a large selection of fragrant appetizers. You can also sample banquet delicacies, but the best dish on the menu has to be the Hot Pot. Go try it.

Chinatown Gerrard Street, Lisle Street and Newport Court, W1

Originally in Limehouse east London, the current Chinatown has been centred round Gerrard Street since the 1970s. The Chinoiserie extends to Lisle Street, where you can find the See Woo Hong Chinese supermarket at number 18–20 and Fung Shing at 15 Lisle Street. New World at 1 Gerrard Street and Wong Kei at 41–43 Wardour Street are both interesting experiences. Y'ming at 35 Greek Street is also popular.

Fuchsia Dunlop

"For lunch or dinner, I love St. John Bread and Wine, because of the honesty and deliciousness of the food, and, for shopping, See Woo in Lisle Street for the Chinese ingredients, and Borough Market for everything else.

Consultant, Bar Shu

Above left
Shredded beef and noodles at Bar Shu.
Right **Cantonese duck viewed through the window of a Chinatown restaurant.**

Gong Bao Chicken with Peanuts
gong bao ji ding

By Fuchsia Dunlop

Serves 2 as a main dish with a simple stir-fried vegetable and rice, or 4 as part of a Chinese meal with three other dishes

2 boneless chicken breasts, with or without skin, weighing about 300–350 g (10–12 oz) in total.

For the Marinade

1/2 teaspoon salt
2 teaspoons light soy sauce
1 teaspoon Shaoxing wine
1 1/2 teaspoons potato flour
1 tablespoon water

For the Stir-fry Mixture

3 cloves of garlic and an equivalent amount of fresh ginger
5 spring onions, white parts only
2 tablespoons groundnut oil
a good handful of dried chillies (at least 10)
1 teaspoon whole Sichuan pepper
75 g (3 oz) roasted peanuts

For the Sauce

3 teaspoons sugar
3/4 teaspoon potato flour
1 teaspoon dark soy sauce
1 teaspoon light soy sauce
3 teaspoons chinkiang or black Chinese vinegar
1 teaspoon sesame oil
1 tablespoon chicken stock or water

Cut the chicken as evenly as possible into 1.5-cm (3/4-in) strips and then cut these into small cubes. Place the chicken cubes in a small bowl and mix in the marinade ingredients. Set it aside while you prepare the other ingredients.

Peel and thinly slice the garlic and ginger, and chop the spring onions into chunks as long as their diameter (to match the chicken cubes). Snip the chillies in half or into 1.5-cm (3/4-in) sections. Discard their seeds as far as possible. Set these ingredients aside on the chopping board while you prepare the other ingredients.

Combine the sauce ingredients in a small bowl and set it aside.

Heat a wok over a high flame, and then add 2 tablespoons of oil. When the oil is hot but not yet smoking, add the chillies and Sichuan pepper and stir-fry them briefly until they are crisp and the oil is spicy and fragrant. Take care not to burn the spices (you can remove the wok from the heat if necessary to prevent overheating).

Quickly add the chicken and fry it over a high flame, stirring constantly.

When the chicken cubes are beginning to turn white, add the ginger, garlic and spring onions and continue to stir-fry them for a few minutes until they are fragrant and the meat is cooked through (test one of the larger pieces to make sure).

Give the sauce a stir and add it to the wok, continuing to stir and toss all the ingredients. As soon as the sauce has become thick and lustrous, add the peanuts, stir them in, and serve.

(Recipe featured in *Sichuan Cookery*, published by Michael Joseph, 2001. Reproduced by permission of Penguin Books Ltd.)

Floridita 100 Wardour Street, W1F 0TN

020 7314 4000 www.conran.com

Based on the original home of the daiquiri and mojito in Havana, this large supper club with dancing, music and cocktails serves Cuban and Latin American dishes including langosta – Cuban lobsters, which are specially flown in. ○

Hummus Bros 88 Wardour Street, W1F OTJ

020 7734 1311 www.hbros.co.uk

We like Hummus Bros because Christian and Ronen, the two friends (not brothers) who set up the business, are devoted to fresh ingredients, flavour and simplicity. With a dash of added humour, the whole concept is slightly eccentric. 'Hummusychology' (their own terminology) proffers interesting customs and behaviour for scooping your hummus with the choice of pitta and toppings. It is still early days for the business – the small Wardour Street operation is the first site – but hopefully the idea will catch on. They don't have a drinks licence at the moment and the beverage list is limited, but if you enjoy chickpeas, tabbouleh, pickles and the like, this is the place to go in Soho. We've always found the service to be charming, witty and informed, too. ○

Imli 167–168 Wardour Street, W1F 8WR

020 7287 4243 www.imli.co.uk

From the people behind Tamarind, another really excellent new-wave Indian restaurant in Mayfair, Imli is a more informal and casual offering. The menu is delightfully small and includes simple Indian street food at great value-for-money prices. The service is slick and the environment is modern without any elaborate nonsense. It is a great place to go after the theatre or for a quick lunch. ○

Right **Imli's Kerala street food presented and served in a modern and colourful environment.**

Mark Hix

The Ivy 1–5 West Street, WC2H 9NQ
020 7836 4751 www.the-ivy.co.uk

Everybody talks about the celebrity clientele and how difficult it is to secure a table at this legendary restaurant, but underneath there is an extremely well-managed business. Whenever we've taken friends who haven't dined at The Ivy before the response is similar: 'Wow, I didn't realize the food was good honest brasserie-style.'

The menu is comprehensive, with everything from bang bang chicken to Beluga caviar available as hors d'oeuvres. The shellfish ranges from oysters to lobster and chips, and the eggs, pasta and rice section provides brunch classics such as eggs Benedict and corned beef hash, or better still, Kedgeree. The fish, roasts and grills, and the entrées section also offer huge choices from far-reaching cuisines. Thai-baked seabass with soy sauce or curried chicken masala are not unusual. (PP) Simply grilled calf's liver or rib steaks are my favourites. Then there is always The Ivy Hamburger. You usually get a choice of at least a dozen side-dish options. In addition, The Ivy is one of the few remaining restaurants still serving great savouries such as Scotch woodcock or herring roes on toast. It isn't haute cuisine, but it most certainly is a long-established great menu that's seasonal, classic and also modern. There is always something that you want to eat.

In 1997 A.A. Gill wrote a book on The Ivy and included many of the recipes that you can still enjoy today. (PP) I regularly refer to my copy. The first pages of the book include a photograph of the then executive chef, Mark Hix. He's now a director of the company and oversees all of the group's restaurants.

Despite the change of ownership over recent years and the much predicted, but never realized, downfall, the main players stay and this surely contributes to the success of the service. The calibre of managers and waiting staff eclipses that of most other restaurants. The dining tables are relatively close together and the staff know intuitively how to glide around the dining room. They seem to communicate with each other on a different level from most other restaurants and the skill at the table is unquestionable. On a recent visit we enjoyed baked Alaska flambéed at the table. Where else can you appreciate such a dish without it being in the slightest bit cheesy?

Upstairs, the private dining room is often host to great gatherings and rumours are circulating that The Ivy will soon open a club and an outpost in the US. ◉

"

Food shopping in London has improved immensely over the years. I remember Elizabeth David in an early book of hers complaining that there were no food shops in London to compare with Peck of Milan or Fauchon of Paris for high quality ingredients. Likewise there was nowhere with the energy of Zabar's, Dean and Deluca or Balducci in New York. Well, things have changed, and a wander around Borough Market or one of the many London farmers' markets would satisfy Elizabeth today, I'm sure.

Chef director, Caprice Holdings

Above **The doorman outside The Ivy getting ready for a night greeting the great and the good, while fending off the paparazzi.**

Lindsay House 21 Romilly Street, W1D 5AF

020 7439 0450 www.lindsayhouse.co.uk

Larger-than-life Richard Corrigan cooks earthy and robust food
in a very sophisticated style with a large dose of Irish flare. The
flavours are not confused and the service is top-class without
being obsequious.

The restaurant is set within a Georgian townhouse conveniently
central to the buzz of Soho, but also just far enough away from the
madness of other Soho streets to make it an ideal location for many
different occasions. The restaurant is spread across a series of small
rooms on different floors and you ring the doorbell to enter. In terms
of special celebrations, luxury foods and high-end dining, We think
this is one of the best restaurants in London. ○

Maison Bertaux 28 Greek Street, W1D 5DQ

020 7437 6007

This is a rickety old French pastisserie and viennoiserie with a
small café that's been part of Soho life for years. The coffee is strong,
the staff true personalities and the self-indulgent éclairs still beat those
in the modern pastry shops. ○

The Neal Street Restaurant 26 Neal Street, WC2H 9QW

020 7836 8368

Originally a Conran-established and designed restaurant, this is
now owned by Terence's sister Priscilla and her mushroom-loving
husband Antonio Carluccio. After over 33 years without a redesign,
the restaurant still looks fresh and has been a firm favourite among the
tenors, baritones, instrumentalists and guests of the neighbouring
Royal Opera House who love its Italian food and fungi. Due to
the development of neighbouring property, the restaurant will
sadly close in the near future, but watch out for a new restaurant
from Antonio. ○

Far left **Outside
Maison Bertaux
Patisserie Française.**
Left **Traditional
French pastries
made on the
premises at
Maison Bertaux.**

Lindsay House | Irish Stew

There is some controversy about whether
carrots should be included in this dish.
Escoffier says no, but then what would
a Frenchman know about Irish stew?
I like them. Cold pickled red cabbage is
a traditional accompaniment in Ireland.

by Richard Corrigan

Serves 4

2 middle necks of lamb, filleted, boned and bones reserved
700 g (1½ lbs) carrots, peeled
450 g (15 oz) floury potatoes, such as King Edward, peeled
450 g (16 oz) waxy potatoes, such as Pentland Javelin or Maris Piper, peeled
1 onion, peeled and thickly sliced
good pinch of fresh thyme leaves
salt and freshly ground black pepper
fresh chives and parsley, chopped to garnish

First, make a well-flavoured stock using the
bones from the lamb and the trimmings
from the carrots and onion, plus any other
vegetables and herbs you like. Add 900 ml
(1½ pints) water and bring everything to
the boil and boil briskly for 30 minutes.
After that strain, discarding the vegetable
trimmings, and the stock is ready for use.

Cut the lamb into large chunks about
3 cm (1 in) square and place them in a heavy-
based saucepan. Set the saucepan over a high
heat and pour in the stock. Bring it to the
boil, skimming off all the impurities from
the surface. Then remove the pieces of lamb
with a slotted spoon and reserve. Take the
stock off the heat and pour it through a fine
sieve into a clean pan. Add the pieces of
lamb and bring it back to the boil. Reduce
the heat, cover and let it simmer gently for
10 minutes.

Meanwhile, cut the carrots into pieces a
little smaller than the pieces of lamb, and
the potatoes into pieces the same size as the
lamb. Add the carrots, onion and floury
potatoes to the pan and simmer for another
10 minutes. Then add the waxy potatoes
and the thyme, and let it simmer for a
further 15–20 minutes or until the lamb is
very tender. The floury potatoes will have
broken down into the sauce, while
the waxy potatoes will keep their shape.

Remove from the pan from the heat,
cover it and leave it, without stirring, for
15 minutes.

Check the seasoning, sprinkle it
generously with the chopped chives and
parsley and serve.

Above **Steamed dim sum at Ping Pong.** Left **A closed jasmine flower about to open when hot water is added.**

Ping Pong 45 Great Marlborough Street, W1F 7JL
020 7851 6969 www.pingpongdimsum.com

Be it baked puffs, steamed dumplings, steamed rolls, steamed buns, fried rolls, crispy prawn balls or other fried morsels, Ping Pong has a great menu, which is particularly well researched and modernized for today. The drinks menu includes a wide selection of cocktails as well as wine and spirits. The dim sum isn't quite as good as Yauatcha, and some say the food is better at the Golden Dragon in Chinatown, but they certainly can't beat the exceptionally low prices and value at Ping Pong. This is democratic dining at its best.

The décor and graphics are suitably simple, with shared tables and atmospheric lighting. When the stacks of bamboo steamed baskets arrive and the jasmine tea is poured the tables come to light.

The prawn toast is some of the best in London and the chicken's feet are an interesting delicacy. Ping Pong operate a no reservations policy so be prepared to queue at busy times, but it is worth the wait.

Randall and Aubin 16 Brewer Street, W1F OSQ

020 7287 4447

Surrounded by sex shops and peep shows, this atmospheric French brasserie, housed in a former butcher's shop, serves great lobster and chips. ◑

Rules 35 Maiden Lane, WC2E 7LB

020 7836 5314 www.rules.co.uk

Opened in 1798, Rules is the oldest restaurant in London. They serve traditional British food with great game, hand-raised pigs, aged beef and a hearty steak and kidney pudding. The ornate interiors are worth viewing, too. ◑

The Savoy Grill Savoy Hotel, The Strand, WC2R 0EU

020 7592 1600 www.gordonramsay.com

Once the preserve of captains of industry, prime ministers and the aristocracy, the new Savoy Grill is managed by the Gordon Ramsay team with Marcus Wareing overseeing the Modern British menu. ◑

J. Sheekey 28–32 St. Martin's Court, WC2N 4AL

020 7240 2565 www.j-sheekey.co.uk

J. Sheekey is often proclaimed as the best fish restaurant in London and we would have to agree. The other comments that usually accompany J. Sheekey is that it's the sister restaurant to The Ivy and Le Caprice, and most people feel that J. Sheekey shines brighter. It is generally assumed that the celebrity count is higher and the level of service is the best it gets. Well, we're not interested in celebrities and we've certainly had friendlier service, if not as efficient. However, we believe J Sheekey is a very good restaurant in fact, it is one of the best.

Service is good in a grown-up and perceptive manner. The seasoned waiting staff make eye contact with the table hosts and communicate in a non-verbal telepathic manner along with an *I've seen it all before* confidence. That's what's good about the service.

As you enter and pass the idiosyncratic doorman and the rather cramped entrance the self-assured reception team hustle you to your table or the bar. The bar is lovely, but don't accept it as a dining location. It is usually offered to those who cannot get a reservation or called too late. The dining tables are located in a series of small alcoves. Generally, they are considered discrete tables, but this can be reversed and become a nightmare if your fellow diners are louder than the small rooms can contain.

The menu is a pleasure to read and includes fresh fish, crustaceans and bivalves from our shores and seas, plus a few from those beyond. All manner of piscine pleasures can be had, from a small selection of caviar for absolute decadence, showing off or just the flavour – whatever applies. The fish pie is a perennial favourite, together with serious Dover sole, lobster thermidor and dressed crab. Steamed Devon cockles with samphire, Evesham asparagus with hollandaise and razor clams are divine seasonal treats.

(PP) For me, one of the negatives is that you always feel rushed. By the time your main course is cleared staff are already thinking about who will occupy the table next. It is for this reason I tend not to have a dessert, despite the magnetism of spotted dick with butter and golden syrup. ◑

Piccadilly Circus at night.

David Thompson

"

When I'm in London I love Locanda Locatelli for everything Italian, Fino for its great Spanish jamon, Royal China and Yauatcha for their gorgeous dim sum and La Fromergerie for the best cheese in the capital.

Chef and cookery writer, Nahm

Above top
Yauatcha waitress with Shanghai Lily and Citrus Rice Queen cakes.
Above and left
The ground floor pastry counter at Yauatcha.

Yauatcha 15–17 Broadwick Street, W1F ODL
020 7494 8888

Another masterpiece by Alan Yau, this all-day teahouse and restaurant has been a success since day one. However, we understand day one was delayed while several redesigns took place. At the time, all manner of rumours circulated about how the client had asked Christian Liaigre, the designer, to change and adjust everything after it was already completed. Whatever happened, it doesn't matter now because the whole operation is a complete and utter success. (PP) Initially, I didn't like the basement space, but others loved it. I now like it very much. Upstairs is unquestionably attractive, as are the staff, who must surely wear the best uniforms in London. Apparently, they were designed by Tom Yip, who also provided art direction for the film *Crouching Tiger Hidden Dragon*.

Most people declare that the dim sum and multitude of cakes and pastries served upstairs are the best in London. ◉

Brick Lane
Spitalfields

Sir Christopher Wren's protégé Nicholas Hawksmoor was commissioned in the eighteenth century to design Christ Church on Commercial Street, and today, after years of disrepair, the restoration is almost complete. While it's an impressive landmark, it is not the reason the area attracts 20,000 people at the weekend. The majority come for the markets and food. A few also come to catch a glimpse of residents Tracy Emin or Gilbert and George.

Just a two-minute walk from Liverpool Street Station, Old Spitalfields Market is open all week, but Sunday is the day it takes off. Hundreds of small market stalls are set up in both the original market and under the new extension. Bargain hunters and browsers throng the walkways before heading for lunch. A short walk from Spitalfields Market is another historic location – the eleven-acre Old Truman Brewery site. Established in 1666, it survived until 1972 as a brewery, but is now a centre for artists, graphic designers, photographic studios and Djs, and has a lively club and bar scene. On Sunday, they also have an energetic market. We suggest that you arrive early, revel in the crowds and take pleasure in the diverse street food.

Brick Lane has long been associated with immigrant populations, who have brought new cultures to London. First there were the Huguenots, following the Revocation of the Edict of Nantes in 1685, then the Jews in the nineteenth century and, latterly, Bangladeshis have made this area the centre of their community. The area's innumerable neon-lit curry houses are cheap and cheerful. Do try them once. While there is different management at each, they are all, in broad terms, the same, and no longer provide the benchmark. However, the food stores are extremely interesting.

Left **Among other things, Brick Lane is renowned as the London home of the most creative (and usually amusing) graffiti art by Banksy and other anonymous artists.**

93 Feet East 150 Brick Lane, E1 6QL
020 7247 3293 www.93feeteast.co.uk

Barbecued food is available in a heated courtyard adjacent to this live music and DJ venue. Impress a Sunday afternoon date with dancing, cool video art or a short film. ○

Ambala 55 Brick Lane, E1 6PU
020 7247 8569 www.ambalafoods.com

From swirls of jelabi to the besan ladoo, made with gram flour, almonds, pistachio and Brazil nuts, to the luminous (thanks to food colourings), marzipan-style kaju fruits, Ambala stocks an impressive selection of traditional sweets from the Indian subcontinent. Baklawa in every possible shape and description is also available.

While the sweet counter is impressive, they are more proud of the rasmalai. It is ideal as an after-dinner dessert on a sweltering hot evening whatever the culinary origin of the food that has preceded it. ○

Left **Indian sweets from Ambala.**

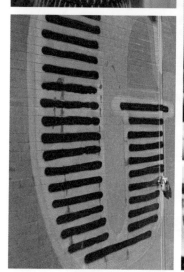

Beigels and doughnuts from Beigel Bake.

Beigel Bake 159 Brick Lane, E1 6SB
020 7729 0616
Open 24/7, Beigel Bake serves *everybody* and has been doing so for decades. Go at 4 am and watch the post-clubbing crowd or the London cabbies enjoying a salt-beef sandwich on a Saturday afternoon. The milky cholla still attracts the Jewish old-timers and the true East Enders come for pastries. They bake over 7,000 bagels a day and sell them for less than 20 pence each, or £1.50 with smoked salmon and cream cheese. ◉

136 **Canteen** 2 Crispin Place, Spitalfields Market, E1 6DW
0845 686 1122 www.canteen.co.uk

Canteen is a recent and very welcome addition to the Spitalfields scene. Located at the heart of the new Foster and Partners extension to the market, and overlooking the traders' trestle tables, the restaurant's interior features simple blond wood communal and democratic bench seats and long tables by BarberOsgerby or angular booths with individual angle-poise lights. It is more akin to a Wagamama than a retro British dining room.

The menu at Canteen respects the British heritage but also delivers modern and stylish cooking, a deftness of touch and well-judged portion size (the latter is all too often incorrectly interpreted at other so-called British restaurants). The chef is committed to providing honest food, nationally sourced, skilfully prepared and reasonably priced. Provenance is paramount, with many ingredients coming directly from producers practising only the best animal husbandry, or fish from the day boats on the south coast.

The kitchen bakes daily-changing pies to order and ensures they are served with good gravy, mash and greens. The choice of fried fish changes daily, according to the best catch. Canteen boasts an enticing range of roast dishes (assuming you allow 48 hours' notice) and an extensive breakfast menu is served all day: think Welsh rarebit, crumpets, black pudding and the best Cumberland sausages.

Since opening in late 2005 the chef has garnered praise from many of the most fastidious critics. Canteen has certainly captured the moment and we're sure this restaurant will last the course. ◗

The Canteen team

We love Bedales at Spitalfields Market – no ordinary wine shop, with excellent, well-priced wines sourced direct from producers, you can drink in for only £5 corkage, plus they serve tasty tapas too and the staff really know their stuff.

Canteen

Above **Barber Osgerby tables and bench seats at Canteen.** Right **A bacon and egg sarnie from Canteen.**

Blackcurrant Jelly with Vanilla Ice Cream and Shortbread

Serves 6

For the Blackcurrant Jelly

5 gelatine leaves
300 ml (1/2 pint) water
150 g (5 oz) sugar
500 g (1 lb) blackcurrants

Place the gelatine leaves in a dish of cold water to soak, and set it aside. Pour the measured water in to a saucepan and set over a high heat. Add the sugar and bring the mixture to the boil. Add the blackcurrants and let them simmer for 10 minutes.

Remove the saucepan from the heat and pour the blackcurrant mixture through a sieve into a large bowl to remove the seeds. Measure the resulting liquid: you should have 600 ml (1 pint). Set the blackcurrant mixture aside while you squeeze the water out of gelatine. Whisk the softened gelatine into the blackcurrant mixture, pour it through the sieve again and then divide the liquid between six glasses.

For the Vanilla Ice Cream

1 vanilla pod
500 ml (17 fl oz) full fat milk
200 ml (7 fl oz) double cream
6 egg yolks
170 g (6 oz) caster sugar

Split the vanilla pod and scrape out the seeds. Cut the pod in to small pieces with scissors. Pour the milk and cream into a saucepan, add the vanilla pieces and place it over a high heat. Bring the mixture to the boil, remove it from the heat and leave it to infuse.

After 1–2 hours, whisk the egg yolks and sugar until they are thick and foamy. Place the infused milk mixture over a high heat and bring it back to the boil, then pour in the egg mixture and turn down the heat. Cook it on a low heat, stirring it continuously with a wooden spoon until the mixture coats the back of the spoon.

Strain the mixture through a sieve and leave it to cool to room temperature. Churn the mixture in an ice cream machine, following the manufacturer's instructions, and place it in the freezer to firm up.

For the Shortbread

420 g (14 oz) plain flour
1/2 teaspoon baking powder
225 g (8 oz) unsalted butter
180 g (6 oz) vanilla sugar

Sift the flour and baking powder together in a bowl and set them aside. In another bowl, cut the butter into cubes. Toss the butter with the sifted flour, and leave it for 30 minutes. In the meantime, line a baking tray with greaseproof paper and set it aside.

Place the flour and butter mixture into the bowl of a KitchenAid or other food processor and process the mixture until it forms crumbs. Then add the sugar and continue processing it until it starts to form small lumps.

Spread the dough out on to the lined baking tray, pressing the dough down and ensuring it is even. Place the dough in the fridge to chill. After an hour, preheat the oven to 180°C (350°F) Gas Mark 4. Place the baking tray in the oven and bake it for 18–20 minutes. Remove the shortbread from the oven and, while it is still hot, cut it into fingers.

To serve, make a small well in the centre of each blackcurrant jelly and place a ball of vanilla ice cream on top. Serve the jelly and ice cream with fingers of shortbread. If the shortbread has cooled off, warm it in the oven for 5 minutes.

Coffee @ 154 Brick Lane, E1 6RU

020 7247 6735

Shade-grown (no trees are cut down) organic coffee beans are the big
thing at this edgy coffee bar. The chai latte is also pretty good on a wet
day – have it with soya milk to complete the feel-good factor. Paninis
and salads are all wrapped or boxed in environmentally conscientious
packaging. The walls are covered with posters announcing the latest
gigs and the furniture consists of comfy, well-worn leather sofas. ○

This page
Inside Coffee @.

Best Sunday Ever!

Start on Brushfield Street with an Italian coffee at Verde & Co. Buy some French artichokes or some Pierre Marcolini chocolate, then step next door to A.Gold and buy some London smoked salmon with pickled cucumbers or Uncle Joe's mint balls.

Then
– One-course lunch at Canteen. Call in advance and order one of the roast dishes like a whole roast chicken.

Then
– Browse the market stalls and pick up some organic green tea or some kalamata olives.

Then
– Cross Commercial Street to The Ten Bells for a quick Guinness and cigarette.

Then
– Collect your sourdough bread and Eccles cakes from St. John.

Then
– Head to the Up Market for a game of carrom with a cup of pan-roasted Ethiopian coffee.

Then
– Have a piece of carrot cake at Story Deli.

Then
– Visit Taj Stores for rare spices and rice.

Then
– Head to the Hookah Lounge for hot almond milk and baklava.

Then
– Go to the Vibe Bar for a cold Margarita.

Then
– Catch an art house short, then a gig at 93 Feet East and dance the night away.

Then
– Pick up a Pieminister steak and kidney pie for the journey home or breakfast, which ever comes first.

Above right **The A. Gold façade dates back to 1880, when the shop was a French milliner's.** Right **The Old Truman Brewery chimney and outside Vibe Bar on Brick Lane.**

A. Gold 42 Brushfield Street, E1 6AG
020 7247 2487 www.agold.co.uk

The shop front dates back to Amelia Gold's French milliner's of 1880. Located next door to Verde & Co., the new A. Gold is a purveyor of traditional foods of Britain, from savoury biscuits to smoked fish, cured meats and unpasteurized cheese, describing themselves as a village shop in the heart of London. They have a fine selection of store-cupboard essentials, jams, marmalades, honey and mustards, plus teas, teabreads and cakes. You can also find cider, perry and Cox's apple juice. Everything British that's GREAT! Uncle Joe's mint balls, acid drops (sour, but without the hallucinogenic effects of the namesake), plus other novelty sweets displayed on shelves in glass jars all add to the charm of this tiny shop. Fortunately, they have an extensive online mail-order system and an interesting range of gifts and hampers to choose from. Closed on Saturday's. ●

Hookah Lounge 133 Brick Lane, E1 6SB
020 7033 9072

Sucking on a hookah can be fun, but most of the regulars sip the cardamom coffee or teas from Afghanistan, Kashmir, Morocco and Turkey, all served in ornate pots. Local politicos plot for and against George Galloway over cocktails influenced by North Africa and kibbe, grilled halloumi, tabbouleh and other mezze. You can also get excellent hot almond milk.

The room is long and narrow with an interesting mix of North African lamps, copper pots and various kasbah objects fused with 1970s suburban house wares or cheap mass-produced art, but it all seems to work. Cool young French staff just back from Glastonbury complete the scene. ●

Pieminister at The Truman Brewery Yard 91 Brick Lane, E1 6QL
www.pieminister.co.uk

Outside Vibe Bar these award-winning West Country piemakers sell steak, kidney and ale pies with rich gravy and Desiree potato mash – the PM Pie. Or maybe you want to try the Heidi pie made with goat's cheese, sweet potato, spinach, red onion and roasted garlic, or a chicken of Aragon pie made with free-range British chicken or the matador pie with free-range beef steak, chorizo and sherry. The unique two pastry pies are all handmade and available with minty mushy peas. ●

Pride of Spitalfields 3 Heneage Street, E1 5LJ
020 7247 8933

Situated just off Brick Lane, this is the archetypal East End boozer – brazenly unmodernized. It serves a good range of ales, and has a cosy coal fire and cantankerous old cockney regulars depressing about the Hammers. Mary's Pantry offers basic pub grub and the wooden interior walls are covered in black and white photographs of a nineteenth-century working Grand Union Canal. ●

Above **Nicholas Hawksmoor's** totemic **Christ Church** on **Commercial Street.** Left **Brick Lane on Sunday afternoon.**

Above left **Gingham table coverings, black and white floor tiles and naff wall art inside S&M Café.**
Above right **The signature dish at Sausage and Mash, with the essential HP Sauce and mug of tea.**

S&M Café 48 Brushfield Street, E1 6AG
020 7247 2252
This mini chain of sausage-and-mash cafés offers a selection of half a dozen sausages from the classic Cumberland, London special or wild boar, to the more adventurous harissa spiced or chorizo style. They even offer a choice of three different mash recipes.

Fentiman's botanical curiosity cola or dandelion and burdock drinks together with gingham table coverings, all add to the retro credentials. Ketchup and HP Sauce are unashamedly placed on the tables. The 1970s and 1980s naff wall art can remind some of us of our parents' bad taste.

The Square Pie 16 Horner Square, South East Corner, Old Spitalfields Market, E1 6AA 020 7377 1114 www.squarepie.com
You can never have too many pie retailers. This established group, with its distinct red livery inside the market, offers a choice of about 15 different pies. You can also get Heinz beans and vegetarian onion gravy.

St. John Bread and Wine 94–96 Commercial Street, E1 6LZ
020 7251 0848 www.stjohnbreadandwine.com

A sibling of the seminal St. John, close to Smithfield Market, Bread and Wine is housed in a former bank and calls on the same no-design design ethic. It has white walls, a reclaimed parquet floor, a few pendant lights, counters clad in stainless steel and an open kitchen with a huge baker's oven.

Fergus Henderson continues the nose-to-tail cooking with the menu set out according to the time of the day. From 9 am you can indulge in porridge and prunes, an Old Spot bacon sandwich or even soft roes on toast. From 11 am, seedcake and a glass of Madeira provide a fillip and the always intensely seasonal best of St. John is rolled out after midday. Although slightly shorter and simpler than the main restaurant, you can still expect duck hearts partnered with pickled walnuts, lamb's tongue with green sauce, simply grilled sardines or veal shoulder with carrots and dumplings. Perfectly ripe cheese and madeleines baked to order end most meals.

Some prefer Bread and Wine for its more edgy and arty crowd. Tracy Emin is a regular and several well-known creatives live on the doorstep and often call in for the weekly sourdough or daily dose of Eccles cakes.

Expect short queues for lunch at the weekend as it can get very busy, but it's certainly worth any wait. The staff, in signature chef-style white jackets, also deserves a mention. ◉

Jeremy Lee

❝

An expression too often used although rarely adhered to is the lovely edict of Monsieur Escoffier, 'Faites simple'. To many, this seems anathema, highly visible presentation and fuss being the proof that much thought and labour have gone into the making of a great culinary creation. Nowhere has this dread way of doing been banished and nowhere has the rule of 'Faites simple' been elevated to a higher degree that has earned worldwide applause and respect, than at St. John. Here, Fergus Henderson pays homage to the ingredient in its natural state through judicious cooking.

Head Chef, Blueprint Café

Above **Inside the utilitarian St. John.**
Above middle **A pig awaiting the oven with foil on its ears so that they don't burn, but can be eaten when cooked.**
Above left **On the step outside St. John.**

Above **Inside
Story Deli.**
Left **The seats
at Story Deli
are sturdy
cardboard boxes.**

Story Deli 3 Dray Walk, The Old Truman Brewery, 91 Brick Lane,
E1 6QL 020 7247 3137

You can't help but feel good about Story Deli; the food looks great and
tastes delicious. It is all certified organic, or wild, and everything's
biodegradable, recycled or from sustainable sources. A brown paper
sign in the window boasts about the composting and recycling of the
restaurant's waste and how they plant trees. It doesn't say, but you can
assume that this is one of the world's first carbon-neutral restaurants.
Add all that to a high-ceilinged small white warehouse at the entrance
to one of London's most edgy locations. This is food for those who care
about what they put in their mouth, with an emphasis on vegetarian
dishes. Large bowls of salads and home-baked cakes are all placed on the
huge central dining table and the wafer-thin pizzas are de rigueur. You sit
on sturdy cardboard boxes set among industrial-sized paper bags of flour,
while dining cheek by jowl. They stock excellent soft drinks, such as hot
ginger beer or Sicilian lemonade, and the wine is served in paper cups. ○

Chocolate Cake

Serves 6

For the Cake Mix

85 g (3 oz) unsalted butter

275 g (9 oz) caster sugar

3 eggs, separated

100 ml (approximately 3 shots) of espresso

175 g (6 oz) plain flour

125 g (4 oz) walnut meal (coarsely broken walnuts)

100 ml (3½ fl oz) crème fraiche

For the Ganache

200 g (7 oz) dark chocolate 70% cocoa solids

220 ml (7½ fl oz) double cream

walnut meal to cover the top of the cake

For the cake

Preheat the oven to180°C (350°F) Gas Mark 4. Cream together the butter and 200 g (7 oz) of the caster sugar. Add the egg yolks and the espresso. Fold in the plain flour, walnut meal and the crème fraiche.

In a separate bowl whisk the 3 egg whites to stiff peaks, then add the rest of the caster sugar and continue to whisk to a stiff meringue consistency.

Pour the egg white mix into the cake mix and gently fold in. Pour into a lightly greased cake tin and bake for 30 minutes. Remove from the oven and leave to cool.

For the ganache

Slowly melt the chocolate with the double cream. If the mixture splits remove from the heat and slowly whisk in a small amount of cold milk.

Allow to cool until the mix reaches a spreadable consistency.

Spread the ganache mix over the cake and then liberally cover with the extra walnut meal.

This page **Inside Taj Stores.**

Taj Stores 112–116 Brick Lane, E1 6RL
020 7377 0061

If you thought your knowledge of rare and unusual fruit and vegetables could match that of most chefs, try naming the ingredients as you enter this cornucopia of foods from India, Bangladesh, Malaysia and Thailand to mention just a few of the sources. Chow chow, turia, ravaja, gourds, muki, and eddoe are just a few of the wonderfully unusual products displayed in large crates alongside the profuse peppers and chillies.

At the rear of the store you will find large chest freezers filled with up to 12 different types of prawns set in blocks of ice. There are also 3 cm-long, deliciously oily, translucent keshi fish or the metre-long and very ugly rita fish and freshwater whole ungutted mirror carp only used in Bangladeshi restaurants.

The halal meat counter includes pheasant, duck, pigeon and goat alongside lambs' brains and chicken hearts. This is a specialist food supplier at its best. Naturally, spices and rice are in abundance, including a special rice for diabetics. If you're thinking about cooking an Indian supper for friends, the starting point is a visit to Taj Stores. Even if you only buy a tarva pan for your chapatti it will certainly impress any guest. ●

The Ten Bells 84 Commercial Street, E1 6LY
020 7366 1721

Sundays are packed out all day and the midweek afternoons attract fashion waifs and DJs connecting with their bohemian side. The beers are nothing special and the bar only stocks a few proprietary spirits on the now rare optic-measure system. But it is the people and nicotine-stained atmosphere that draws everyone in. What will it be like after the smoking ban hits London?

In the shadow of Hawksmoor's Christ Church, The Ten Bells has links to Jack the Ripper. However, it's best not to talk about that – it only attracts the tourists and morbid Ripper geeks. ●

Up Market Food Stalls Up Market, Hanbury Street,
Old Truman Brewery, E1 6QL Sundays 10 am–5 pm

The local carrom (an easy to understand board game, believed
to have originated in India hundreds of years ago, it is often
compared to billiards, marbles or air hockey) league meets
regularly every Sunday so pick up an herbal lassi and wait your
turn. Everybody is welcome.

Street food, from sushi to paella or empanada to falafel, rules
at the Up Market. You can even buy a healthy jungle juice from
Caribbean Momma's. My personal favourite is the Ethiopian stalls.
Soya shuroh and gomen (Ethiopian greens) are wrapped in soft
injera bread, made with four different flours. Ethiopian coffee is
roasted in small pans over charcoal, crushed, and then placed in a
jebena pot with hot water.

A trailer kitchen outside the market sells cheap Lao and Thai
staples like tom yum, phad Thai and red curries. ◉

Above left **An
Ethiopian jebena
coffee pot on coals.**
Right **Street food
rules at the Up
Market on Sunday.**

FARM EGGS
FRESH BREAD
··
TOFFEE SHOP FUDGE
LEMON CURD
CIDER BRANDY.

This page
**Verde & Co. sells
the very best
quality ingredients
in season.**

Verde & Co 40 Brushfield Street, E1 6AG
020 7247 1924

This boutique continental grocer was set up by Harvey Cabaniss, a former St. John chef, on the ground floor of a beautifully restored Georgian building owned by the writer Jeanette Winterson. Save for a few specialist items, the produce is exclusively sourced from small co-operatives and family-run firms. Italian farmhouse eggs, French artichokes and other premium prime-condition fruit and vegetables are displayed on the pavement outside. They also stock the fantastic Pierre Marcolini chocolate. ◐

Vibe Bar The Old Truman Brewery, 91 Brick Lane, E1 6QL
020 7426 0491 www.vibe-bar.co.uk

One of the original and most innovative bar-meets-club venues, and part of the founding team behind the revamped Truman Brewery, this is a centre for the creative arts. It is still cutting edge and a hive of activity for young graphic designers, architects and musicians. ◐

Chelsea
Kensington

According to the 2001 census, the Royal Borough of Kensington and Chelsea is the most densely populated local authority in the UK with a population of almost 160,000 spread over 12 square kilometres (7½ square miles). Strictly speaking, the borough also incorporates sections of Notting Hill, Belgravia, Knightsbridge and areas of the Fulham Road that, for the purposes of this book, have been listed separately. Another interesting fact about RBKC, as it is often abbreviated, is that it has the highest number of high earners (over £60,000 per annum) in the country. We certainly weren't surprised to learn about this last fact. Kensington and Chelsea has transcended gentrification to achieve a residential zone that is the envy of the world.

Owning and operating a restaurant in an area of such wealth should be a restaurateur's paradise. However, we know from experience that a large proportion of the population have second homes in other countries or the Home Counties. Therefore, a mass exodus generally occurs on Friday afternoon. Furthermore, these high net-worth individuals are busy people and either work late in the City during the week or attend corporate events. This makes it a particularly tricky area in which to operate a restaurant. On the one hand you must offer exceptional service and food standards to attract the key residents, but when doing this your prices automatically start to increase, thus alienating other markets.

Kensington Place is one of the best restaurants in London and has managed to balance these factors perfectly by creating a smart brasserie that is suitable for all occasions.

Pascal Aussignac

11 Abingdon Road W8 6AH

020 7937 0120

Opened only recently, this well-liked neighbourhood restaurant serves
modern European food in a stylishly restrained and self-confident space
displaying interesting art. ◉

Tom Aikens 43 Elystan Street, SW3 3NT

020 7584 2003 www.tomaikens.co.uk

Tom is renowned as an unruly taskmaster with some infamy to his
name, but the more important facts relate to his achievements and
numerous awards, not least two Michelin stars at Pied à Terre. His
eponymous Chelsea restaurant currently has one star, which we fail
to understand. Surely it deserves at least two. We are not fans of the
Michelin system, but this restaurant seems to stand out from several
other one-star places and demonstrates all the characteristics you
would associate with other two-star places. This further demonstrates the need for an overhaul of the Michelin system or
maybe just a trashing. Perhaps Tom Aikens will have two stars by
the time this book is published. We wish you good luck with
that, Tom.

Anouska Hempel has designed the restaurant and the tableware
is particularly desirable to own (a light-hearted joke referring to the
large amount of stock that disappears from the tables).

It's a rather basic way to view the food, but one of the more
enjoyable aspects of Tom's dishes is that you get plenty of sauce on
your plate. It is particularly annoying when other chefs merely provide
a drizzle to accompany a large piece of protein. But then, this is just a
personal view.

It's more than a rumour that a new, more informal offering called
Tom's Kitchen will soon open just up the street from the restaurant.
Early reports sound really enticing, with news of a mainly organic British
menu, a purpose-built hanging room for the meats – not the chefs – plus
a huge rotisserie and wood oven. ◉

Above **Tom Aikens
in his kitchen.**
Opposite **Inside the
Anouska Hempel-
designed Tom
Aikens restaurant.**

Bibendum Restaurant and Oyster Bar Michelin House,

81 Fulham Road, SW3 6RD 020 7581 5817 www.conran.com

Like many Londoners we rate Bibendum as one of the best places to dine
in the capital. Starting with the handsome architecture, the excellent
location and the building's previous use as the headquarters for the
Michelin Tyre Company from 1909, it is always a pleasant experience,
whatever the occasion. (TC) Since 1987, when Paul Hamlyn and I
created its new format and reopened the building, it has provided a
joie de vivre that is still hard to equal.

The Coffee Bar on the ground floor opens early and serves freshly
baked Viennoisserie and milky bridge rolls, the house speciality. A small
counter selling wet fish and various crustacea, plus a working florist
and the Conran Shop next door help establish the forecourt as a hub
of activity at the axis of Chelsea and South Kensington.

Lunch at the Oyster Bar is one of the essentials for anybody visiting
London. The original tiled floors and walls depicting motor-racing scenes from the Art Nouveau and Deco periods don't hold

the grandeur of Grand Central Station in New York. But, somehow,
the modest scale is more British and the French undertones add a note
of sophistication.

The smell of freshly baked baguettes and the sight of plateau de fruits
de mer served by well-trained staff in the essential black and whites are so
appealing. The menu also includes salads, smoked fish, a house terrine,
vitello tonnato and it even has space for decadence in the form of Sevruga
caviar with a good selection of Champagne.

Upstairs the atmosphere is more elegant, but without a hint of
pretension. The armchairs are comfortable and change their colour
every season. Space between the white linen covered tables is conducive
to a sociable ambience and you bathe in an abundance of natural light.
Monsieur Bibendum the iconic Michelin man, in the form of several
colourful stained-glass images, oversees everything that occurs. Fun and
quirky references to his corpulence and love of cigars are evident
throughout. The decanters, flower vases, table legs, the bar, art, coat
stands and the best ashtrays in the world all characterize his peculiar shape.

Simon Hopkinson, the founding chef and inspiration for many
of London's top chefs, together with his successor, Matthew Harris, have
consistently delivered classic dishes with a French bias and an occasional
contemporary twist. The portions are always generous and the flavours
more so.

Above **The upstairs
restaurant's stained-
glass window
featuring Monsieur
Bibendum.**

Not to be confused or connected with the London wine company
of the same name, the restaurant has an award-winning wine list. ●

This page
**The Bibendum
Oyster Bar.**
Left middle **Scallops
a la Provençale.**

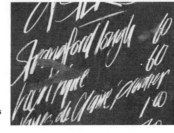

Ceviche of Oysters with Cucumber and Dill

Serves 4

1 cucumber, peeled
2 bird's-eye chillies, seeds removed
1 red onion, diced down to 2.5 mm (1/8 in)
juice of 3 limes
1 bunch of dill, chopped
1 dessertspoon olive oil
salt and freshly ground black pepper
24 rock oysters
4 teaspoons crème fraîche

Cut the peeled cucumber in half lengthways and remove the seeds with a teaspoon. Now cut the remaining flesh into a fine 2.5 mm (1/8 in) dice and set aside. Chop the seeded chillies finely and place them in a bowl. Add the cucumber and the diced onion and combine. Then add the juice of the limes, the chopped dill and the olive oil. Season it with salt and pepper and set it aside for 10 minutes to macerate.

Open the oysters and divide them between four plates. Spoon a heaped teaspoon of the cucumber mixture on to each oyster. Allow the oysters to sit for 10 minutes before serving at room temperature.

To serve, top each oyster with a small blob of crème fraîche.

Above **Grilled rabbit with sauce vierge and pappardelle.** Right **Poire William parfait with blackcurrant poached pear and madeleines,** another speciality from Bibendum.

Bibendum

Grilled Rabbit with Sauce Vierge and Pappardelle

Serves 4

2 farmed rabbits (head and shoulders removed)
8 tomatoes
2 cloves of garlic, finely chopped
4 shallots, finely chopped
1 bunch of basil, leaves picked and finely chopped
150 ml (¼ pint) olive oil
zest and juice of 1 lemon
salt and freshly ground black pepper
400 g (13 oz) pappardelle

To prepare the rabbit for grilling, first remove the livers. Then cut the legs away from the saddle by following the ball and socket joint with your knife. With a small, sharp knife, next remove the outer membrane that covers the loin by cutting just below the surface and dragging your knife along the saddle. You will have to repeat this two or three times on each side of the saddle to remove it all. You will be left with a clean looking loin and a little pile of scraps. Now cut the loin in half with a large chopping knife. Having done both rabbits, you will be left with four portions, each being one leg and half a saddle. The liver can be cut in half as well and served. Cover and place in the refrigerator while you prepare the other ingredients. (Alternatively, you can ask your butcher to do this for you if you do not feel confident to do it yourself.)

Make the sauce vierge by scoring the tomatoes and blanching them in boiling water to remove their skins. Then cut them into four, remove the seeds with a knife and discard them. Cut the remaining flesh into 5-mm (¼-in) dice and put it in a bowl. Add the chopped garlic, shallots, basil and olive oil. Grate the zest of the lemon and add this to the bowl, along with the lemon juice, and combine. Season the mixture with salt and pepper. Allow this dressing to sit for 20 minutes before using it.

Preheat the grill. Put a large pan of salted water over a high heat and bring it to the boil for the pappardelle. Season the rabbit with salt and pepper, brush with olive oil then place on a grill rack and set it under the grill. (If it starts to get too dark under the grill, finish it in the oven at 200°C (400°F) Gas Mark 6.) Prepare the liver in the same way, then, when the rabbit is almost cooked, add the liver, as it will not take as long to cook as the rabbit. The rabbit is cooked when it becomes firm to the touch and cooked through like a chicken breast, but still juicy and moist.

Meanwhile, when the water comes to the boil, add the pappardelle and cook it following the directions on the package. When it is cooked al dente, drain it through a colander.

To assemble the dish, divide the cooked pappardelle among four plates with half a saddle, a leg, and some liver on each plate.

Dress the dish with the sauce vierge and serve.

Chelsea / Kensington

155

Mark Broadbent, the chef at Bluebird, has probably one of the largest and most difficult assignments in London. With a bustling ground-floor café, forecourt barbecue, 200-seat brasserie, a new two-floor Épicerie, an outside catering company, private members club and his blue-ribbon British Dining Room, jobs don't come much bigger.

(PP) I must immediately declare a fondness for Bluebird. As general manager of the original-format building, it is the gastrodrome where I started my career with Conran Restaurants. I know from experience that the 50,000 square foot (15,240 square metre) building is terrifically challenging to manage, yet enormously rewarding when you see the place bustling with shoppers, diners and drinkers.

Throughout, the design makes subtle reference to the building's past, especially the period between 1927 and 1935 when it was home to the original Malcolm Campbell Bluebird cars that broke the world land speed record at 301.129 mph. The forecourt that once accommodated the fuel pumps is the place on the King's Road for a pit stop and refuel with meats from the barbecue, a hamburger or a summer salad, whilst watching the world go by. Over the summer months, the tables are turning from breakfast to dusk.

The new Épicerie is particularly good, with a fine selection of luxury delicatessen products, and the basement houses a small wine shop that regularly hosts tastings. On the first floor you will find a huge bar, brasserie and private dining room located amongst the steel eaves. Next door in the Dining Rooms and Club, Mark cooks his own distinctive upmarket British menu in surroundings to match. The studio-like space features a large collection of Paul Slater's colourful illustrations with a strong food and drink identity. Several specially commissioned and valuable Jack Vettriano pieces also hang in the club.

Terence acquired the building in an almost derelict state in 1995 and it reopened in 1997. It is now living its new life as a King's Road landmark, literally, as many use Bluebird as the compass point for other premises.○

Top right **The art deco enamel tiled wall bordering Bluebird forecourt on the King's Road.** Right middle **The elegantly appointed Bluebird Dining Rooms with hardwood and leather arm chairs, large tables, white linen and generous distance between each table.** Right **An Ingo Maurer light fitting in the centre of the glass ceiling in the Dining Room. A recipe or cooking tip is featured on each piece of parchment.**

Far left **Fresh fruit and vegetables beautifully displayed in the Bluebird Épicerie.** Above left **The popular forecourt barbecue at Bluebird.** Left **Legs of cured ham and garlic hanging above the counter in the Épicerie.**

New Season's Lamb Rump with Pearl Barley and Yellow Leg Mushrooms

by Mark Broadbent

Serves 4

Here, we've taken a risotto idea and replaced the rice with pearl barley – the result? Delicious!

olive oil
4 trimmed lamb rumps
salt and freshly ground black pepper
100 g (3½ oz) butter
5 shallots, finely chopped
3 cloves of garlic, finely chopped
220 g (7½ oz) yellow leg mushrooms (girolles)
300 ml (½ pint) mushroom stock
250 g (8 oz) pearl barley, cooked
200 g (7 oz) broad beans, skinned
120 g (4 oz) Parmesan cheese, grated
zest of 1½ lemons, finely grated
5 stalks parsley, finely shredded
4 globe artichokes, cooked
200 ml (7 fl oz) lamb stock (brown)

157

Preheat the oven to 200°C (400°F) Gas Mark 6. Place a little oil in to a large ovenproof pan and put it on a high heat. Season the lamb and fry it until it is golden brown all over. Then place the lamb in the oven and, depending on how well you want it to be cooked, leave it there for 6–12 minutes for rare, 8–12 minutes for medium rare or 16–20 minutes for well done. Then take the lamb out of the oven, remove it from the pan and allow it to rest on a wire rack.

Meanwhile, heat half of the butter in a saucepan over a medium heat. Add the shallots, garlic, mushrooms and sauté for 2 minutes. Pour in the mushroom stock and let it reduce by half. Add the pearl barley and let it warm through.

Add the broad beans, the remaining butter, the Parmesan cheese, lemon zest and parsley, and season it to taste. The mixture should be firm and creamy and not too wet. Allow it to rest for 2 minutes.

Meanwhile, pour the lamb stock into a saucepan and place it over a medium heat to warm.

Now carve the lamb and set it aside. To arrange the dish, divide the pearl barley mixture into four bowls, keeping it to the left-hand side. Fan the lamb rump slices to the right-hand side of bowl, allowing them to overlap the barley mix. Place the cooked artichoke leaves top of the barley mix to add some height. Pour the lamb stock over everything and finish the dish with a drizzle of olive oil and a sprinkle of sea salt.

Paul Slater's colourful illustrations adorn the walls in the studio-like Bluebird Dining Rooms.

Summer Potage of Broad Beans, Green Gammon Hock and Soft Herbs

by Mark Broadbent

Serves 4

150 g (5 oz) butter
8 shallots, finely chopped
4 cloves of garlic, peeled and grated
4 sprigs of lemon thyme
2 bay leaves
2 litres (3½ pints) ham stock (or vegetable stock)
1.5 kg (3 lb) broad beans, fresh or frozen
salt and freshly ground black pepper

For the Garnish

smoked gammon hock
broad beans, podded
handful of mint, parsley and lemon thyme, finely shredded
zest of ½ lemon
olive oil, to drizzle

Melt the butter in a heavy-based saucepan over a medium heat. Add the shallots, garlic, thyme and bay leaves. Allow them to sweat slowly, without covering the pan, for 5 minutes. Then add the ham or vegetable stock, and turn up the heat. Bring the mixture to the boil, and let it simmer. After 5 minutes have gone by, add the broad beans and let them simmer for 2 minutes.

Pour the soup through a sieve or colander into a large bowl. Place the solid ingredients in to a food processor and blitz them. Slowly add the reserved liquid to the solid ingredients until you reach a pouring consistency. Season the soup to taste and then pass it through a fine sieve.

For the garnish, boil the smoked gammon hock until the meat comes away from the bone, then shred the meat. To serve, reheat the soup if necessary and top with the shredded gammon hock, podded broad beans, finely sliced, mint, parsley, thyme, grated lemon zest and a drizzle of olive oil.

Cambio de Tercio 163 Old Brompton Road, SW5 OLJ
020 7244 8970 www.cambioetercio.co.uk

The Spanish government awarded the founders Abel Lusa and David Rivero the 'Premios Alimentos de Espana 2004' for being the best Spanish restaurant in any country of the world outside Spain. Generally quiet at lunch, the restaurant comes to life in the evening. The room features strong colours and the artwork by Luis Cañizares has a bullfighter identity.

Across the road the management have opened a really good tapas bar and small delicatessen called Tendido Cero. We prefer this place.

Le Cercle 1 Wilbraham Place, SW1X 9AE
020 7901 9999

We don't normally like restaurant interiors designed by Keith Hobbs – in particular Galvin at Windows on the World, Pearl and Nobu – but this one is quite acceptable. Barring the overuse of sheer curtains, we like the combination of leather, heavy and crafted timbers, Scandinavian-style dining chairs, the cheese conditioner, cosy corners and the bar surface. Although, I've heard on the grapevine that most of the good ideas come from Pascal Aussignac, the chef proprietor.

The food comes from the Club Gascon team, although the point of difference is that they have created a 'grazing' menu, which allows diners to order several smaller portions of traditional French favourites. For us, the overall effect is better than Club Gascon.

The bar is also a good place to meet friends and share a bottle of wine and order a few small plates of smartly presented but rustic-flavoured foods.

Clarke's 122 and 124 Kensington Church Street, W8 4BH
020 7221 9225 www.sallyclarke.com

Following a four-year stint in California and forming a friendship with Alice Waters at the seminal Chez Panisse, Sally returned to London in 1984 and established Clarke's. Like Chez Panisse, the restaurant originally offered a no-choice daily-changing menu based on what was good, fresh and seasonal. (PP) For me, sadly, this policy has recently changed and they now offer more choices – I suppose that this is what the public wants and after 20 years I assume Sally has proved her point. That said, I would still hope to open a humble place myself one day with just one menu based on the same principles.

In 1988 the adjoining shop was opened and has flourished ever since. The bakery is renowned across London, with many of the leading delis, hotels and restaurants serving the breads and pastries. The shop includes an extensive range of excellent fruit, vegetables, larder essentials, sauces, salads and much more. They also offer a seasonal menu of sweet and savoury cakes and tarts that change twice a week from apricot clafoutis and bitter chocolate cake to oven-dried vine tomato, goats cheese and basil tart and asparagus, leek and Parmesan tart.

Above **Sally Clarke**. Left **Tarts and strawberry meringues from Clarke's.**

160

Eight Over Eight 392 King's Road, SW3 5UZ
020 7351 5157 www.eightovereight.nu

Will Ricker seems to own a pan-Asian eatery on every corner in every cool neighbourhood in London. Eight Over Eight serves good dim sum, sushi, sashimi and tempura. Success is due to the quality of the food, good design and killer cocktails. •

The Fish Shop at Kensington Place 201–209 Kensington
Church Street, W8 7LX 020 7243 6626 www.egami.co.uk

This is an impressive fish shop that also sells prepared meals, soups and sauces, along with other goodies. •

Kensington Place 201–209 Kensington Church Street, W8 7LX
020 7727 3184 www.egami.co.uk

Designed by Julian Wickham, also responsible for the original Vth Floor at Harvey Nichols and Bank Restaurant, the dining room of Kensington Place is immediately reassuring, with its distinctive chairs and fabulous shop-front glass window. Kensington Place opened in 1987 and was one of first contemporary brasseries. Rowley Leigh, the chef on opening night, is still at the piano today. One of the most respected guys in the business, Rowley has a weekly column in the *Financial Times* that is extremely informative and a pleasure to read.

Not to be forgotten, the wine list at Kensington Place has many virtues of its own. •

A.A. Gill

"

Kensington Place has one of the best menus in the world: food that can be eaten three or four times a week. Rowley Leigh's cooking is contemporary rather than fashionable, simple where it needs to be, with dextrous flourishes, thoughtful combinations and, above all, seasonality. If you haven't tried the chicken and goat's cheese mousse or the griddled scallops with pea purée and mint vinaigrette, you just don't understand what you're missing.

From AA Gill's Sunday Times weekly column

Above left **A large marlin outside the Fish Shop at Kensington Place.** Above right **Rowley Leigh – one of the best chefs and food writers in London.**

Charlotte Pennington

"After collecting your meat at Lidgate's, you might want to take in a few Italian specialities from Speck delicatessen around the corner – they are the only place, that I know, in London that stocks Cipriani products, including a great canned peach juice for making the perfect Bellini. Nearby, Jeroboams stocks good cheese, including Vacherin Mont d'Or in season, and Maison Blanc have plenty of French fancy cakes. Then walk to the Saturday morning Notting Hill Farmers' Market (on the car park behind Kensington Place restaurant and fish shop) for breads, vegetables and fruit.

Notting Hill Gate resident and Peter Prescott's dining-out companion

Above **Lidgate's ornate façade on Holland Park Avenue.**

C. Lidgate 110 Holland Park Avenue, W11 4UA
020 7727 8243

David Lidgate runs this fourth-generation family butcher's that understands customer service, with nothing being too much trouble. When I visited recently three successive customers each requested something unusual or difficult; the butchers wearing straw boater hats and bow ties unflappably and courteously fulfilled the demand. They sell the best quality meats, poultry, game in season, sausages and Kelly's turkey's at Christmas. If you want heather-fed Shetland lamb, a haunch of wild boar or teal and other wild ducks this is the place to come.

The Shepherd's and Cottage pies are very tasty and made on the premises. The pre-marinated meats, meat balls, kofta kebabs and jerk chicken are all ideal for mid-week meals when you haven't got time or the inclination to roast a large piece of meat. ●

162 **The Pig's Ear** 35 Old Church Street, SW3 5BS

020 7352 2908   www.thepigsear.co.uk

This is one of the best gastropubs in London today: the food here is good, the atmosphere is welcoming and the interior has been sensitively and respectfully fashioned. It's been said before: they have created *a silk purse from a sow's ear*. They have a good daily-changing bar and dining room menu. The deep-fried pig's ear with sauce ravigote should be mandatory on every visit. ○

Restaurant Gordon Ramsay 68 Royal Hospital Road, SW3 4HP

020 7352 4441   www.gordonramsay.com

The apotheosis of fine dining, the Gordon Ramsay flagship restaurant has retained its three coveted Michelin stars since 2000. Mark Askew is the executive head chef and Jean-Claude Breton the maitre d'. Both have been with Gordon since the early days at Aubergine.

The dining room and kitchens were refurbished during August 2006 so if you've been before, it's maybe time to go again. The restaurant is located adjacent to the Chelsea Physic Garden, which is also worth a visit. ○

Randalls 113 Wandsworth Bridge Road, SW6 2TE

020 7736 3426

Favoured by several high-profile chefs, this is one of London's top five butcher's. It specializes in organic and free-range meat and dairy products but it also sells a range of home-made pies and cheese. ○

Ashley Hancill

"

Passion, commitment and consistency are everything in my business. That is why my favourite restaurant of all time would be Harvey's. Sadly, it is no longer open. I worked with Marco Pierre White in these hailed times and the experience still influences my cooking today.

Head Chef, The Pig's Ear

Above left **A well stocked waiter station at The Pig's Ear.**
Above **The upstairs dining room at The Pig's Ear.**
Opposite **A regular in the bar at The Pig's Ear.**

Rasoi Vineet Bhatia

Grilled Lobster with Curry Leaf, Lobster Jus and Broccoli Khichdi

Serves 2

For the Lobster

2 lobsters, each cut in half
1 sprig curry leaves, chopped
1 tablespoon fresh chopped ginger root
salt to taste
a knob of butter

For the Broccoli Khichdi

3 tablespoons vegetable oil
3 tablespoons butter
1 teaspoon mustard seeds
2 sprigs curry leaves
2 shallots, sliced
1 teaspoon chopped fresh ginger
1 teaspoon chopped garlic
1 teaspoon chopped green chillies
3 tablespoons chopped broccoli
200 g (7 oz) basmati rice
600 ml (1 pint) shellfish stock
salt to taste
3 tablespoons Greek yoghurt, whipped

For the Lobster jus

4 tablespoons vegetable oil
1 onion, roughly chopped
2 cloves of garlic, crushed
3 tablespoons coarsely chopped carrots
1 celery stick, coarsely chopped
3 lobster shells
4 tablespoons tomato purée

For the Roux

30 g (1¼ oz) butter
30 g (1¼ oz) flour
salt to taste
40 ml (1½ fl oz) cream

First, blanch the lobster claws by putting a saucepan of water over a high heat and bringing it to the boil. Immerse the claws in the water, reduce the heat and simmer for 5 minutes. Then drain the claws and wash under cold runnng tap water. Pat them dry on kitchen paper and crack the claws with the back of a knife, to expose the meat.

Preheat the grill. Mix the curry leaves, ginger and salt together in a bowl and rub the mixture in to the lobster. Grill the lobster tail and claw in a nonstick ovenproof pan. Add a knob of butter and finish them off in the oven at 180°C (350°F) Gas Mark 4.

For the broccoli khichdi, heat the oil and 2 tablespoons of the butter in a stockpot. Add the mustard seeds and when they start to crackle, add the curry leaves. Add the sliced shallots and sauté until translucent. Add the ginger, garlic and green chillies,

and sauté them for two minutes before adding the chopped broccoli. Cook everything for a further 2 minutes.

Pour in the basmati rice and stir it until the rice is coated with the oil and butter. Add the stock and salt. Bring the mixture to the boil and reduce the heat to simmering. Cover and simmer until the rice is half cooked. Stir in the whipped yoghurt, replace the lid and cook the rice until it is fully done. To serve, stir in the remaining tablespoon of butter. Set the rice aside in a warm place until you have made the lobster jus.

To prepare the jus, heat the oil in a stockpot. Add the onion, garlic and celery and sauté them until the onion is slightly coloured. Add the lobster shells and cook them until they turn red. Stir in the tomato purée and sauté. Add just enough water to cover the lobster shells and bring the mixture to the boil. Turn down the heat, cover the pan and let it simmer for 15–20 minutes.

Meanwhile, in a separate pan prepare a roux to thicken the jus as follows. Place the pan over a medium heat and add the butter. When it melts, add the flour and cook it, stirring constantly on a slow heat. When it becomes blond in colour, blend the roux into the jus and bring it to the boil. Take the jus off the heat and strain it through a sieve. Season it with salt and finish it off by stirring in the cream.

To assemble the dish, place a ring mould in the centre of a large soup plate and spoon the broccoli khichdi into it. Pour the jus around the khichdi. Lift out the ring mould and place the grilled lobster on top of the khichdi. Serve with the rice.

Right **Masala crab cake, crab chutney.**

Tom Conran

I would much rather shop in a specialist food store than a supermarket, although you may have a broader choice in the bigger shops the actual experience can leave you cold. I like to take my time and enjoy the process: discuss the virtues of a certain cheese and why I should choose the 18 month over the 12. There are a number of local shops that I love, the Athenian Grocer on Moscow Road for Greek provisions and fresh vegetables and salads imported direct from Cyprus. Tawana on Chepstow Road for eastern ingredients (it's a bit scruffy but always has what you need at the right price). I like the Lisboa Deli on Golbourne Road for Portugese cheeses, wine and charcuterie and their patisserie over the road for orgasmic custard tarts. But if I had to choose one shop as an all time favourite it would have to be Garcia's on Portobello Road.

Owner, The Cow, Crazy Homies

Rasoi Vineet Bhatia 10 Lincoln Street, SW3 2TS
020 7225 1881 www.vineetbhatia.com

Progressive, visionary, contemporary twists, innovative – all these are words one associates with Rasoi (meaning kitchen) Vineet Bhatia. Having grown up in Bombay, as it was known then, Vineet gained a classical training. But he became frustrated and has now formed his own style of new-wave Indian food. Initially earning a name for himself in the 1990s at South Kensington's Star of India, he then launched Zaika, where he became the first-ever Indian chef restaurateur to be awarded a Michelin star. His new restaurant, which is close to Sloane Square, has also been granted the same accolade. The latter is hardly surprising given the use of luxury ingredients and the presence of a nine-course tasting menu, as well as his amazing creativity.

(PP) Personally, I find the presentation on the plate verging on tricksy and the choice of plate ware sometimes completely over the top, nor am I keen on the restaurant's interior, but you can't deny that the flavours are completely sublime. ○

Troubadour 263–267 Old Brompton Road, SW5 9JA
020 7370 1434 www.troubadour.co.uk

The first coffee-and-café-culture revolution to arrive in London happened in the late seventeenth century and continued throughout the eighteenth century. Think of Dr Johnson and his dictionary, and Edward Lloyd and the insurance market, formed as an extension of the café discussions. The second revolution occurred in the 1950s. The Troubador opened in 1954 as a destination for the cultured and the intelligentsia, along with a large bohemian element. The historic site is now the antithesis of what must be the third coffee revolution in the form of Starbucks, Caffè Nero, Prêt et al. Clearly, none of these places will be included in this book.

The Troubadour includes a café, delicatessen, art gallery and underground club, allowing it to continue its strong links with new emerging musical talents. An impressive list of past troubadours have performed here, including Jimi Hendrix, Paul Simon, Bob Dylan and Joni Mitchell. ○

Zaika 1 Kensington High Street, W8 5SF
020 7795 6533 www.zaika-restaurant.co.uk

Although the second site for this restaurant, the original being on Fulham Road, it was one of the first top-flight new style Indian restaurants. The current site was once a rather grand bank and much of the internal architecture has been retained and fused with a rich colour palette.

Zaika translates quite literally as 'sophisticated flavours' and this is the ethos behind a menu that includes the use of prime ingredients to create dishes such as coconut prawn curry, grilled masala duck breast, Indian home-smoked salmon and tandoori monkfish with curry leaf risotto. ○

The City

Ten to fifteen years ago good restaurants simply didn't exist in the Square Mile. All this has changed and it is now alive with high-quality eating establishments. Five-star hotels, in the form of the Great Eastern Hotel and Threadneedles, have also arrived and brought their own collection of restaurants and brasseries. We're not saying that residents from all over London are rushing to Bank or Bishopsgate for gourmet experiences, but it is no longer a case of mass departure at 5 pm. Office staff and company directors are now staying close to their offices and are entertaining in the City in the evening.

Over the same period the City has also changed its personality in many other ways. The trading floors have all but disappeared, the venture capitalists have realized it isn't vital to be located in the City and new tenants have arrived in the form of overseas banks and insurance brokers. Some of the traditional trades have completely disappeared and the explosion in the number of people who now work from home or the virtual office, has also had an impact on the transformation.

The Corporation of London, the authority that governs the City, has overseen this change by encouraging the new in the form of world-beating architecture, but, thankfully, they have also retained a sense of tradition. Most lampposts and public buildings carry the heraldic shield of St. George with the dragon to indicate the Corporation's existence. The Lord Mayor's Parade, the annual banquet, along with the Guildhall and Mansion House, with all their frills, are good examples of the pomp and circumstance that continue to permeate.

1 Lombard Street EC3V 9AA

020 7929 6611 www.1lombardstreet.com

As the retail and online banking world has changed over recent years many restaurants and bars have been formed in old banking halls or local branches. The grandest example of such a conversion must be 1 Lombard Street, which also boast an address opposite the ultimate bank: The Bank of England. The neoclassical building is Grade II listed, and features an internal domed ceiling by Pietro Agostini.

Soren Jessen, a former banker himself, together with evergreen chef Herbert Berger, has created a buzzing brasserie with a central bar under the dome and an adjoining fine-dining restaurant. The brasserie confidently serves old-fashioned classics while the dining room serves more Michelin-focused European dishes. ○

Barcelona Tapas Bar 1 Bell Lane, E1 7LA

020 7247 7014 www.barcelona-tapas.com

The surrounding streets are not exactly smart and the interior is very much similar, but the food here is the real thing and typical of the tapas bars of Barcelona or Madrid. ○

This page **A glimpse of the Pietro Agostini dome at 1 Lombard Street.**

This page **French service, good wine and a long lunch at The Bleeding Heart.**

The Bleeding Heart Bleeding Heart Yard, Off Greville Street, Hatton Garden, EC1 8SJ 020 7242 2056 www.bleedingheart.co.uk

Located in a historic courtyard close to Hatton Garden, the renowned London diamond district, The Bleeding Heart is said by many to offer the finest French cuisine in London. (PP) I positively revelled in a main course of Broadside Farm suckling pig 'Four Ways'. The setting is quaint and moderately romantic for a City establishment.

More than the food, The Bleeding Heart restaurant and bistro has a very strong connection with the grape and its juice. The wine list is extensive, with over 450 bins, and you can tell that the proprietors devote much endeavour in this area. (PP) On two recent occasions when I have visited I was glad to see a handful of conspicuous late-lunch tables that appeared to be enjoying the sommelier's labour. As restaurateurs, we say long may this tradition continue. Clean living and mineral water don't have to be unanimous and clients do still need to be vinously entertained. ◗

Mickael Weiss

"

I always look for the best produce available and have a general hatred of supermarket food. We shop locally if possible, at the fishmonger at 326 Norwood Road, who always has fresh fish. Opposite there is a small vegetable store open every day from early morning to late. For meat I'll go to William Rose Butchers in East Dulwich. They supply wonderful fresh organic meat. Once a month we go to Battersea, where there is a great health shop called Dandelion on Northcote Road who supplies everything from wheat-free muesli to all types of dairy-free milk. We also go to the market on Northcote Road, which is open most of the time apart from Sundays.

Head Chef, Coq d'Argent

Boisdale of Bishopsgate Swedeland Court, 202 Bishopsgate, EC2M 4NR 020 7283 1763 www.boisdale.co.uk

Cubaphile Ranald Macdonald of Clanranald runs this idiosyncratic old City club and restaurant. Enjoy the Scottish tartan interiors, decent beef, live jazz – and plenty of Cuban cigars, while it's still possible. ○

Coq d'Argent No.1 Poultry, EC2R 8EJ
020 7395 5000 www.conran.com

If you work in the City then you must have been to Coq d'Argent. Set on the top floor of James Stirling's bold postmodern building at the heart of the City, with capacious gardens designed by Arabella Lennox-Boyd and a Conran-designed restaurant it was destined to be a success. Since opening in 1998 it has proved to be a perennial favourite with City dealers and big shots who love it.

Superstar Conran chef and all-round good guy Mickael Weiss has been the chef at Coq d'Argent since 2001 and has also spared the time to assist with the opening of several other new Conran eateries, including Paternoster Chop House and The Royal Exchange. He's become a City specialist, knowing exactly how to deal with the 1pm rush and what the City boys and girls really want to eat. Somehow Mickael manages to cope with a 150-cover formal dining room with an outside terrace, a large grill restaurant and barbecue terraces, a busy bar and a buoyant party and events business. Le Coq, as it is known, is a stunning destination for a celebration.

When the summer weather fades you can always rely on Mickael's deftly prepared regional French menu. Coq au vin is the signature dish and they always feature frogs' legs and snails, serving over 1,000 escargots per week. As you would expect, it has a huge menu with oysters, crustaceans, Châteaubriand, great fish, delicious desserts and a well-stocked cheese trolley. Needless to say, the wine list is primed for bonus day.

Like the menu, the interior of the restaurant is modern, with black and white photographs of French artisans to remind you of its terroir plus a rampant coq by Anthony Caro. ○

Opposite **Snails with garlic butter.** Above **Mickael Weiss in his kitchen at Coq d'Argent.** Right **The lawns and gardens atop No.1 Poultry.**

Côtelette de Veau au Pesto, Fondue de Tomates et Olives

(Veal Cutlet with Pesto, Tomato and Olive Compote)

Serves 4

For the Tomato and Olive Fondue

100 ml (3¹/2 fl oz) olive oil
salt and freshly ground black pepper
1 red onion, cut in 1 cm (¹/2 in) dice
2 cloves garlic, quartered and blanched in milk
1 sprig fresh thyme
6 plum tomatoes, skinnned and quartered
100 g (3¹/2 oz) mixed Provençal olives, pitted
handful of basil leaves, shredded

For the Coarse Pesto

150 g (5 oz) basil leaves, shredded
30 g (1 oz) pine nuts, toasted and crushed
pinch of salt
pinch of cracked black pepper
40 g (1¹/2 oz) Parmesan cheese, grated
120 ml (4 fl oz) extra-virgin olive oil

4 veal cutlets, each weighing 250–280 g (8–9 oz)
a knob of butter

To make the tomato and olive fondue, place a saucepan over a medium heat and add the olive oil. Season the red onions and place them in the pan and bring slowly to a light simmer. Simmer for 5 minutes then add the garlic and thyme and simmer for a further 5 minutes. Add the tomatoes to the ingredients in the pan. Cover the pan, remove it from the heat and set aside.

Make the pesto by placing all the ingredients together in a bowl. Mix them together but do not stir them too much. Your aim is to keep a coarse texture. Set aside.

Season the veal cutlets. Place a frying pan over a high heat and add a teaspoon of olive oil. Place the cutlets in the pan and fry them, reducing the heat once the cutlets start to colour. After about 3¹/2 minutes add a little butter and turn them over to fry the other side. Continue basting your meat. It should take about 7 minutes altogether to cook and still be pink on the inside. (Alternatively, fry for 5 minutes each side for medium; 7 minutes each side for well done.). Remove the pan from the heat. Set it aside and cover with foil. This will keep your meat warm and rest it.

Turn on the grill. Put the fondue back on a gentle heat to warm it. Add the olives and basil. Spread some pesto evenly on to each cutlet and place under a hot grill for 1 minute.

To serve, drizzle some pesto around the edge of the plate. Place some tomato fondue in the middle and top with a veal cutlet.

Coq au Vin

Serves 4

| 4 corn-fed chicken legs and 2 breasts on the bone |
| 1 litre (1³/4 pints) red wine |
| 1 each of carrot, onion and stick celery, diced |
| 1 spring onion |
| 1 sprig of thyme |
| 1 clove of garlic |
| 1 bay leaf |
| plain flour, for dusting |
| 2 tablespoons olive oil |
| 500 ml (17 fl oz) chicken stock |
| salt and freshly ground black pepper |

For the Garnish

| 100 g (3¹/2 oz) unsmoked streaky bacon, cut into lardons |
| 200 g (7 oz) button mushrooms |
| 12 baby onions, peeled |
| 2 slices white bread, crust removed |
| 2–3 tablespoons olive oil or clarified butter |
| 1 clove of garlic, peeled and finely chopped |
| 1 handful of flat-leaf parsley, finely chopped |

Cut the chicken legs in two through the joint, separating the drumstick from the thigh. Cut the breast through the bones in four pieces.

Place the diced vegetables, herbs, garlic and wine in a bowl and add the chicken making sure they are well covered in the marinade.

Cover the bowl with cling film and set it in the refrigerator overnight. Or, leave it to marinate at room temperature for 6 hours.

After marinating, preheat the oven to 170°C (340°F) Gas Mark 4. Remove the chicken from the bowl and dry it with kitchen paper. Dust the chicken with flour, shaking off any excess. Place a casserole dish over a medium heat and add the olive oil. Brown the chicken pieces until they are golden all over. Pour the marinade with the vegetables into the casserole over the chicken. Turn up the heat and bring to the boil. Once boiling add the stock.

Place the casserole in the oven. After 55–60 minutes, remove the chicken and strain the sauce into a bowl. Pour the sauce back in to the casserole and then reduce the liquor to your desired consistency. Put the chicken back into the sauce and bring it to a slow simmer before serving.

Meanwhile, place the lardons in a frying pan over a medium heat. Fry until they colour and release their fat. Add the mushrooms and baby onions and stir to coat them in the fat. Cook them until they gain a bit of colour.

To make the croutons, add the oil or clarified butter to frying pan over a medium heat. Cut the bread slices into 4 triangles each and add them with the garlic to the pan and fry until they are crispy and brown. Remove the croutons from the oil and drain on kitchen paper.

To serve, place the coq in a serving dish. Top it with the bacon and mushroom garnish, and place the croutons on top. Sprinkle with the chopped parsley and serve.

Passion Fruit Tart

Serves 8

| 200 g (7 oz) sweet shortcrust pastry |
| 12 passion fruit |
| 9 eggs |
| 400 g (13 oz) caster sugar |
| 250 ml (8 fl oz) double cream |

For the Decoration

| icing sugar, for dusting |
| crème fraîche, to serve |
| 4 passion fruit, quartered |

You will need a 25 x 4 cm (10 x 1¹/2 in) tart tin.

Preheat the oven to 180°C (350°F) Gas Mark 3¹/2. Roll out the sweet pastry on a floured work surface to a thickness of about 3 mm (just less than ¹/4 in). Lay the pastry into tart tin and blind bake.

While the tart case is baking, remove the flesh from the passion fruit by cutting the them in half and scooping the flesh out with a spoon. Place the passion fruit flesh in a blender and blitz, pulsing it a couple of times to make a pulp. Pass the passion fruit purée through a sieve in to a bowl, and discard the pulp.

Whisk the eggs and sugar together in a large bowl and set them aside. Place a saucepan over a medium heat, add the cream and heat it until it is nearly boiling. Remove the cream from the heat and whisk it in to the egg and sugar mixture, then whisk in the passion purée.

Turn the oven down to 110°C (225°F) Gas Mark ¹/4. Fill the tart case with the filling and place it in the oven. Bake for 50 minutes or until the filling has nearly set.

When it is done, remove it from the oven and leave it to cool for a couple of hours. To decorate the tart, cut it into servings and place on a heatproof surface. Sprinkle each piece individually with icing sugar and then burn with a blowtorch (if you don't have a blowtorch, flash each slice under a very hot grill) just until the sugar caramelizes. Set the pieces of tart aside.

Keep 8 of the passion fruit quarters to the side. Remove the pulp from the rest, and place it in a bowl. Whisk it lightly to separate the seeds. Place a slice of passion fruit tart on a serving plate. Top each slice with a teaspoon of crème fraîche. Drizzle some of the pulp around the slice and finish with one of the reserved passion fruit quarters.

The Don Restaurant and Bistro The Courtyard, 20 St Swithins Lane, EC4N 8AD 020 7626 2606 www.thedonrestaurant.com

Here, on the site of the old Sandeman port cellars, you can enjoy high-quality Gallic fare and a far-reaching wine list. The atmospheric rooms and friendly staff make this a preferred destination for City dining. ⬤

Energi Box 5 Philpot Lane, EC3M 8AQ
020 7626 5690 www.energibox.com

We're not suggesting that everyone should go GI-diet mad, but we do think it is wise to understand more about the chemical processes and reactions that occur in our bodies as we consume foods. Of all the recent diets and fads that have hit the headlines we think everyone should be more aware of the importance of a balanced daily intake giving attention to the Glycaemic Index. This small takeaway food and drink shop founded by ex-Goldman Sachs high-flier Viki Cornish, has many merits. First, the foods are delicious. They are freshly made using low-GI foods, which keep your blood-sugar levels even throughout the day and at the same time provide a natural energy boost.

Hopefully Energi Box will help reduce the many City boardroom coups and the all-too-frequent CEO outburst directed towards the defenceless PA. ⬤

Great Eastern Hotel Liverpool Street Station, EC4M 7QN
020 7618 5000 www.great-eastern-hotel.co.uk

Unlike most other hotels in this country, the Great Eastern Hotel boasts a collection of individually successful restaurants that are all popular with both residents and non-residents. They include: Miyabi a really good Japanese restaurant, probably the best in the City; Fishmarket and its adjoining Champagne bar; Terminus, an all-day informal brasserie and bar; George, a good pub with British ales and simple foods; and Aurora, an architecturally stunning setting for fine prandial pleasures. Set up and designed by the Conran group, the hotel is now under the management of Hyatt Hotels. ⬤

Left **The all-day brasserie Terminus at The Great Eastern Hotel.** Above **The mini Guggenheim, the atrium beyond the hotel lobby.**

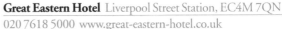

Above **Formal dining at Aurora Restaurant.** Above right **the crustacea and caviar display in Fishmarket.** Right **A Miyabi sushi chef.**

Opposite **Horace Jones's Leadenhall Market with cobbled walkways, glass roof and a collection of retailers with a small food market on a Friday afternoon.**

Leadenhall Cheese 4–5 Leadenhall Market, EC3V 1LR
020 7929 1697 www.cheeseatleadenhall.co.uk

If you work in the City of London this place must be a blessing. You can call in and choose from over 100 different cheeses, plus chutneys, biscuits, ports and a few carefully selected wines. Presumably you could buy your chilled product at lunch and store it in the briefcase until after the train home by which time it should be perfectly ripe for supper.

Friday morning is the best time to visit the market when they have a few extra stalls selling charcuterie, olives, antipasti and other snack options. The architecture isn't too bad either. The Horace Jones (Victorian architect du jour) building dates back to 1881. Its also interesting to note that in 1397 cheesemongers from the countryside were bound by trade law to bring all of their cheese to Leadenhall Market for onward sales. We wonder if the owners of this cheese shop were aware of the sites long connection with the cheeses of Britain? ●

Leon 12 Ludgate Circus, EC4M 7LQ

020 7489 1580 www.leonrestaurants.co.uk

Dairy-free, good carbs/good sugar only, no or low animal fat, vegetarian, wheat-free, lactose-free, fair trade, organic, locally sourced, fresh and just made, antioxidant, naturally low GI, superfoods: a list of the many politically correct labels that appear on the menu at this really excellent fast-food takeaway/quick-service restaurant. And it is all done with an enormous helping of style and relevance. The quality doesn't end with the written menu. The Mediterranean food with a splash of British is fresh, seasonal and reasonably priced.

This is the second site of the chain started by John Vincent, Allegra McEvedy and Henry Dimbleby, and hopefully they will have many more in the future, so move over McDonald's, the new phenomenon to hit the high street is Leon. Unlike other chains, the individual design of the Leon premises seems to hold more integrity. They also have branches in Spitalfields, Great Marlborough Street and Brompton Road. ●

Henry Dimbleby

❝

I love the Turkish Food Centre in Dalston. They sell parsley in great bales, bake their own bread and stock sweetbreads. They also give eccentric free gifts. 'Anatolian wafers or spun sugar fluffs, sir?'

Co-founder, Leon

This page **Inside Leon the management give significant attention to the menu and interior design details.**

Left above
Sir Christopher Wren's dome over St Paul's Cathedral viewed from outside Paternoster Chop House.
Left below **The Corinthian-style Paternoster Square column adjacent to the restaurant and the new London Stock Exchange.**
Right **A rib of beef with a 'healthy' amount of fat for flavour; fresh horseradish and beetroot sauce.**

Paternoster Chop House, Warwick Court, Paternoster Square, EC4M 7DX 020 7029 9400 www.conran.com

Paternoster Square is a historic location and before it was rebuilt at the turn of the millennium the development was much lambasted, especially from royal quarters. Today it has a bustling office community and the venerable London Stock Exchange has found a new home on the square. St Paul's is just a short walk through the rebuilt Temple Bar, where the dining chamber is a popular venue for receptions and business meetings, and the Millennium 'wobbly' Bridge is just a few hundred yards beyond Sir Christopher Wren's masterpiece.

With heritage like this in the area it was only fitting that in 2004 Conran Restaurants launched a chop house with a gutsy British menu. Peter Weedon's menu includes a beast of the day, a fine selection of meats from the spit roast and grill, line- and diver-caught fish and shellfish, a back to basics Sunday lunch menu, along with much more from the farms and fields of Great Britain. ◐

Wild Fennel and Lemon Stuffed Mackerel

Serves 4

We buy mackerel from Marshall Vinnicombe who, during the winter months, fishes Falmouth Bay in his Gaff rig cutter (under sail power) to harvest the wild native oyster from the last remaining natural fishery in the country. In the summer he fishes for bass and mackerel under cover of darkness.

8 x 250–350 g (8–11 oz) very, very fresh mackerel gutted, washed and patted dry

For the Stuffing

1 cup of breadcrumbs
2 tablespoons Lilliputian capers
2 tablespoons chopped preserved lemon
1 handful of chopped spring onions
1 handful of roughly chopped parsley
2 handfuls of roughly chopped wild fennel fronds
freshly ground black pepper (already plenty of salt from the other ingredients)

4 lemon wedges, to serve

Preheat the oven to 175ºC (340ºF) Gas Mark 3½. Mix all the stuffing ingredients together in a bowl. Open each mackerel and stuff with the stuffing. Season the outside of the stuffed fish and lay them on a greased baking tray. Bake in the oven for 15–20 minutes until the flesh turns opaque and comes easily away from the bone. Remove from the oven and serve with fresh lemon wedges.

Strawberries and Cream with Rhubarb Sorbet

Serves 4–6

For the Rhubarb Sorbet

1 kg (2 lb) rhubarb	
50 ml (2 fl oz) grenadine	
300 g (10 oz) sugar	
juice of half a lemon	

250 g (8 oz) of all-butter puff pastry	
600 ml (1 pint) of whipping cream	
1 vanilla pod	
75 g (3 oz) sugar	
500 g (1 lb) strawberries, washed (We use strawberries from Kent, Essex or Herefordshire chosen for flavour not just look.)	
icing sugar, for dusting	

To make the rhubarb sorbet, preheat the oven to 140°C (275°F) Gas Mark 1. In a roasting pan, add the rhubarb, the grenadine and a splash of water and bake until soft.

Meanwhile, in a medium-sized saucepan, add the sugar and 300 ml (½ pint) water and dissolve to a clear syrup over a low heat. Once the rhubarb is cooked, chop it up into chunks and place in a blender or food processor and purée. Add the puree mix to the sugar syrup with a squeeze of lemon juice. Leave to cool to room temperature then churn in a sorbet machine following the manufacturers instructions.

To make the pastry; increase the oven to 190°C (375°F) Gas Mark 5. Roll out the pastry dough 3–4 mm thick (just under ¼ in) into a deep oblong shape. Then divide this between the number of guests. We bake off these puff pastry oblongs (or any shape you like) brushed with egg yolk and a pinch of salt for a nice finish and placed on a lightly greased baking sheet – bake for 15–20 minutes. Allow the pastry to cool then cut in half horizontally and set aside.

Meanwhile, make the cream filling by whisking the whipping cream with the seeds scraped from the vanilla pod and the sugar until just soft. Set aside in the fridge.

To serve, spread the bottom half of the pastry with cream and top with strawberries, then place the remaining half on top like a lid. Dust with icing sugar to give the puff pastry the dry, sweet edge which brings out the best in the strawberries and cream. Serve with scoops of rhubarb sorbet on the side.

Gary Rhodes

Rhodes 24 Tower 42, 25 Old Broad Street, EC2N 1HQ
020 7877 7703 www.rhodes24.co.uk

This is the flagship restaurant from Gary Rhodes OBE, located on the twenty-fourth floor of Tower 42, the tallest building in the City of London. It might be the tallest – surely for not much longer, but the view from the restaurant is direct towards Lord Foster's Gherkin, a far more engaging edifice.

Some might not favour Gary's television appearances and endorsements, but his food remains popular and staunchly seasonal British. His playful use of ingredients and flavours has earned him national recognition, even without the spiky haircut. The Jaffa cake, jam roly poly with custard and bread and butter pudding are all worth ordering. It is also notable that Gary is the only chef to achieve a Michelin star for a restaurant serving British food. We highly recommend Rhodes 24, but please allow sufficient time to enter the building and progress to the 24th floor past all the security barriers and lift changes. Also, you might want to ascend further to Vertigo 42, the Champagne bar at the top of the building. The views are amazing! ○

"I Love Le Gavroche restaurant. One of my favourite dishes on the menu is the souffle suissesse – it's just a dream to eat. Le Gavroche holds a wonderful menu, with the French classics that have never been lost, but always with something new, inventive and real on offer from Michel Roux Junior.

Chef and restaurateur

Above left **Richard Seifert's 1980 NatWest Tower, now called Tower 42, was built in the shape of three chevrons in a hexagonal arrangement to copy the NatWest logo.** Above right **Sir Norman Foster's Swiss Re Building the 'Erotic Gherkin'.**

Bread and Butter Pudding

Serves 6–8

12 medium slices white bread, crusts cut off
50 g (2 oz) unsalted butter, softened
1 vanilla pod or few drops of vanilla essence
400 ml (14 fl oz) double cream
400 ml (14 fl oz) milk
8 egg yolks
175 g (6 oz) caster sugar, plus extra for the caramelised topping
25 g (1 oz) sultanas
25 g (1 oz) raisins

You will need 1 x 1.5 – 1.8 litre pudding dish/ basin buttered.

Pre heat the oven to 180ºC (350ºF) Gas Mark 4.

Butter the bread. Split the vanilla pod and place in a saucepan with the cream and milk and bring to the boil. While it is heating, whisk together the egg yolks and caster sugar in a bowl. Allow the cream mix to cool a little, then strain it on to the egg yolks, stirring all the time. You now have the custard.

Cut the bread into triangular quarters or halves, and arrange in the dish in three layers, sprinkling the fruit between two layers and leaving the top clear. Now pour over the warm custard, lightly pressing the bread to help it soak in, and leave it to stand for at least 20–30 minutes before cooking to ensure that the bread absorbs all the custard.

The pudding can be prepared to this stage several hours in advance and cooked when needed. Place the dish in a roasting tray three-quarters filled with warm water and bake for 20–30 minutes until the pudding begins to set. Don't overcook it or the custard will scramble. Remove the pudding from the water bath, sprinkle it liberally with caster sugar and glaze under the grill on a medium heat or with a blowtorch to a crunchy golden finish.

When glazing, the sugar dissolves and caramelizes, and you may find that the corners of the bread begin to burn. This helps the flavour, giving a bittersweet taste that mellows when it is eaten with the rich custard, which seeps out of the wonderful bread sponge when you cut into it.

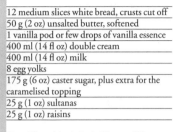

Above **Bread and butter pudding, one of Gary Rhode's signature dishes.** Right **Seared scallops with hot mustard shallot sauce.**

The City

183

The Royal Exchange, Grand Café and Sauterelle Bank, EC3V 3LR
020 7618 2483 www.conran.com

This is an impressive all-day café and oyster bar located in a large courtyard previously used as a trading floor. A French restaurant and a collection of bars can also be found on the mezzanines of this truly impressive building. Grade I listed and the former home of LIFFE, the complex now includes luxury retailers, offices and private dining rooms. In 1565 Sir Thomas Gresham first launched the site as a centre for trade and commerce, but the original and a second building on the same site were both destroyed by fire. The current building first opened for trade on 1st January in 1845.

The restaurant's logo features a grasshopper and if you look up to the roof of the building you will notice that the weathervane has the same detail, both relate to the Gresham's family crest.

(PP) I recommend lunch in the courtyard consisting of a plate of charcuterie, some langoustines and possibly a crab tartine with a cold glass of Chablis. ◗

Above left **Crustacea and fish stew from the Sauterelle menu.**
Above right, top **The view from the Coq d'Argent viewing platform towards the Royal Exchange portico.**
Above right, below **The courtyard inside the Royal Exchange.**

Tom
Martin

"

I love Royal China (Docklands)
for its consistently good dim sum,
quick and attentive service,
reasonable prices and the worst
background music in the world!
The White Swan, The Gun and
The Well

Sweetings 39 Queen Victoria Street, EC4N 4SF
020 7248 3062

The term 'institution' is generally too often and easily applied to
restaurants, but in Sweetings case this accolade is fully justified. It has
been trading since 1889 with few apparent changes and it is still full
most days.

Word has it that the Queen Victoria Street entrance was bombed
during World War II forcing the loss of the wet fish counter and
the installation of a large window instead. In the 1980s, when the
City started to become the global financial centre it is today the rumour
extends to a compensation cheque for £10,000 being delivered by
a recently relocated German bank. It might be an apocryphal story,
but it fits very nicely with the legend that is Sweetings.

The food is pure nursery stuff with a piscine emphasis so you
can gorge on potted shrimps, cod's roe, skate wings with brown butter,
crab and smoked salmon. Over recent years many chefs have featured
old English puddings on their menu, but obviously in a lighter and
less liberal manner – not at Sweetings. The steamed syrup pudding
and baked jam roll are vast.

They only open for lunch Monday to Friday, you can't make
a reservation, nor do they serve coffee, but it is still worth a visit.
Take your godson to explain how things were done in yesteryear. ○

The White Swan 108 Fetter Lane, EC4A 1ES
020 7242 9696 www.thewhiteswanlondon.com

Once the Mucky Duck pub, the site has been tastefully refurbished
by gastropub specialists Tom and Ed Martin, who also run The Well
in Clerkenwell and The Gun in Docklands. The change of plumage
and breed has retained a good pub on the ground floor with a daily-
changing menu serving dishes such as braised pig's cheeks with
horseradish mash, pint o' prawns and steak and kidney pudding.
There is also a smart dining room upstairs. ○

Far right
**The downstairs bar
at The White Swan.**
Right above **Rib eye
steaks on the grill.**
Right below
**Essential fish
and chips.**

Clerkenwell
Highbury
Islington
Stoke Newington

Islington features extensively in English literature – past and present – both as a subject and as the home of distinguished writers. Evelyn Waugh, George Orwell, Sir Francis Bacon, even Sir Walter Raleigh, have all resided in the area. Various satirical publications, not least *Private Eye* magazine, have implied that the area is the spiritual home of New Labour (Tony Blair lived in Islington before moving to Number 10), Champagne socialists and *Guardian* readers. The clientele is discerning and expects the best from its restaurants and food stores. Since the 1980s and gentrification, Upper Street has been the desirable address for new branded or group restaurant concepts, often meaning that the more interesting independent operators have been squeezed out. Any new restaurant that doesn't meet the grade very quickly disappears and is readily replaced by a new idea.

Two places that have lasted the course are the fishmonger's Steve Hatt, which we consider the best in London, and the butcher's James Elliott, both of which are on Essex Road. Their fish and meat would grace the table of any literary luncheon or left-leaning dinner party.

The writer Nick Hornby also resides in the area and his book and the film *Fever Pitch* is based on Arsenal Football Club, the next important thing in Islington. On big game days all of the local restaurant activity takes on a new life, often providing an excellent afternoon fillip.

Exmouth Market, just two minutes' walk from Sadler's Wells Theatre, is a pleasant microcosm of London as we would all like to see it. The market has excellent restaurants, food stores, art galleries, interior design shops and a few small independent fashion boutiques.

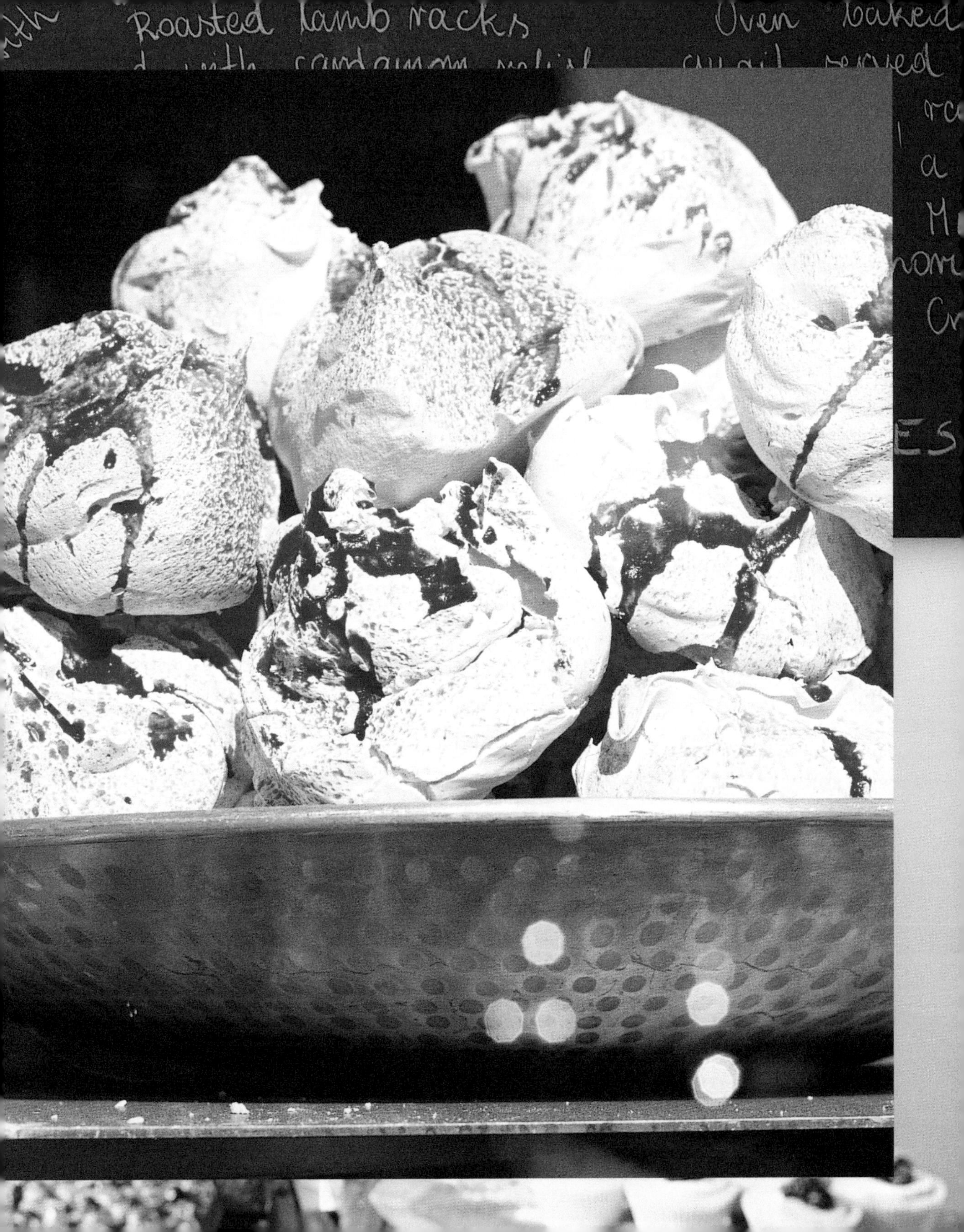
Roasted lamb racks
Oven baked

Almeida 30 Almeida Street, N1 1AD

020 7354 4777 www.conran.com

The Almeida restaurant is directly opposite the Almeida Theatre and the two complement each other perfectly, yet they both stand out as excellent examples of their own art. Favoured by distinguished thespians, the Almeida Theatre puts on a diverse programme of drama, Shakespearian plays and mini operas. When partnered with a pre- or post-performance meal at the Almeida Restaurant, you can't imagine an urban night out being any more sophisticated.

The bustle of Upper Street at the end of Almeida Street offers a plethora of dining and drinking destinations (most come and go within a few years), which creates a challenging competitive market for the Almeida. Yet this perfect neighbourhood restaurant triumphs on all levels.

From his munificent Rorgue kitchen, the self-effacing Ian Wood crafts some of the finest, yet simplest, French regional cooking in London. As head chef since the day the restaurant opened, he quietly plies his trade with a confidence that, if you didn't know the man, you would imagine he had inherited it from a family that has kept a French restaurant for centuries.

Escargots à la Bourguignonne, half a dozen oysters with sausages, steak tartare and seasonal asparagus with hollandaise sauce are just a few of the first-course options. The pièce de résistance, however, is the trolley with terrines, rillettes, chicken liver parfait, Jésus de Lyon and Rosette de Lyon saucisson and charcuterie. Main courses could include a salad Niçoise, Landes duck, spit-roast pork or an extremely good-value Châteaubriand with pommes frites. Even the side dishes of gratin dauphinoise, petits pois à la Française and simple tomato salad deserve a mention. The trolley returns for dessert with a fine selection of tarts. Tarte Tatin, crème brûlée or rhubarb financier appear from the kitchen in a properly prepared and respectful fashion. Olivier Eynard, the general manager, also part of the original management team, presides over the down-to-earth professional service with typical French aplomb. Olivier's head sommelier has created an unrivalled collection of over 400 mainly regional French wines. An exceptional selection is available by the glass and pot Lyonnais. Friendly and efficient service is also a special feature at the Almeida.

Terence Conran personally designed the dining room with its low-hanging modernist pendant lampshades, timber-frame chairs, synonymous with the early days of Habitat, and generous tabletops. The lighting is soft and mellow, yet allows the summer evening light to flow through the large windows gazing towards the white angular façade of the theatre opposite. The restaurant's identity and logo adopt the French *drapeau tricolore* and the emblematic character style and graphics employed on the menu and wine list exude la Française.

Above **Large table tops and linen runners on a window table at Almeida.** Opposite **The enticing trolley of French tarts.**

The small adjoining sunken bar adorned with Hulton Getty 'Funny Peculiar' photographs serves small plates of French tapas from the south-west of France. Anchoïade en croûte, manchons de canard, cuisses de grenouilles persillées or coeurs d'artichauts fondant are excellent with a glass of wine before a memorable performance at the theatre. ●

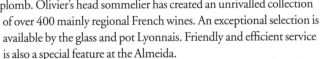

Sea Bass Barigoule

Serves 4

For the Sea Bass

plain flour, for dusting

4 fillets of sea bass, weighing about
180–200 g (6–7 oz) each

2 knobs of butter

For the Barigoule

100 g (3½ oz) butter

200 g (7 oz) girolle mushrooms

2 shallots, sliced

1 clove of garlic, peeled and finely sliced
(optional)

2 carrots, sliced and cooked

8 baby artichokes cooked

1 bunch picked parsley, roughly chopped

100 ml (3½ fl oz) olive oil

Put the flour on to a plate. Roll the fillets
in the flour until they are lightly coated,
shaking off any excess. Discard the unused
flour and set the fillets aside. Add a knob of
butter to a frying pan and place it over a high
heat. Place the fillets skin-side down in the
pan and cook them until they are golden in
colour. Add another knob of butter to the
pan, turn the fillets over and fry them for a
further 1–2 minutes

While the bass is cooking, put the 100 g
(3½ oz) butter into a separate pan. Add the
girolle mushrooms, the shallots, garlic,
artichokes, carrots and parsley and fry over
a high heat for 2 minutes. Drizzle with a
little olive oil, and season to taste.

To serve, place the barigoule on to a
plate and lay the bass fillet on top.

Navarin Lamb

Serves 4

1.5 kg (3 lb) lamb neck or shoulder,
chopped into cubes

plain flour, for dusting

salt and freshly ground pepper

vegetable or groundnut oil, about 100 ml
(3½ fl oz)

3 litres (5 pints) lamb stock

a bouquet garni (1 sprig thyme,
3 cloves of garlic, 1 bay leaf tied together
in a muslin bag)

8 button onions, peeled

8 baby turnips, peeled

8 baby carrots, peeled

8 baby leeks, blanched

200 g (7 oz) mange tout, blanched

Place the flour on a large plate and season it
with salt and pepper. Roll the cubed lamb in
the seasoned flour to coat it. Then give each
piece of lamb a shake until it is left with a
fine dusting of flour. Set the lamb aside and
discard the unused seasoned flour.

Preheat the oven to 180°C (350°F) Gas
Mark 4. Add a drizzle of oil to a large, roomy
frying pan and place it over a high heat. Add
the lamb, a few pieces at a time, being careful
not to overload the pan. Fry the lamb until it
has browned on all sides. When all the lamb
is browned place it in a large flameproof
casserole. Pour the lamb stock over the meat,
and add the bouquet garni. Place the
casserole over a high heat and bring it to the
boil. Then cover the casserole with a lid and
place it in the oven.

After 30 minutes, remove the casserole
from the oven and add the onion, carrots
and turnips to the lamb. Replace the lid
and put the casserole back into the oven to
simmer. After another 30 minutes or when
the lamb is tender, remove the casserole
from the oven and strain the liquid into a
pan. Leave the meat and vegetables in the
casserole, covered, and set aside.

Bring the lamb stock to the boil,
skimming off the fat. Allow it to reduce a
little, season it and then pour it back into
the casserole pan. Add the blanched leeks
and mange tout and serve.

The Ambassador 55 Exmouth Market, EC1R 4QL
020 7837 0009 www.theambassadorcafe.co.uk

Exmouth Market probably didn't need another place to eat. However, the Ambassador Café has recently arrived and is certain to be a success. The menu principally consists of simple, well-executed upscale European café classics. It is not food one immediately imagines worth making a detour for; other charms make this place special. An air of understated sophistication and self-confidence prevails in the simply decorated dining room.

The menu size is just right. Pleasingly, it is not overwhelmingly large and all the dishes have been planned to provide balance and contrast.

Clive Greenhalgh, the owner, has crafted a modestly priced wine list of interest. It is light on the New World, overflowing with flavours and offers value for money from the classic territories. You can drink a decent glass of wine for £3, a 50 cl carafe for a tenner and have plenty of choice under £20. ●

The Best Turkish Kebab 125 Stoke Newington Road, N16 8BT
020 7254 7642

Most people only venture to a kebab shop post the pub and a few too many alcoholic beverages. It is certainly not health food, but this small takeaway outlet is worth a visit when sober. Expect queues, especially later in the evening. For west Londoners Kebab Kid on New King's Road is also good. ●

Brindisa Shop 32 Exmouth Market, EC1R 4QE
020 7713 1666 www.brindisa.com

Home-cooked and simply prepared Spanish food is, in our opinion, the best manifestation of the Iberian culinary soul. However, Spanish food is increasingly gaining a reputation for experimental and boundary-pushing cuisine. Ferran Adria's El Bulli on the Costa Brava has regularly been voted the best restaurant in the world. It is a laboratory-meets-dining-adventure restaurant and boasts year-long waiting lists for a table. We've heard and read plenteous articles about El Bulli, but not a word has stimulated a desire to explore this new 'phenomenon' in cooking. (PP) I can't help drawing comparisons with the nouvelle cuisine craze of the 1980s and how deeply unfashionable that became.

In our opinion, food should be about tasty nourishment in relaxed, comfortable, sociable surroundings. It should be about limited preparation time and excellent natural ingredients that speak for themselves and do not need manipulation. The traditional Spanish ingredients available at Brindisa satisfy these criteria and serve as excellent family food.

The Ortiz range of tinned foods, from anchovies to various tuna options are available in abundance. The Padrón peppers, Manchego cheese, chorizo and arroz Calasparra are all excellent. The Spanish vinegars, olives and olive oils are kitchen essentials and the different cured hams, from Joselito to Serrano, are kept in perfect condition. You can also buy a fine range of Spanish cookery books and paella pans. The torta de aceite, which are traditional handmade sweet olive-oil biscuits, are delicious as a late-morning snack with a small glass of fino. ●

From top to bottom
The bar at The Ambassador Café; Poached halibut with hispi cabbage and Alsace bacon at The Ambassador Café; Spanish olives at Brindisa; Joselito and Jabugo cured hams being sliced to order at Brindisa.

Cicada 132–136 St. John Street, EC1V 4JT

020 7608 1550 www.cicada.nu

This is another pan-Asian eatery with a large cocktail bar from serial restaurateur Will Ricker. ●

The Eagle 159 Farringdon Road, EC1R 3AL

020 7837 1353

Having opened in 1991, The Eagle is reputedly the first gastropub, a 'fact' confirmed on the Internet by Wikipedia.

Over the years a metamorphosis and proliferation have occurred in the gastropub sphere, yet The Eagle remains thankfully the same and true to its original idea. This is probably the best format for a business of this type; let the pubs remain pubs, with good inexpensive grub, and the restaurants can be restaurants. The ground-floor open kitchen sets the tone of the place, and everything is stripped back, possibly a little too scruffy for some. There are no airs and graces, yet the place is packed with integrity. Robust in every sense with a generally faultless kitchen.

Original chef, David Eyre, has now set up a new restaurant with his brother at 70 Leonard Street, EC2 www.eyrebrothers.co.uk. ●

James Elliott Butchers 96 Essex Road, N1 8LU

020 7726 3658

Rosy-cheeked James Elliott is always on hand to afford his regulars a special and very personal greeting. James seems to know an unusually large number of his customers personally. Occasional visitors might start to believe the expression 'some people are more equal than others' is particularly relevant here, yet still receive excellent service themselves. He offers sage-like advice on the best and most suitable cuts available.

James Elliott Butchers specializes in free-range dry-plucked ducks and chicken, Suffolk pork, aged foreribs of beef and Lincolnshire lamb. A thoughtfully selected range of condiments, a few cheeses, butter, quails' eggs and a small collection of black puddings are also stocked. ●

David Eyre

"

The Bife Ana steak sandwich recipe has been on the menu since day one. Not to be confused with the Portuguese fried pork escalope of the same name, this (beef) steak sandwich is named after Dona Ana, a larger-than-life mafiosa who owned a cattle ranch, bakery and bar in Mozambique.

David Eyre, original chef at The Eagle

Left and right **James Elliott breaks down a whole beast.**

Bife Ana – The Eagle Steak Sandwich

Serves 2

For the Marinade

1 onion
1 clove of garlic, chopped
1 small dried chilli, crushed
1 bay leaf, broken up
1 tablespoon chopped parsley
1 teaspoon dried oregano
2 tablespoons red wine
3 tablespoons olive oil
freshly ground black pepper

For the Sandwich

500g (1lb) rump steak, thinly sliced (the original would have used fillet)
2 large crusty rolls (we use stone-baked Portuguese rolls called carcaças)
2 tablespoons olive oil
1 cos lettuce
salt

Mix all of the marinade ingredients together in a large bowl. Add the steak, cover with cling film and refrigerate. Leave the steak to marinate for a few hours (but no longer than 8). Remove the steaks from the marinade and set on a plate. Strain the marinade and set aside.

Preheat the oven to a medium heat and place the rolls in it for a few minutes to warm.

Heat a heavy-based frying pan until it is very, very hot, and add the olive oil.

Then add the steaks and fry them very quickly. If your pan was hot enough, the steaks will need to be turned in 1 minute.

Cook the other side for one minute. Remove the steaks and keep warm, then add the marinade ingredients to the pan with a pinch of salt over a medium heat.

Add the strained marinade liquid to the pan and let this bubble and reduce a little. Meanwhile, remove the rolls from the oven and cut them in half. Arrange the Cos lettuce on the bottom halves of the rolls and then add the steaks. Pour the reduced marinade into the top halves of the rolls. Close the sandwich and eat immediately, using both hands.

193

Above **The Bife Ana – steak sandwich at The Eagle.**

Euphorium Bakery 202 Upper Street, N1 IRQ
020 7704 6905 www.euphoriumbakery.com

This is an emphatically French bakery and patisserie with top-quality breads, Viennoisserie, savouries and cakes. The pain de campagne and pain paysan are classic. They also bake a pure rye bread, made with 100% rye flour from Germany, a speciality that is difficult to find, plus Fougasse-Provençale from the south of France, Scandinavian bread, focaccia and the classic baguette.

The Euphorium ovens also serve excellent slices of pizza with French-inspired toppings, choux pastry éclairs, quiche, chocolate delights and much more. ○

Fredericks Camden Passage, N1 8EG
020 7359 2888 www.fredericks.co.uk

Trading for over 20 years, Fredericks has witnessed the Islington boom and at the same time managed to retain its position as an excellent location for business entertaining, social gatherings and special events. The restaurant is family-run and you can tell. The main dining room is located at the rear of the building under a glass-vaulted conservatory. They also have a small space for al fresco dining and a seriously attractive wine list. ○

Fresh and Wild 32-40 Stoke Newington Church Street, N16 0LU
0207254 2332 www.freshandwild.com

Now owned by Whole Foods, one of the world's leading retailers of natural and organic foods, Fresh and Wild has six stores in London and one in Bristol. The original direction of the company was to provide foods without artificial colourings, hydrogenated fats, flavourings, sweeteners or preservatives. The Stoke Newington branch is a blessing to locals.

Watch out for a flagship Whole Foods Store that is due to open in 2007 on Kensington High Street. (PP) I visited the New York version and it promises to be excellent, when it eventually opens in London. ○

Opposite top
**Preparing apple
tart at Euphorium
Bakery.**
Left **Preparing
French-style pizza.**

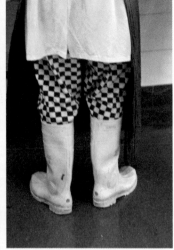

Ian Wood

"Steve Hatt is the best fishmongers in London. The selection and quality of fish is always exceptionally high and you can be assured of fair prices.

Head Chef, Almeida

Steve Hatt Fishmonger 88–90 Essex Road, N1 8LU
020 7226 3963

The queues from early on a Saturday morning speak volumes about the freshness of the fish available here. This no-frills shop is small, but the stock displayed on mounds of crushed ice is exhaustive. Hatt offers everything from tuna for sushi suppers to monkfish, turbot and sea bass for elegant Islington dinner parties. This is a place to buy proper Palourdes clams for your spaghetti vongole or oysters and prawns to make your loved one swoon. They also smoke a fine range of fish on site. ◉

Medcalf 40 Exmouth Market, EC1R 4QE
020 7833 3533 www.medcalfbar.co.uk

Medcalf occupies the site of a former esteemed butcher's shop. They now serve distinctly British food from a daily-changing menu in a long, narrow room with stylishly appointed, mostly reclaimed, furniture. The art and creative music policy also hold the interest on a Friday evening. ◉

Left **The wet fish display at Steve Hatt, the best fishmonger in London.** Right **Medcalf's former life as a cash butcher's is evident from the front window.**

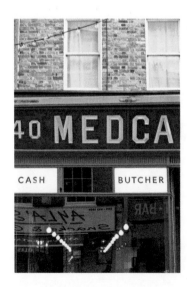

Chilled Gazpacho with Tomato and Olive Oil Sorbet

Prepare this the day before you want to serve it.

Serves 8

For the Soup

3 cucumbers, peeled and chopped
10 tomatoes, peeled and chopped
3 cloves of garlic, peeled and chopped
3 red peppers, chopped
3 shallots, peeled and chopped
100 ml (3½ fl oz) of red wine vinegar
100 ml (3½ fl oz) extra-virgin olive oil
salt and freshy ground black pepper

For the Sorbet

5 beef tomatoes, chopped
1 tablespoon of chopped fresh thyme
5 tablespoons of extra virgin olive oil
1 tablespoon of glucose

For the Crouton

1 aubergine
8 slices of crusty bread, toasted

Place the cucumber, tomatoes, garlic, red pepper and shallots in a large bowl. Pour over the vinegar and olive oil, and season with salt and pepper. Leave to marinate in the fridge covered with cling film.

After 24 hours, pour the mixture into a liquidizer, and blend. Then pass the liquid through a fine sieve into a large bowl. Cover with cling film and place in the fridge.

For the sorbet, place the chopped tomatoes and the thyme in a saucepan over a medium heat. Simmer them until you get the consistency of a sauce. Remove the pan from the heat and pour the tomato mixture into a blender. Add the olive oil and glucose and blend until combined. When ready, turn the tomato mixture into an ice-cream maker and follow the manufacturer's instructions for making sorbet.

Preheat the oven to 150°C (300°F) Gas Mark 2. Place the aubergine on a baking tray and bake the aubergine for about 2 hours. When it feels soft, remove the aubergine from the oven. Cut it in half and scoop out the flesh. Roughly chop the flesh, place it in a bowl and season it. Then set it aside to cool. Create a crouton by covering a slice of the bread with the aubergine purée.

To serve, pour the chilled soup into serving bowls. Place an aubergine crouton into each bowl and add a scoop of tomato sorbet on top.

Right **Inside Morgan M.**

Morgan M 489 Liverpool Road, N7 8NS
020 7609 3560 www.morganm.com

Morgan Meunier is a chef with a vision and high ambitions for his food, which he describes as 'a modern approach to cooking rooted in classical French cuisine'. His meticulous artistry on a plate is embodied with his signature dessert, chocolate moelleux. This is the type of serious cooking that sets out to attract the attention of the Michelin inspector. A shelf reverentially stocked with past editions of Michelin guides might also catch any inspector's attention.

Liverpool Road is an unusual address for cooking of this calibre. Surely Mayfair or St. James's is calling in the future. At the moment, the intimate dining room seats 48 and is subtly decorated with cream walls, oak floors and comfortable green upholstered armchairs. ●

Clerkenwell / Highbury / Islington / Stoke Newington

197

Moro 34–36 Exmouth Market, EC1R 4QE
020 7833 8336 www.moro.co.uk

This restaurant is 'Moorish' in every way. According to the first Moro cookbook, the menu was born out of a desire to cook within the wonderful traditions of the Mediterranean, yet still explore new and exciting flavours. From its inception in 1997 Moro has been cooking excellent Spanish food with more than a hint of North African flavours and ingredients. When the Moors occupied Spain between the eighth and fifteenth centuries a culinary link was established, it is this influence that now prevails with twenty-first-century reserved style. Moro is certainly not a 'concept' restaurant, but as a culinary direction, nothing similar or close to this standard of cooking exists in London today. Some chefs introduce an occasional dish that might also make use of the link between saffron, cinnamon, paprika or cumin, but at Moro it is the entire menu and it's a delight.

Prior to opening on Exmouth Street, the recently married Sam and Sam Clark, the restaurant's proprietors, set off in a camper van to explore Spain and Morocco to the Sahara. Clearly the journey was worthwhile. The food that the Clarks serve shows their previous experience at the seminal River Café and they adopt the same relaxed idiom, yet have created a lively dining room and open kitchen. Charcoal-grilled meat, poultry or fish, together with dishes such as wood-oven roasted pork with green mojo sauce and wrinkled potatoes, form the heart of the menu. Along with the River Café, Moro is one of the few restaurants that really understand excellent wood-oven cooking. The vegetable mezze plate and other vegetable accompaniments coursing through the first and mains selection are all superb.

The lively long zinc bar is the ideal spot to enjoy tapas, cured hams and a glass of sherry. ◉

Above and opposite
Sweet and sour poached spring vegetables with labneh on toast.

Tuna with Pomegranate Molasses

Serves 4

4 tuna steaks, 2–3 cm (about an inch) thick, weighing about 200–250 g (7–8 oz) each

For the Marinade

1 clove of garlic, peeled
4 tablespoons pomegranate molasses
1 level teaspoons ground cinnamon
2 tablespoons chopped fresh coriander
a good pinch ground black pepper
1 tablespoon extra-virgin olive oil

To serve

4 teaspoons pomegranate molasses
2 tablespoons extra-virgin olive oil
4 tablespoons fresh coriander leaves
seeds of 1 pomegranate (about 4 tablespoons)

Make the marinade by crushing the garlic in a mortar with a pinch of salt until smooth. Stir in the pomegranate molasses. Transfer to a large bowl and add the cinnamon, coriander and pepper. Rub all over the fish. Drizzle on the olive oil. Leave to marinate in the fridge covered with cling film for at least an hour or two.

If you are grilling the fish over charcoal, light the barbeque 45 minutes before you wish to cook, or use a very hot griddle pan or frying pan. Grill (or fry) the fish for about 2–3 minutes either side, basting with any excess marinade, until the outside is slightly charred but the inside is still pink and juicy. Drizzle the extra pomegranate molasses and olive oil over the fish, and scatter the coriander leaves and pomegranate seeds on top.

(Recipe featured in *Casa Moro* by Sam and Sam Clark published by Ebury. Reprinted by permission of The Random House Group.)

Sam & Sam Clark

Opposite **Tuna with pomegranate molasses.**
Above **Toros en Sevilla 2005 by artist Anthony Fry – Samuel's father.**

"

Persepolis (28–30 Peckham High Street, SE15 5DT 020 7639 8007) is an inviting Aladdin's cave, over flowing with wonderful produce, ceramics and curiosities from Iran. The food is aromatic and visual: seasonal fruits, a kaleidoscope of spices and nuts to mention a few. There is a little of everything crammed into this truly Persian emporium and definitely worth a visit.

Restaurateurs, Moro

Ottolenghi 287 Upper Street, N1 2TZ

020 7288 1454 www.ottolenghi.co.uk

Following the success of the Notting Hill branch, Ottolenghi opened in
Islington. This not-inexpensive delicatessen serves Mediterranean foods
with an occasional North African influence, all made with the very best
ingredients. All the food is made onsite in the kitchen below the shop.

　　The all-white room is dominated by an elongated all-white dining
table positioned in the centre and surrounded by white iconic 1968
Verner Panton chairs. To the sides of this long thin space the salads,
prepared traiteur foods and bakery items are beautifully displayed.
Everything looks as though it is straight from the pages of *Vogue
Entertaining* magazine. The epic display of meringues in the window
garners patronage from elegant Islington ladies who lunch. ○

Portal 88 St John Street, EC1M 4EH

020 7253 6950 www.portalrestaurant.co.uk

Modern European food with a strong Portuguese accent, served in
a light and spacious dining room. Or you can take pleasure in a few
petiscos (Latin tapas), at the bar. ○

Rasa and Rasa Travancore 55 Stoke Newington Church Street,

N16 0AR 020 7249 0344 www.rasarestaurants.com

The Rasa group specializes in Keralan food from southern India. Rasa
Stoke Newington is a strictly vegetarian version and Rasa Travancore
across the road serves meat, seafood and vegetarian dishes. In these
simple, but authentic, restaurants you must remember to eat with your
hands. While the bright pink façade would not be out of place in an
Indian temple or market, it is possibly considered garish by some on a
wet Wednesday in north-east London. Despite the exterior, the food
offers exceptionally good value for money and is very tasty. ○

Stoke Newington Farmers' Market Stoke Newington Church Street,

N16 0NX Saturday's 10am–2.30pm

Located within the playgrounds of the William Patten School, this
market was the first in the UK to be totally organic, biodynamic and
wild with most of the produce coming from within 100 miles of
Hackney. The produce on sale is being sold by the people who grew,
or reared it. The market was initially set up to enable local people to
buy locally produced food, grown or raised in a way that benefits
the environment. ○

**Lemon &
blackberry
cup cake**

**White chocolate
& lemon tart
£2.40**

Paul A. Young – Chocolaterie 33 Camden Passage, N1 8EA
020 7424 5750 www.payoung.net

A regular on TV, former head pastry chef for Marco Pierre White, and winner of a gold medal at the World Chocolate Awards, Yorkshireman Paul Young has now opened his eponymous boutique chocolaterie on the beguiling Camden Passage. This is the place where the semi-professional patissier comes to buy the best-quality pure Amedei or Valrhona chocolate. The chocolate truffles, all hand-made in the shop, are delicious and gracefully crafted, especially the sea-salted caramel and chocolate truffles. The small bars of chocolate with complementary ingredients, such as Szechuan chilli paired with 70% cocoa, or pink peppercorn and white chocolate, are ideal for mid-afternoon snacks. Over the summer months the shop offers Paul's homemade ice cream with hot 70% chocolate sauce. Closed on Mondays. ☉

Left **A selection of chocolate truffles and tarts at Paul A. Young's chocolate boutique.**

Paul Young

Chocolate Vodka Sorbet

Serves 6–8 portions

This intense and chilling sorbet laced with smooth warming vodka is a real adult's dessert. With the huge selection of flavoured vodkas on offer, this frozen and exquisite version will not disappoint even the most discerning palate.

25 g (1 oz) dark pure cocoa powder
450 ml (3/4 pint) water
150 g (5 oz) dark bitter chocolate
125 g (4 oz) caster sugar
50 g (2 oz) glucose syrup
100 ml (3 1/2 fl oz) vodka

Place the cocoa powder and the water in a saucepan and simmer for 5 minutes. Cut the chocolate into small pieces and place it into a mixing bowl with the sugar and glucose syrup. Pour the hot cocoa liquid onto the chopped chocolate mixture. Combine it well so the chocolate melts evenly and then set it aside to cool.

After it has cooled to room temperature, stir in the vodka. Place the mixture in an ice-cream machine and churn it, following the manufacturer's instructions. Or, pour the chocolate and vodka mixture into a plastic container with a lid. Seal and place it in the freezer. After 30 minutes remove it from the freezer and give it a stir. Repeat this every 30 minutes until it is smooth and frozen.

Place some small glasses in the freezer until they are totally cold. Offer this wicked sorbet on its own, scooped into the frozen glasses, and serve with a teaspoon.

Left and above
A simple, but beautiful dining room at the Zetter overlooking St. John's Square.

The Zetter St. John's Square, 86–88 Clerkenwell Road, EC1M 5RJ
020 7324 4455 www.thezetter.com

Born out of the Zetter Pools building, this trendy and surprisingly affordable hotel, with noteworthy environmental credentials, has a first-rate restaurant adjunct.

We love the simplicity of the restaurant layout and general arrangement. A sweeping black marble bar leads the way as you enter the space and from the slightly elevated position above Clerkenwell Road you get to gaze out of the sizeable windows overlooking St. John's Square – not that it's much to view, but the natural light brings satisfaction. Simple black chairs, white table coverings and white walls are always a winning formula.

When the restaurant opened it had strong Italian roots and has now started to become more broadly Mediterranean. The cooking is of a high standard and the presentation on the plate is loose and very similar to that at Moro or The River Café. ○

Farringdon
Smithfield

Only hardened foodies should chart a course to Smithfield, but those who do venture to this *bloody cool and offaly good* corner of London won't be disappointed. Synergistically juxtaposed, the meat market and some of the coolest bars, clubs and restaurants in the capital enjoy the perfect symbiosis. As the nightclubs empty at 4 am, the goggle-eyed clubbers are greeted by the sight of colliding guts, flesh and bones together with men in white coats – incomprehensible if you don't know the area before you enter the nightclub and disconcerting if you do. By breakfast a fleet of white vans are discharging their bovine, porcine, ovine and avian consignments. Shortly afterwards, the market porters slip away for a pint of ale and a slap-up English breakfast, before heading home for a hard day's sleep. The butcher's shop opens in the morning, chefs are taking deliveries and piggy treats start to appear by lunch. By dinner your favourite slab of beef arrives on the plate and the cyclical process begins again. New York's meat-packing district has achieved similar notoriety for its hip bars and eateries, but somehow the sight of a few random carcasses in the open warehouses between Ganesvoort and West 15th doesn't deliver the same concentrated carnivorous hit. And Sir Horace Jones's Victorian temple is a sight on its own.

St. John with its offal, Smith's with its rare breeds and Club Gascon with its foie gras all contribute to the area's new heritage. Even Saki, a Japanese offering, steps up to the plate with its monkfish liver sushi.

Rivers of blood and gore don't run through the streets, but please don't go to Smithfield and ask for the vegetarian option.

Club Gascon 57 West Smithfield, EC1A 9DS

020 7796 0600

Pascal Aussignac has created a multiple award-winning and Michelin-starred eatery devoted to the food of south-west France. The house speciality is foie gras, and the menu includes about half a dozen slightly ditzy variants generally served on small plates. Cassoulet, sweetbreads and pork belly also appear, the latter served with a bizarre-sounding mustard ice cream.

The dining room has a City boy atmosphere, seats about 60 people and has dark woods, marble and linen napery.

Cellar Gascon next door is a busy wine bar with a nonpareil list of wines from Gascony. Serious bar snacks follow the same robust duck, foie gras and porcine direction. ●

Comptoir Gascon 61–63 Charterhouse Street, EC1M 6HJ

020 7680 0851

The Club Gascon team offers more duck, goose, pork and other meats in this small, rustic 30-seat bistro with a few bakery and deli items also available. ●

Pascal Aussignac

For simple canteen-like meals I adore Café Brindisa at Borough Market (see page 299), Busaba Eathai on Bird Street (see page 14) and Ottolenghi on Upper Street (see page 202).

Head Chef, Club Gascon

Above left **Pascal Aussignac inside Club Gascon.** Above right **Club Gascon next door to a Tudor-style building on West Smithfield.** Right **Foie gras and papaya.**

Club Gascon

Cassoulet

by Pascal Aussignac

Cassoulet is a rich combination of beans and meats. There are several recipes, but here is the easiest to cook.

Serves 6

4 'confit' (preserved) duck legs
1 leek, sliced
1 stick of celery, roughly chopped
1 onion, roughly chopped
1 carrot, roughly chopped
2 cloves of garlic, peeled but left whole
$^1/_2$ teaspoon fresh thyme leaves
1 bay leaf
500 g (1 lb) dried white beans, soaked overnight in cold water (I prefer to use Tarbais beans as they retain their shape and flavour after being cooked)
1 $^1/_2$ teaspoons salt
$^1/_2$ teaspoon freshly ground black pepper
500 g (1 lb) pork sausages
500 g (1 lb) pork spare ribs
500 g (1 lb) unsmoked bacon rashers

Preheat the oven to 160°C (325°F) Gas Mark 3.

Place the duck legs skin-side down on a baking tray and bake in the oven for 10 minutes or until the fat round the legs melts and the skin becomes crisp. Remove them from the oven and set them aside.

Heat a large ovenproof sauce pan with a lid over a medium heat. Add a tablespoon of the fat from the confit duck legs, then add the vegetables and sauté them for just a few minutes with one of the cloves of garlic, the thyme and bay leaf.

Take the beans and pour them with their soaking water in with the vegetables. Crush the remaining clove of garlic and add it to the pot with some salt and pepper. Cover the pan with the lid and place it in the oven for 1 hour 30 minutes.

Meanwhile, fry the sausages in a frying pan over a medium heat and set them aside. Cut the spare ribs into four, season with salt and pepper and set them aside.

Once the vegetables have finished simmering, add the sausages, spare ribs and bacon, then recover the pan and place it back in the oven and bake until no liquid is left (this may take up to 2 hours). You may like to remove the lid after an hour to let a crust form on top.

Cut the confit duck legs into portions and arrange them on top of the pan. Serve the dish making sure each portion gets a bit of everything.

This cassoulet tastes better when reheated.

Bon appetit!

Farringdon / Smithfield

209

Flâneur 41 Farringdon Road, EC1M 3JB

020 7404 4422 www.flaneur.com

A flâneur is someone who idly strolls in arcades, shops, in the markets and hangs out at cafés to demonstrate their wealth. You can certainly take time to do the same at this well-stocked deli.

If you live in Clerkenwell, or in a nearby loft apartment, this is the place to come for high-quality victuals from France, Spain, Italy, the UK and USA. It is a perfect one-stop shop, offering everything from morning pastries to a fine selection of wine, beautifully merchandized fruit and vegetables, cheese, artisanal pasta, fresh fish and meats.

The restaurant offers breakast, brunch, lunch and dinner, with all of the menu including well-sourced seasonal foods at reasonable prices. Mellow lighting, soft hues and attractive furniture help create an authentic French aura. They also offer an extensive take away menu including salads, quiches and hand-made pies, scones, cakes and tarts. ○

Ayako Watanabe

"I love St. John, especially the bar area. Knowing its past as a smokehouse makes it very special and the food is unique.

Managing Director, Saki Bar and Food Emporium

Above **Cheese, charcuterie and pastries on display in Flâneur.**

Left and above left
**Japanese products
for sale in Saki's
Food Emporium**
Above right
**Making sushi
in the basement
restaurant of Saki.**

Saki Bar and Food Emporium 4 West Smithfield, EC1A 9JX
020 7489 7033 www.saki-food.com

Saki means happiness in Japanese, and should not be confused with sake,
the Japanese rice wine. Saki Bar and Food Emporium is an innovative and
modern concept that is bursting with technology. The surroundings are
modern and immediately make you think about a healthy, balanced diet.

On the ground floor they have an advanced noodle-making machine
and take away sushi and sashimi. At the rear of the food boutique the
shelves are stocked with wasabi, nori, miso, soy sauce, pickled things,
sake, shochu, Japanese cookery books, tableware and even rice cookers.

The basement has a lively bar with creative cocktails and a Kobachi
menu – the Japanese equivalent of tapas. Wi-Fi access is available
throughout and the lavatories have heated seats and a paperless 'service'.

The basement restaurant has a small sushi bar and about 70 seats,
with an extensive menu that includes sea urchin and the rare monkfish
liver (when in season) – foie gras of the sea as it is sometimes known. ◎

Smithfield Meat and Poultry Market Charterhouse Street, EC1A 9PQ
020 7236 8734

Meat and poultry has been sold on this site for over 800 years, making it one of the oldest markets in London. A livestock market occupied the site as early as the tenth century. In 1860 an act of Parliament decreed that a permanent market was to be established here and Sir Horace Jones was commissioned as the architect. The new market cost almost a million pounds and was opened in 1868. Although the building suffered a fire in 1958 and was replaced in 1962, much of the original Victoriana remains and it has a Grade II listing.

The market still influences the cost of meat and poultry in the UK today with hundreds of butchers and suppliers visiting on a weekly basis.

You can visit the market and shop there, but access to certain areas is restricted unless you are wearing clean protective clothing in accordance with hygiene standards. As an alternative there is a very good butcher on Charterhouse Street selling meats directly from the market. ○

Above **The porters outside Smithfield Meat Market.**

John Torode

"

I just love my fried eggs with crisp edges, and the way to make that happen is to heat some oil, preferably olive for flavour, until it is quite hot in a nonstick pan, drop your egg in and let it start to spit and splutter – that is all part of the plan. Now reduce the heat to low so the yolk sets, and then right at the last minute turn the heat up to full and cook for 30 seconds. There you have it: crispy-edged fried egg, fantastic on hot buttered toast with a couple of rashers of bacon. But then you knew that already.

Chef and restaurateur

Above right
The downstairs café at Smith's of Smithfield.
Above **Field mushrooms on toast.**

Smith's of Smithfield 67–77 Charterhouse Street, EC1M 6HJ
020 7251 7950 www.smithsofsmithfield.co.uk

John Torode, the personality behind Smith's, is a distinguished Australian chef, TV personality and restaurateur who cut his British teeth at Quaglino's and Mezzo. He now possesses a relaxed style that is absolutely at one with the Smithfield vibe and this former warehouse building opposite the meat market offers a multitude of dining and drinking options. The common thread that connects the five floors here, each with its own distinct characteristic, is a passion for unpretentious and great-tasting food.

On the ground floor the décor is simple, with bench seats, leather sofas and a long bar. An open kitchen serves up an excellent all day breakfast, along with club sandwiches, meat pies, sausage and mash, brunch, freshly squeezed juices and smoothies. Good beer is the order of the day.

As you progress upstairs the New York warehouse feel continues – the first floor is a smart cocktail bar, the next floor is a private dining and events space. A 130-seat dining room is located on the second floor, with heavy timber chairs and tables and a semi-open kitchen that offers food prepared in a range of cooking methods from the wok to clay ovens and charcoal grills. The menu crosses several continents and includes a grill section and a 10-oz beef burger with mature Cheddar and Old Spot bacon.

On the top floor you reach the peak in culinary terms with a glass-walled dining space overlooking the market rooftop and a decked terrace. The menu is dedicated to the best of British meat, rare breeds, organic additive-free foods, fresh fish and seasonal vegetables. ●

Steak Béarnaise

Smith's of Smithfield

by John Torode

The two classic steak dishes that will never go out of fashion are steak with béarnaise sauce (similar to hollandaise, but made with tarragon) and pepper steak – both served with a bowl of crisp, freshly cooked chips.

Béarnaise sauce is one of the great, great sauces of both modern and traditional cookery. Used as flavouring for meat and fish it is always served at room temperature and should have a good kick to it. As with mustard or horseradish, Béarnaise should be served in small quantities either along side the meat, fish or eggs but never served over.

Béarnaise is an emulsified sauce, which means that it is held together with an emulsifier in the same way that mayonnaise and hollandaise are held together. Egg yolks are cooked slowly but not scrambled and then butter is added slowly. This fat wraps itself around the warm protein strands (the egg) and the sauce holds together for a short period of time.

Serves 4

For the Sauce

a few stalks of fresh tarragon
100 ml (3½ fl oz) white wine vinegar
1 shallot, chopped
peppercorns
2 egg yolks
120 g (4 oz) warm melted butter
salt and freshly ground black pepper

For the Steak

4 rump or sirloin steaks, each weighing about 300 g (10 oz)
a little olive oil
bunch of watercress, to serve

Strip the tarragon leaves from the stalks, chop them and set them aside. Crush the stalks in your hands to release the oils and set aside.

Put the vinegar, shallot, peppercorns and tarragon stalks in a heavy-based saucepan over a high heat and bring to the boil. Continue to cook until the liquid has reduced in volume by about ¾. Remove from the heat and allow the liquid to cool. Then strain it in to a non-reactive stainless-steel or heatproof glass bowl.

Set up a bain marie by bringing a pot of water to the boil over a medium heat. Then reduce the heat so the water is not quite simmering. Place a bowl over the pan of just-simmering water so it is not touching the water and add the egg yolks. Start to whisk until you can see the whisk leaving a pattern in the sauce – this is known as ribbon stage.

Place a folded cloth on your work surface. Remove the bowl from the heat and set it on the cloth (to keep the heat in). Start to add the melted butter, little by little. Make sure that the egg mixture has taken up each amount of butter you add. If the sauce gets too thick, add a little hot water from the saucepan. Continue to whisk, adding all the butter or until your arm has fallen off! Season the mixture well with salt and freshly ground black pepper and set aside. Remember that this sauce is to provide flavouring for a piece of meat or fish so it should be sharp, well seasoned and have a good punch of salt to it.

Preheat a griddle plate over a high heat. Alternatively heat a little butter in a heavy frying pan, and preheat the oven to 200°C (400°F) Gas Mark 6. Season the steaks with lots of salt and pepper and rub them well with olive oil. If using the griddle plate, cook for 3–4 minutes on a very high heat, turn and cook for a further 3–4 minutes on the other side, to produce medium-rare steaks. Increase or decrease these times by a minute if you prefer your steaks well done or rare respectively Alternatively, place a frying pan over a high heat and add a little butter.

Add the steak and seal it quickly on both sides. Then transfer the steak to the oven for about 5–10 minutes, depending on how rare you like your meat.

Allow the steaks to rest briefly in a warm place, then serve with a little watercress and béarnaise sauce on the side.

Slow Roast Belly Pork with Salsa Verde

by John Torode

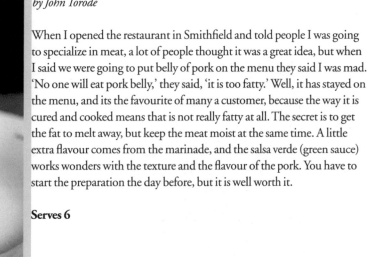

When I opened the restaurant in Smithfield and told people I was going to specialize in meat, a lot of people thought it was a great idea, but when I said we were going to put belly of pork on the menu they said I was mad. 'No one will eat pork belly,' they said, 'it is too fatty.' Well, it has stayed on the menu, and its the favourite of many a customer, because the way it is cured and cooked means that is not really fatty at all. The secret is to get the fat to melt away, but keep the meat moist at the same time. A little extra flavour comes from the marinade, and the salsa verde (green sauce) works wonders with the texture and the flavour of the pork. You have to start the preparation the day before, but it is well worth it.

Serves 6

2 kg (4 lb) piece of belly pork, bone in, rind on
1 teaspoon salt
4 cloves of garlic
2 teaspsoons paprika
30 ml (1 fl oz) vegetable oil
juice of 1 lemon
4 large potatoes

For the Salsa Verde

Traditionally served with boiled meats, this is great with pork as the sourness of the vinegar goes so well with the sweetness of the meat. Also delicious with fish and chicken, it can be made the day before if you wish and it will hold for a few days in the fridge.

handful flat-leaf parsley
handful basil
2 cloves of garlic, peeled and crushed
1 hard-boiled egg
handful fresh white breadcrumbs
1 tablespoon white vinegar
1 tablespoon capers
50 ml (2 fl oz) olive oil
pinch of salt

The day before

With a very sharp knife, score the skin of the pork in a criss-cross fashion at 1-cm (½-in) intervals. In a mixing bowl combine all the remaining ingredients except the potatoes. Rub the pork with the marinade and leave for 12–24 hours covered with cling film in the fridge.

The next day

Preheat the oven to 150°C (300°F) Gas Mark 2. Peel the potatoes and place them in a large roasting dish. Lay the pork over the top. Pour over any remaining marinade and add half a cup of water to the bottom of the tray. Cover it with foil and place it in the oven for 3 hours.

After 3 hours have passed, remove the foil and increase the temperature of the oven to 180°C (350°F) Gas Mark 4. Cook the pork for a further 40 minutes until the skin is crisp.

Remove the pork from the oven, set it on a plate and leave it to rest for 30 minutes. While it is resting, take the potatoes from the roasting dish and mash them.

Next make the salsa verde by placing the parsley, basil and garlic in a food processor and blending them to a paste. Add the remaining ingredients, blend for a further 2 minutes and set aside.

Remove the bones from the pork – they should easily pull away from the flesh – and trim the edges to keep for a snack later. Cut the pork into six portions and return to the oven for 10 minutes to heat through again. Serve the portions of pork on top of the mash with the salsa verde spooned over.

St. John Bar & Restaurant 26 St. John Street, EC1M 4AY
020 7251 0848 www.stjohnrestaurant.com

Its now over ten years since Trevor Gulliver tempted Fergus Henderson
and Jon Spiteri to set up a new restaurant close to Smithfield Meat Market.
Jon was instrumental in the early years and has subsequently moved on.
He can now be found at Bentley's, whilst Fergus's Nose to Tail menu has
gained a global reputation.

When Trevor hit upon the building its previous use had been a
smokehouse, amongst other things. He simply painted the walls white,
put in a skylight, installed a kitchen and dropped in some tables and chairs.
This no-fuss approach is a major reason for the success of the place.

Of course, the food is beyond reproach. Laconic and to the point
describes the menu-writing style, but they also apply to what appears on
the plate. Nobody cooks to this standard and uses the range of ingredients
pioneered by Fergus. It should be said that his parents have a lot to answer
for. Brian Henderson has always enjoyed the best food and wine in
generous quantities. Elizabeth is a fine cook, very much in the Henderson
tradition. Fergus learnt at her stove but originally trained as an architect.

We thoroughly recommend a visit as many times as possible, whether
you are calling in for a morning fillip, a long lunch or a simple supper.
Or why not just collect a few Eccles cakes or a seed cake from the bakery.

(PP) I recently celebrated my thirty-fifth birthday there with a
raucous party for eighteen. We shared a whole suckling pig, followed by
chocolate tart – it's just a wonderful place to be. ◗

Trevor Gulliver

"

There was a time maybe 12–16 years
ago when people from outside those
traditional sources of British chefs
and cooks, restaurateurs and the like
started turning up. Dare I say they
tended to be educated, certainly not
'trade', often successful in business
and who had travelled, more Elizabeth
David than Fanny Craddock. Terence
Conran, Rowley Leigh, Alastair
Little, the River Café, us with our
Fire Station (before St John), a new
use for old premises, Oliver Peyton
with the Atlantic and the guys at
The Eagle giving a different future
to existing pub culture. It allowed for
people like Monica to start Brindisa,
Dominic Ford even put a restaurant
at the top of a department store!

Restaurateur

Above **Trevor
Gulliver (seated)
and Fergus
Henderson in the
bar at St. John.**

Roast Bone Marrow and Parsley Salad

Serves 4

This is the one dish that does not change on the menu at St. John. The marrowbone comes from a calf's leg; ask your butcher to keep some for you. You will need teaspoons or long thin implements to scrape your marrow out of the bone.

Do you recall eating Sultana Bran for breakfast? The sultana to bran-flake ratio was always a huge anxiety, to a point, sometimes, that one was tempted to add extra sultanas, which inevitably resulted in too many sultanas, and one lost that pleasure of discovering the occasional sweet chewiness in contrast to the branny crunch. When administering such things as capers it is very good to remember Sultana Bran.

12 pieces of middle veal bone marrow, 7–8 cm (3–3½ in) long
generous bunch of flat-leaf parsley, picked from its stems
2 shallots, peeled and very thinly sliced
1 modest handful of capers (extra-fine if possible)

For the Dressing

juice of 1 lemon
extra-virgin olive oil
pinch of sea salt and pepper
toasted coarse sea salt, to taste

Preheat the oven to 220°C (425°F) Gas Mark 7. Put the bone marrow in an ovenproof frying pan and place it in a hot oven. The roasting process should take about 20 minutes depending on the thickness of the bone. You are looking for the marrow to be loose and giving, but not melted away, which it will do if left too long. Traditionally the ends would be covered to prevent any seepage, but I like the colouring and crispness at the end.

Meanwhile lightly chop your parsley, just enough to discipline it, mix it with the shallots and capers, and at the last moment, dress.

Recipe featured in *Nose to Tail Eating*, published by Bloomsbury, 2004

St. John's Chutney

There is nothing finer, after having a good stock up your sleeve, than having a reserve of chutney.

Makes enough to fill a dozen jam jars

1.5 kg (3 lb) apples, peeled, cored and chopped
1 kg (2 lb) bag of shallots, peeled
10 cloves of garlic, peeled
1.5 kg (3 lb) tomatoes, chopped
1 kg (2 lb) dates
1 kg (2 lb) raisins
200 g (7 oz) fresh ginger, peeled and coarsely grated
1 kg (2 lb) soft dark brown sugar, or to taste
600 ml (1 pint) malt vinegar, or to taste

Tie together in a stockinet bag

whole black peppercorns
whole coriander seeds
whole white peppercorns
whole chillies
allspice
mace
bay leaf
celery seeds
cloves
fennel seed
mustard seeds

Take a large stainless-steel pot, with a thick bottom so as not to be affected by the vinegar, and add all the ingredients together. Cook on a gentle heat, stirring occasionally to avoid sticking at the bottom, for approximately 1 hour. What you want is a brown-chutney look and consistency – this may take some more cooking, but be careful not to go too far. You do not want to end up with a brown, jammy consistency. When satisfied, remove the spice bag and bottle the chutney in clean, sealable sterilized jars. Store them in the fridge for at least 2 weeks before eating.

Recipe featured in *Nose to Tail Eating*, published by Bloomsbury, 2004

St. John's Eccles Cakes

Should easily make a dozen cakes. Any leftover pastry freezes very well.

I stress the St. John in our Eccles cake, as I am sure Eccles cake bakers in Eccles will not recognize them as an Eccles cake they know.

Oddly enough, for a restaurant with a certain carnivorous reputation, we serve a vegetarian Eccles cake, omitting to use the traditional lard in the pastry. Instead, we use puff pastry, so apologies to Eccles, but this recipe's results are delicious and particularly fine when consumed with Lancashire cheese.

For the Pastry

125 g (4 oz) unsalted butter (butter A), cold from the fridge

500 g (1 lb) strong white flour

a pinch of sea salt

250 ml (8 fl oz) water

375g (12 oz) unsalted butter (butter B), cold from the fridge

For the Filling

50 g (2 oz) unsalted butter

110 g (4 oz) dark brown sugar

220 g (7³/4 oz) currants

1 teaspoon ground allspice

1 teaspoon ground nutmeg

For the Glaze

3 egg whites, beaten with a fork

a shallow bowl of caster sugar

To make the puff pastry, mix butter A with the flour and salt using your fingers until the mixture resembles breadcrumbs. Then cautiously add the water and mix until you have a firm paste. Pat the pastry into a square and wrap it in cling film. Leave it to rest in the fridge for at least one hour before using.

To make the filling, melt the butter and sugar together, Place all the dry ingredients into a bowl and then add the butter and sugar mixture. Mix them well. Leave the mixture to cool and rest before using it. Once rested, roll the pastry dough into a rectangle about 8 mm (¹/3 in) thick, then beat butter B between greaseproof paper into a rectangle a wee bit smaller than half the dough rectangle. Lay the butter on the dough, leaving a space at the end. Fold the unbuttered half over the butter and fold the edges over, so you now have butter-in-dough package. Pat it square, wrap it in cling film, and allow to rest in the fridge.

After the pastry has been in the fridge for at least 15 minutes, roll it out into a rectangle in the opposite direction to your initial major fold. (Each time you roll out the pastry to fold, turn your pastry and roll across the previous direction you rolled. You will have to sprinkle flour on the surface of your rolling pin, however, it is very important to dust the flour off the pastry before folding it at every turn in the process.)

Once the pastry is approximately 1–1.5 cm (¹/2–³/4 in) thick, fold it like a traditional letter, with one end of the rectangle to the halfway mark, and the other end over this. Pat it square and place it in the fridge for at least 15 minutes to rest again. Repeat this process twice more, but no more than that! This is essential for successful puff. Return it to the fridge to rest for 1 hour or more. Do not be deterred. In writing this, it seems like a more complicated process than it is in practice.

To make the Eccles cakes, preheat the oven to 220°C (425°F) Gas Mark 7. Roll the puff pastry out to 8 mm (¹/3 in) thick and cut circles approximately 9 cm (3¹/2 in) in diameter. On half of these spoon a blob of your filling mixture in the centre of the circle, then place the other pastry circles on top. Pinch the edges together, gently press to flatten the cakes, then slash the top three times. (I'm told it is very significant how many times an Eccles cake is slashed.)

Paint the top with the egg white, then dip it into the sugar. They are now ready to bake for 15–20 minutes in the oven. Keep an eye on them so that they don't burn.

They can be eaten either hot or cold and, as I mentioned earlier, are particularly marvellous with Lancashire cheese.

Recipe featured in *Nose to Tail Eating*, published by Bloomsbury, 2004

BAKERY TAKE AWAY

WHITE LOAF 2 80

BROWN LOAF 2 80

LIGHT RYE 2 70

WHITE SOUR DOUGH 3 -

BROWN SOUR DOUGH 3 -

SODA 2 20

RAISIN 3 20

WHOLE SEED CAKE 5 -

ECCLES CAKE 1 80

CHOCOLATE BROWNIE 1 80

MERINGUE 1 -

CHEESE CRACKERS (bag of 10) 2 80

London Dining

Shopping for dinner in London

As diverse as the restaurant and bar scene, London has a wealth of specialist food and drink stores. When preparing for an important dinner party or the arrival of weekend house guests, whatever appears on your menu plans, you can be sure that any unusual or premium foods can be found in London.

We heartily recommend the following;

Champagne and wines

The historic site of Berry Brothers & Rudd with its Georgian vaulted cellars has been trading as a wine shop since 1698. They now hold 20,000 bottles with a choice ranging from as little as a fiver to £4,000 (and probably more given the recent attention shown towards the 2005 clarets). Their own label claret is great value. Berry Brothers & Rudd, 3 St. James's Street, SW1A 1EG, 020 7396 9600 www.bbr.com.

Specialist spirits

Surprise your guests with an unusual Lillet aperitif or maybe an after-dinner Absinthe. Gerry's Wine and Spirits, 24 Old Compton Street, W1D 4UV, 020 7734 421.

Olives and nibbles

For olives, go for the Spanish variety with a few slices of Joselito before dinner. Brindisa, Exmouth Market (see page 191) Or
Excellent Italian antipasti can be sourced at the long-established and beguiling Lina Stores, 18 Brewer Street, 020 7437 6482.

Sushi

You can purchase sushi from Saki (see page 211) or Arigato (see page 124)

Bread

Try Poilâne (see page 84) or Clarke's (see page 159) for different varieties. For a more British loaf you could try St. John Bread and Wine (see page 142) and collect some Eccles cakes or a seedcake at the same time.

Fishmongers

The best fishmonger in London is undoubtedly Steve Hatt (see page 196). The Fish Shop at Kensington Place (see page 160) is particularly handy when preparing dinner with friends and Bibendum (see page 152) has a Saturday morning lobster sale. Pick up some oysters while you are there.

Butchers

Lidgate (see page 161) and The Ginger Pig (see page 20) are equally good.

Cheese

La Fromagerie (see page 18).

Sweet things

Macaroons from Ladurée in Harrods (see page 80).

Chocolate

After-dinner truffles can be purchased from the quintessentially French chocolatier La Maison du Chocolat at 45–46 Piccadilly, W1J 0DS, 020 7287 8500.

Coffee and tea

Tea Palace (see page 279) or Monmouth Coffee Shop, Monmouth Street, Covent Garden, WC2H 9EH, 020 7379 3516 www.monmouthcoffee.co.uk

Cuba's finest

To top it all, buy a few of the finest Cuban cigars (nothing but Cuban should be considered), from Casa del Habano, 100 Wardour Street, W1F 0TN, 020 7314 40 01.

One-stop shop

If you don't have time to travel across London then Villandry (see page 34) or Flâneur (see page 210) are great food halls. Selfridges (see page 33), Harrods (see page 78), Vth Floor at Harvey Nichols (see page 79) and Bluebird Epicerie (see page 156) are also more than reliable.

Home delivery

Don't support the supermarkets (maybe Waitrose is OK). A better option is Abel and Cole, 0845 2626262; www.abel-cole.co.uk, who deliver organic produce all over London.

Vinoteca 7 St. John Street, EC1M 4AA

020 7253 8786 www.vinoteca.co.uk

The emphasis is intended to be the wine, yet the food prepared by Carol Craddock is certainly worth a visit. Carol trained at Bibendum under Simon Hopkinson and she has started to make a name for herself with a regularly changing menu that includes seasonal ingredients with strong flavours. Pork and prune terrine, roast quail with wet polenta, bavette steaks and Welsh rarebit with grilled bacon, soft egg and watercress are all good examples. They also import cured meats from Jabugo in south-west Spain, including Pata Negra. The cheese is first rate.

Each of the menu items has a recommended wine or the staff can guide your choice from the list containing over 220 bins. Once you've tasted you can also buy a case to take home – a very interesting and enjoyable concept devised by three independent wine merchants. I'm sure they have a success on their hands. •

Vivat Bacchus 47 Farringdon Street, EC4A 4LL

020 7353 2648 www.vivatbacchus.co.uk

The sibling of legendary wine restaurant Browns of Rivonia in Johannesburg, the London site has three wine rooms – Champagne, white and red – with around 250 labels for the diners to explore before ordering. They also have a cheese room with up to 80 different cheeses to choose from. •

Above **Inside Vinoteca black boards detail the menu specials.**

Fulham
Hammersmith
Shepherd's Bush

Sophie's Steakhouse appears in this section of *Eat London*, but in reality has a Chelsea postcode and address. This buzzing restaurant and bar is located in pure Fulham territory occupying a prominent 'beach' position, referring to a specific stretch of the Fulham Road, that has since the 1980s been associated with Sloane Rangers; a word play on Sloane Square and the Lone Ranger. Sloanes, Sloaneys or Trustifarians, as they are sometimes referred to, were immortalized by style barometer Peter York and Ann Barr in 1983 when they created *The Official Sloane Ranger Handbook* and its companion, *The Sloane Ranger Diary*. York was at the time style editor of *Harpers and Queen*, the society magazine that was responsible for identifying this right-wing pseudo cult (and also became the first to recognize the term 'foodie'). A Sloane is a public-school educated young wannabe who spends most of his or her time spending Mummy and Daddy's money or strutting their stuff at 'The Cod' (the Admiral Codrington – a pretty good gastropub) and hanging out at the The Sloaney Pony (real name: The White Horse) barbecue and pub on the edge of Parsons Green.

Hammersmith and Shepherd's Bush are more closely aligned with the headquarters of large corporations, including Coca-Cola, Disney, EMI, AOL, Sony Ericsson and the BBC. The forthcoming White City multi-billion-pound development intends to transform much of this part of London with a huge mixed-use retail, leisure and business complex. Until this time, the area's bar and drinking scene is heavily by influenced transient Antipodeans.

Angelsea Arms 35 Wingate Road, Hammersmith, W6 0UR

020 8749 1291

Given the choice, we would certainly prefer a restaurant environment to a gastropub, but we also recognize that in the right hands a good gastropub can serve some very enjoyable food and drink – often better than many restaurants where the food is over-garnished and too fussy. This excellent example seems to call on proven classic dishes and earthy ingredients, such as duck liver parfait, pork belly, duck confit and char-grilled onglet steaks, amongst others. Oysters from France, Ireland and Colchester feature alongside an excellent pint of prawns with lemon aioli and crusty bread. ○

Chez Kristof 111 Hammersmith Grove, W6 0NQ

020 8741 1177 www.chezkristof.co.uk

The menu may not have the qualities of Racine or Almeida, but it certainly has similar aims and Chez Kristoff is one of the better restaurants in this corner of London. The dining room is pleasant and the service fine, if not overly professional. You can get fresh crustacea or bivalves and the main-course options include simple grills, braises and a very tasty pot au feu with Morteaux sausage and pork belly. The definition of a good neighbourhood restaurant is that it should deliver simple dishes that involve good purchasing, and respectful preparation with a few accompaniments that enhance the natural ingredients. The menu should include a few strongly flavoured 'comfort' dishes which demonstrate that the chef has taken the time that you can't afford, and the technique that you haven't received the professional training to master. ○

Above right **Whole Dorset crab with celeriac rémoulade from Chez Kristoff.** Opposite **Potted pâté de campagne from Chez Kristoff.**

The Gate 51 Queen Caroline Street, W6 9QL 020
020 8748 6932 www.gateveg.co.uk
Considered by many the best vegetarian restaurant in London. Dishes
include root vegetable ale stew, aubergine teriyaki and carciofi. ●

The Nutcase 352 Uxbridge Road, W12 7LL
020 8743 0336
This is a very unusual shop that specializes in Arabic sweets, nuts and
fruits that have been dry-roasted on the premises. Everything from
mulberries to lupin or pumpkin seeds, plus baklawa and Turkish jellies
can be found here. ●

Sid Kassabian

" I believe the only way to survive as a butcher in London is to be honest with your customers and provide excellent quality produce with friendly service. That's my policy.

Olympia Butchers

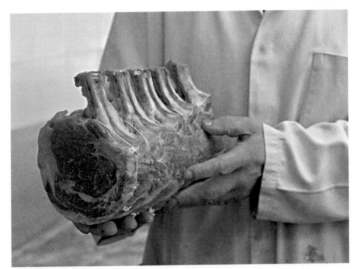

Olympia Butchers 70 Blythe Road, W14 0HB
020 7602 4843

Of all the top butchers in London, this is, by some distance, the best value for money. Armenian Cypriot Sid Kassabian and his family have operated butcher shops for over 100 years and his experience is at your disposal. We understand Simon Hopkinson is a regular visitor and his books are proudly displayed in the shop. That's good enough recommendation for us. So, even if you don't live in the immediate neighbourhood or if you find The Ginger Pig and Lidgate's too expensive, make a beeline for Olympia Butchers; you can be assured of excellence. ◉

Planet Organic 25 Effie Road, SW6 1EL
020 7731 7222 www.planetorganic.com

This small chain of organic supermarkets has an array of retail awards to its name including the Soil Association Organic Industry Award for Best Large Organic Store 2005. ◉

Opposite **Orange and strawberry salad with crushed pistachios, watercress, basil, mint and rocket.** Left **Inside The Gate vegetarian restaurant.** Above right **Sid Kassabian holding rib eye beef inside Olympia Butchers.**

River Café Thames Wharf, Rainville Road, W6 9HA
020 7386 4200 www.rivercafe.co.uk

What started out with the intention to operate mainly as a canteen for the neighbouring architecture practice is now within most foodies' top five London restaurants. However, it was no ordinary architects office. It was that of Lord Rogers, and the shell of the building was a nineteenth-century warehouse on the north bank of the Thames. Since those early days in 1987, Rose Gray and Ruth Rogers have set the pace in terms of modern Italian cooking.

This is the kitchen where the TV production company responsible for *The Naked Chef* first spotted Jamie Oliver and the same kitchen where Hugh Fearnley-Whittingstall worked before his TV career took off. I recently heard that they now have a waiting list for chefs willing to work in the hallowed kitchens for virtually no pay.

Ruth and Rose are passionate about their search for the finest ingredients, especially those from Italy. It is this continual research and tireless procurement that have become respected across the industry. Due to the phenomenal success of the *River Café Cookbooks*, their style of cooking is well known and the books have deservedly achieved global renown.

The River Café chocolate nemesis has also entered the chef vernacular and become a byword for flourless chocolate cake (even when the recipe in the book doesn't work). Another much-copied dish is the squid with chilli and rocket; somehow, others don't seem to quite deliver the same excellence.

Menus always start with the aperitivo of the day in the form of a variation on the bellini made with Prosecco; Charentais melon, pomegranate and grapefruit are sometimes exchanged for the white peaches that usually form the core ingredient.

Detractors and fans alike usually comment about the high menu prices. It might be cucina povera style, but it certainly isn't poor kitchen ingredients. Anyway, the diaries remain busy and it is always difficult to secure a table at short notice. For me, I trust that the proprietors only apply the same margins as other restaurants and would find cupidity vulgar. I'm sure the high prices are due purely to the quality of ingredients (and the generous portions) and the normal costs of running a high-quality restaurant. (PP) My only reservations about the costs are in relation to the cab journeys to and from the Hammersmith location, especially when most of my business is in the West End or more easterly locations and the fact that they have to empty the restaurant by 11 pm because of local residents. For these reasons, I don't visit as often as I would like, but maybe that is a blessing for the wallet. ◉

Left **Rose Gray picking herbs from the gardens outside the River Café.**

Marinated Fresh Anchovies with Rosemary and Red Wine Vinegar

Serves 6

1 sprig rosemary, finely chopped
1 tablespoon salt
1 teaspoon fennel seeds, ground
1 dried chilli, crumbled
freshly ground black pepper
juice of 2 lemons
extra virgin olive oil
500 g (1 lb) fresh anchovies
3 tablespoons red wine vinegar

Mix the chopped rosemary immediately with the salt. Scatter some of the rosemary, fennel seeds, chilli and black pepper over the surface of a serving dish. Drizzle with lemon juice and olive oil.

Place a layer of anchovies skin-side up in the dish, packing them closely together. Sprinkle them with a little more of the rosemary, fennel seeds, chilli, black pepper, lemon, red wine vinegar and olive oil. Make further layers, repeating the process. Make sure the final layer is submerged. Cover with clingfilm and leave to 'cook' in the marinade for at least an hour.

Serve on warm bruschetta.

Recipe featured in *The River Café Cookbook* published by Ebury, 1995

Skye Gyngell

"The extraordinarily amazing River Café has got to be my favourite London restaurant. It's uniquely relaxed and convivial. Unlike other successful restaurateurs, Ruth and Rose continue to work in the kitchen and ensure the standards are maintained at all times even after 20 years at the top of the business.

Petersham Nurseries Café

Right **Rose Gray in the River Café kitchen.** Below **Almond and apricot tart.**

Above **The outside terrace at The River Café.** Left and right **Making ravioli.**

Zucchini Soup
Zuppa di Zucchine

Serves 6

1 kg (2 lb) medium zucchini, trimmed
25 ml (1 fl oz) olive oil
2 cloves of garlic, peeled and chopped
sea salt and freshly ground black pepper
500 ml (17 fl oz) chicken stock or water
140 ml (4½ fl oz) double cream
1 small bunch basil, chopped
1 small bunch flat-leaf parsley, chopped
120 g (4½ oz) Parmesan, freshly grated

For the Crostini

6 slices ciabatta bread, cut at an angle
115 g (4 oz) black olives, stoned and chopped
1 large fresh red chilli, seeded
extra-virgin olive oil

Cut the zucchini lengthwise into quarters, then into 2.5 cm (1 in) pieces. Heat the oil in a heavy saucepan and cook the garlic and zucchini slowly for approximately 25 minutes until the zucchini are brown and very soft. Add salt, pepper and the stock and simmer for another few minutes. Remove from the stove.

Put three-quarters of the zucchini in a food processor and puree. Return to the pan, add the cream, basil, parsley and Parmesan.

To make the crostini, toast the bread on both sides. Mix the olives and the chilli with some extra virgin olive oil and spread thickly on the crostini. Serve the soup with the crostini at the side of the plate.

Recipe featured in *The River Café Cookbook* published by Ebury, 1995

Grilled Peaches with Amaretto
Pesche Gratinate con Amaretto

Serves 6

8 ripe peaches
1 vanilla pod
2 tablespoons caster sugar
120 ml (4 fl oz) Amaretto
crème fraîche, to serve

Preheat the oven to 190ºC (375ºF) Gas Mark 5. Preheat a char-gill or griddle pan. Slice the peaches in half and remove the stones, trying to keep the cut as clean as possible. Carefully place the peach halves cut side down, and grill until each peach half has become slightly charred.

Thinly slice the vanilla pod lengthways and put into a mortar with the sugar. Pound with a pestle until broken up and combined.

Place the peach halves face up in a shallow ovenproof baking dish.

Scatter the vanilla sugar over the peaches and pour in some of the Amaretto. Place in the preheated oven and bake for 10 minutes or until the peaches are soft. Pour over the remaining Amaretto and serve hot or cold with crème fraîche.

Recipe featured in *The River Café Cookbook* published by Ebury, 1995

Giuseppe de Wilde

" I love the River Café! Why? Because that is were my wife, Nicole, took me for our first date (yes, she did… not me!), also the taste of the chocolate nemesis is still in my mouth, simply voluptuous! A perfect lunch and most memorable! I try to return as often as possible.

General Manager, Le Pont de la Tour

Opposite
Grilling peaches at The River Café.
Above right **Exposed ceiling-mounted ducting and light fittings at Sophie's Steakhouse express a Manhattan vibe.**
Above far right **Half-eaten chocolate brownie at Sophie's.**

Sophie's Steakhouse 311–313 Fulham Road, SW10 9QH
020 7352 0088 www.sophiessteakhouse.co.uk

SW10 is officially a Chelsea address, but Sophie's feels like a Fulham restaurant and certainly feeds the Fulham crowd. This stretch of the Fulham Road is traditionally difficult to trade from, but get it right and you have a huge target audience that consists mainly of young boys and girls with a large disposable income, mostly thanks to Mummy and Daddy.

The bar is always busy and seems to serve whopping martinis and other cocktails. The surroundings are very Manhattan with the exposed brickwork, ceiling electrics and ducting. It feels like a warehouse, but it isn't.

As the name implies the menu includes ample choice of beef with six different cuts available, all of which have been aged for at least 28 days. These include: a 15-oz Châteaubriand (a traditional French cut that comes from the top end of the long fillet); a 27-oz porterhouse (t-bone) steak, including both sirloin and fillet; a 24-oz côte de boeuf, from the fore rib, (this is the Sunday lunch special); 10-oz rib eye, which is fattier than others, but with the fat comes flavour; an 8-oz fillet with hardly any fat ((PP) whilst popular in top restaurants and favoured by many, I prefer something with more flavour); and a 10-oz contre fillet, also known as sirloin, which is my favourite.

The menu also has a Black Angus Burger made with chilli, garlic, capers and mixed herbs. It may be very tasty, but it is not exactly for the burger purist. Rotisserie chicken, fish pie, tuna steak, fish and chips and many other salads and sandwiches also appear on the menu. ●

Une Normande á Londres North End Road Market, SW6

This Fulham street market is not exactly typically French. The ingredients are not of any discernable standard either. However, this is one stall that is worth a visit. The French cheese selection is first rate, especially the Camembert and Saint Marcellin. The same people/cheeses also appear at Portobello Market on Friday and Saturday, as well as at the Chapel Road Market on Friday, Saturday and Sunday. ●

Hampstead
Highgate
St John's Wood

Home to numerous thespians and awash with actors from the big screen, it is rather surprising that the restaurant scene in this area of London is not more exciting than it is. Hampstead is supposedly the intellectual suburb in London and a large proportion of the residents say that they are dedicated foodies, but it doesn't seem to show on the high street. Hampstead and Highgate are lovely places to live; the history, large residential properties, proximity to Hamsptead Heath, its elevated status (theoretically), are all strong assets, but until the restaurant scene improves these attractions won't be enough to persuade real food-lovers to live in the area. Some good news might be on the horizon as it is rumoured that a new restaurant from Will Ricker, the man behind E&O, the Great Eastern Dining Room and Eight Over Eight, will open soon another pan-Asian restaurant on Belsize Lane called XO.

Some relief can be found in the vast open spaces of Hampstead Heath and Parliament Hill, with its amazing view over the London skyline. Given the opportunity to picnic, I would certainly navigate a course to north London. It is more enjoyable if you prepare the foods yourself and pack a rug, proper plates, cutlery and glassware, a bottle of Champagne and a few English strawberries, but if this is inconvenient Villandry (see page 34) make great food hampers as well as delectable cakes, tarts and petit fours to take away. Or put together your own feast from the local delis and collect fresh antipasti from Carluccio's on Rosslyn Hill or charcuterie, pies and cakes from The Rosslyn Delicatessen.

The idyllic
Kenwood House.

Brew House Kenwood, Hampstead Lane, NW3 7JR

020 8341 5384 www.companyofcooks.com

On a good-weather day, head north to Hampstead Heath to celebrate the
Englishness when you take mid-afternoon tea and cake in the shadow of
Kenwood. The terraces, café and event catering are professionally managed
by The Company of Cooks, who also oversee Kensington Palace.
Kenwood is an idyllic setting for summer evening concerts; start with a
glass of Champagne at the Brew House and have a picnic afterwards. ◐

Left **Hampstead
Heath on a glorious
summer's day.**
Right **Inside Brew
House at Kenwood.**

Lisa Linder

"

I love my fruit salad and cappuccino at Café Base in the morning despite there often being too many Arsenal supporters for my liking.

Photographer and
Hampstead resident

Above **Fruit jellies
and tea cake at
Brew House.**

Café Base 71 Hampstead High Street, NW3 1QP
020 7431 2224
This is an inexpensive neighbourhood restaurant that is popular with locals and offers a range of freshly prepared Mediterranean-style food.

Carluccio's St. John's Wood High Street, NW8 7SH 020 7449 0404
and 32 Rosslyn Hill, NW3 1NH 020 7794 2184 www.carluccios.com
These two branches in north London are both extremeley popular – the Hampstead shop offers both a café and deli on the ground floor.

Gaucho Grill 64 Heath Street, NW3 1DN
020 7431 8222 www.gaucho-grill.co.uk
This book purposely avoids 'multi-site', branded restaurants, but not because we disagree with the approach. The reason is simple: the food and service at virtually all branded restaurants in London, and the UK generally, are habitually dreadful. This reference mainly refers to restaurants with the same menu and similar interior designs at each property. Notwithstanding the above, we do think that two groups of restaurant – Carluccio's and Gaucho Grills – have done much better than others. Some concepts are simply not suited to being rolled out to every high street in the country, while others are eminently so. The critical element is the motivation of the management and their experience. What invariably starts in London as a new and exciting concept rapidly gets over-managed by the financiers.

Gaucho Grills are serious restaurants that are slightly more expensive than most other branded operations and are not always found on the high street. They have integrity, as well as an interesting concept. The first site opened over ten years ago, and therefore they do not seem to be mandated by investors. Instead, they have expanded gradually and in a controlled fashion (there are currently six Gaucho Grills in London and one in Manchester). While the design at each has a common thread, including high-quality furnishings, there are significant differences.

The main reason for their success is the excellent quality of the Argentinean beef they use. Due to the adequate moisture, mild climate, rich soil and vast terrain on which the cattle graze, as well as the process in which the meat is aged, Argentinean beef develops its own distinctive flavour. The Argentine Aberdeen Angus that grazes freely over grassland contains less cholesterol and has less intra-muscular fat. At Gaucho Grill the meat is cooked in the traditional Argentine manner whereby the steak is only turned once so that there is a greater caramelization, which forms a delicious crust and enhances the flavour. Their menu also has many other facets, not least an all-Argentinean wine list.

Antonio Carluccio

" There's a separate market within the Nine Elms general food market which sells mainly British produce like vegetables and some other foods. I like it because the food doesn't have a lot of mileage.
Carluccio's

Above **Inside Café Base.**
Right **A French crêpes stall on Hampstead High Street.**

Ecuadorean Gambas Ceviche with Ecuadorean Sauce

Serves 2–3

For the Ecuadorean Sauce

100 g (3½ oz) red jalapeño pepper	
200 g (7 oz) romero peppers	
500 g (1 lb) red bell pepper	
550 g (1 lb 2 oz) Spanish onion, chopped	
500 g (1 lb) plum tomatoes, chopped	
100 g (3½ oz) cloves of garlic, peeled and finely chopped	
Kosher salt and freshly ground black pepper	
5 ml (¼ fl oz) Tabasco sauce	
50 ml (2 fl oz) extra-virgin olive oil	
5 oranges, juiced	
5 lemons, juiced	
5 limes, juiced	
75 ml (3 fl oz) ketchup	

Lightly grill peppers and jalapeños until their skins blacken. Then place in a bowl, cover with cling film and set aside. This will cause the peppers to shrink and will make it easier to remove the skin. Once cool, peel the peppers and deseed.

Preheat the oven to 200°C (400°F) Gas Mark 6. Toss the onion, tomatoes and garlic together in a roasting pan and season them. Place them in the oven and roast for about 30 minutes or until they are slightly soft.

Now place them, along with the roasted peppers, Tabasco sauce and olive oil, into a blender and whizz until you have a smooth sauce. Blend in the citrus juices and tomato ketchup then set the sauce aside while you prepare the shrimp (gambas).

For the Gambas

1 tablespoon oil	
5 g (¼ oz) popcorn kernels	
a pinch of Kosher salt	
1 lemon	
a pinch of crushed red chilli flakes	
16–20 shrimp (gambas), weighing 125 g (4 oz)	
juice of 5 limes	
a bunch of coriander	
1 red onion, sliced thinly	
⅛ haas avocado, sliced, for garnish	

Place the oil in a saucepan with a lid over a high and heat until it is smoking hot. Pour in the popcorn and cover. Once the corn begins to pop shake the pan and hold the lid down. As soon as speed of the popping begins to slow, remove the pan from the heat to prevent it burning and sticking to the bottom of the pan. Pour the popped corn in to a bowl and season with salt to taste and set aside.

Place a large pot of water over a high heat. Add a pinch of kosher salt and bring to the boil. Add the lemon juice and chilli flakes, then add the shrimp (gambas). Boil for approximately 1 minute, then remove the shrimp and plunge them into a bowl of iced water to stop the cooking process. Once cool, cut them in half and clean.

Place the cleaned shrimp into a large bowl and season with salt and lime juice. Add in the Ecuadorean sauce, coriander, sliced red onion and toss to combine. Arrange the salad on plates or in glass coupes. Garnish with slices of avocado, coriander leaves, popcorn and season with salt.

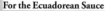

Above **Argentinean beef – the house speciality at Gaucho Grill.** Right **Ecuadorean gambas cocktail.**

Joelle Marti-Baron

"
I love Vinoteca (page 221) for the atmosphere and it's the perfect example of good food and good wine offered in a very friendly, professional environment. This is a great modern wine bar that is always busy and you can rely on the food. We need more authentic places like this.

Director of Wine,
The Great Eastern Hotel

Opposite **The bar at The Horseshoe has its own micro-brewery.**
Right
An abundance of natural light inside The Horeshoe.

Giraffe 46 Rosslyn Hill, NW3 1NH
020 7435 0343 www.giraffe.net

This is part of a group and brand, but it is very much a family restaurant and good for kids – ideal for the area. Visit for brunch and enjoy stacked pancakes with banana and blueberries or try their evening menu, which includes firecracker chicken and egg noodle stir-fry and grilled citrus salmon tostada, plus they offer great salads and burgers. ●

The Highgate 53–79 Highgate Road, NW5 1TL
020 7485 8442

A gastropub of a vast size (formally a car showroom) with a great bar menu and a downstairs restaurant serving British and European dishes. ●

The Horseshoe 28 Heath Street, NW3 6TE
020 7431 7206

This is a stripped-back gastropub with stripped-back food and a decent fish (pollack) and chips. A very popular haunt with the Hampstead locals and they also have a micro-brewery on site. ●

Jinkichi 73 Heath Street, NW3 6UG
020 7794 6158

Eternally busy, probably because it only has about 20 seats, it's a little scruffy, but the sushi and yakitori are good. ●

Brian Lay-Jones 36 Heath Street, NW3 6TE

020 7435 5084

This traditional local greengrocer's offers a wide array of fresh and exotic produce at very reasonable prices. ●

Louis Patisserie 32 Heath Street, NW3 6TE

020 7435 9908

A Hungarian café with old-fashioned pastries and endearing grumpy old ladies with a few charms. Its interior hasn't changed over the years – a welcome relief from the blandness of coffee shops we see on every high street. ●

Harry Morgan's 29–31 St. Johns Wood High Street, NW8 7NH

020 7722 1869 www.harryms.co.uk

It's important that you know about Harry M's, but less important that you eat on the premises. The room is not attractive and the service is pretty poor, especially from the young kids (the slightly more mature staff aren't bad). Established for many years, the diner, deli and takeaway service has perennially attracted the great and the good from the north-west London Jewish community, plus many other religious faiths and communities. The chicken soup and salt beef are said to be the best in London. Other heimishe foods include pickled tongue, chopped liver, gefilte fish, pickled cucumbers, potato latka and the lokshen pudding and apple strudel. The hot salt beef sandwich and the smoked salmon bagels are also good to go. ●

Above **The fruit and vegetables on sale at Brian Lay-Jones.** Right **Harry Morgan's salt beef sandwiches on rye.**

Lisa Linder

" Just like my mother, I continue to return to J. A. Steele the butcher's because it's simply the best-quality meat and the service is always friendly.

Photographer and Hampstead resident

The Rosslyn Delicatessen 56 Rosslyn Hill, Hampstead, NW3 1ND
020 7794 9210 www.delirosslyn.co.uk

This delicatessen is independently owned and locally supported. They stock a vast range of foods sourced from all over the world including cheese, charcuterie, oils, vinegars, herbs, spices, pasta, sauces, tea, coffee, cake and biscuits. They can make up delicious picnics and will provide the basket, flasks and blankets, and they offer a dinner party service where a chef will come to your home to cook your chosen dishes.

Royal China 68 Queen's Grove, NW8 6ER
020 7586 4280 www.royalchinagroup.co.uk

Part of the burgeoning chain of Chinese restaurants, specializing in excellent dim sum.

J. A. Steele 8 Flask Walk, NW3 1HE
020 7435 3587

This is a long-established butcher's that has served several generations of Hampstead residents.

Every Christmas Eve there is a massive queue outside the shop that snakes down Flask Walk and into the high street. The staff from the shop come out with tumblers full of whisky and everybody starts happily chatting for hours while they wait their turn. It is at this point that you know Christmas has arrived and you can merrily stagger home with a huge bird under one arm and a fantastic ham under the other.

Left **The impressive shop window of J. A. Steele.**

Left **Maki rolls at Sushi-Say.** Right **Katsuhara (Katsu) Shimizu chef and owner with Mrs Yuko Shimuzu at Sushi-Say.**

Sushi-Say 33b Walm Lane, NW2 5SH
020 8459 2971

Although this restaurant is quite northerly and not exactly located in one of the finest areas of London, it is actually easy to reach. The Jubilee Line tube goes directly from Green Park to Willesden Green station in about 20–25 minutes. From the station the restaurant is just a one-minute walk. The ambrosial food at Sushi-Say is certainly worth a little inconvenience, so forget the car and take the tube.

This is a small traditional and authentic Japanese restaurant run by a husband and wife team. Yuko is the manageress whilst Katsuhara (Katsu) presides over the sushi bar. The menu doesn't appear to reveal anything unusual or unique; it just offers the best execution of age-old classics from the Japanese repertoire. After a really excellent lunch recently Yuko started talking with us about the modern new-wave Japanese restaurants and the modern Japanese dishes that, thanks to Nobu, have entered the menu vernacular. Yuko was clear that the furthest Katsu will go in this direction is California rolls and soft shell crab tempura – thankfully, not very far.

Katsu's recent recommendations allowed me to try razor clam, whelk and freshwater eel nigiri sushi, plus a really excellent o-toro – fatty tuna belly. The lustre evident on all of the fish denotes an extreme freshness and unlike in many other Japanese restaurants, the proportion of rice to fish is just right at Sushi-Say. The fish is far more dominant than the rice, which is not overpowered by the wasabi, but instead exposes a subtle sweetness. If you don't like sushi, there is still a fine choice of tempura, yakitori, pickled vegetables, bean curd and grilled fish, along with rice and noodle dishes. The gyoza and shumai are excellent appetizers.

We first heard about Sushi-Say via a London restaurant guide website when various diners were giving negative feedback on another well-known central London restaurant. Several blogs kept comparing the shortcomings of this very expensive restaurant to the contrasting qualities at Sushi-Say. Many other bloggers also agreed. We wholeheartedly support their comments. Sushi-Say has the best sushi in London. ◗

Above **Sashimi platter.** Right **A young local enjoying edamame beans.**

Top left **The Wells's downstairs bar.** Above and above left **The upstairs restaurant is a cluster of small dining rooms.** Left **The Georgian façade.**

The Wells 30 Well Walk, NW3 1BX

020 7794 3785 www.thewellshampstead.co.uk

Not exactly a gastropub, but a professionally managed, comfortable ground-floor bar with a couple of small upstairs dining rooms. Given the sedate and semi-rural charm of the area and its location – a classic Georgian building perched about halfway between the heath and the village high street, it's a good place to stop for a light lunch and a good beer. The dinner menu is not complicated, just proven classics and good everyday dining. ○

Mayfair
Piccadilly
St. James's
Westminster

If we have to be truly objective, this is the very best area of London, superior to any other neighbourhood. It has the wealth, tradition and assets to eclipse any other. It may not be everybody's favourite, but nobody can challenge its pre-eminence. The homeland of haute cuisine in this country, the requisite address to occupy if you are a noble wine merchant and the quintessential setting for a cigar shop. For us, it conveys the conduct of an English gentleman, a locale defined by its bespoke Savile Row suits, full-handle umbrellas from Swaine Adeney Brigg, shirts from Jermyn Street, tweeds from Cordings and antique guns from James Purdey and Sons. If bowler hats were still fashionable they would be sold in this area.

According to Monopoly, the board game patented in 1935 by Charles Barrow, Mayfair has the most expensive property in London. Recent reports have suggested that a small bolthole in the Albany, the aristocratic chambers next door to the Royal Academy, can set you back a cool million. Then this is considerably less than the £30million for a 5-bedroom townhouse close to Grosvenor Square that was also in the news recently.

Green Park, St. James's Park and Hyde Park are verdant oases providing large open space for leisurely walks after lunch or summer picnics. For the tourist attraction minded, there is also the fine collection of palaces and stately property: St. James's Palace, Spencer House, Lancaster House, Clarence House, Bridgewater House, the Palace of Westminster and Buckingham Palace.

The solitary Achilles' heel can only be its shortage of the humble things in life.

Allen's 117 Mount Street, W1K 3LA
020 7499 5831

Butcher to the 'Mayfair Set' for almost 200 years, Allen's sell top-grade meats, poultry and game. It is one of the few remaining places where you can find gulls' eggs during the short season between the May Bank Holidays. The worn octagonal butcher's block in the centre of the shop dominates the space and unusually very little meat is actually on display. It is better to call ahead and place an order or build up a relationship with the staff. ⊙

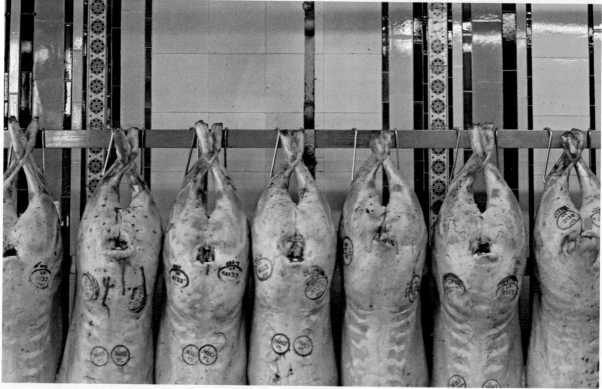

Vicki Conran

" Bellamy's is one of my favourite places largely because it offers no resistance – you get a warm welcome, an unchallenging menu and delightful service – its club-like atmosphere is friendly and discreet, you could eat there every day and never tire. I love it.

Cookery writer

Opposite **Whole beasts awaiting the butcher's block and knife.** Far right **Bellamy's prawn and avocado salad.**

Bellamy's 18–18a Bruton Place, W1J 6LY
020 7491 2727

Rustic French menus delivered with poise and 'je ne sais quoi'. Incongruous among the simple dishes such as salade oeuf en gelée or salad Lyonnaise, the centrepiece of the menu card is a selection of Beluga, Sevruga and Oscietra caviar with 125 grams of the Beluga priced close to £400. I'm not sure how much caviar they sell, but its inclusion in this manner seems to illogically degrade the value of the overall experience. The owner, Gavin Rankin, has previously been involved with various private members' clubs owned by the infinitely refined Mark Birley and it is clearly evident that many of the 'society' clientele have followed him to his new venture. ●

Benares 12a Berkeley Square House, Berkeley Square, W1J 6BS
020 7629 8886 www.benaresrestaurant.com

Atul Kochar's subtly spiced Indian recipes are perfectly executed with a menu that includes a large proportion of fish, and they are all premium catch at that. Lobster, John Dory, seabass and turbot all appear, but are never overwhelmed by the Indian seasonings and accompanying ingredients. Other dishes include an excellent lamb rogan josh or chicken biryani.

While the location of this restaurant at a prestigious Berkeley Square address makes for a restaurateur's delight, the space does not have any windows. Despite this shortcoming, the designers have created a very attractive series of rooms. Many of the top restaurant critics believe that Atul Kochar is the best Indian chef in London. ●

Bentley's Oyster Bar and Grill 11–15 Swallow Street, W1B 4DG
020 7734 4756 www.bentleys.org

Given new life by Richard Corrigan, Bentley's is a civilized, mainly fish and crustacea restaurant, conveniently positioned on a narrow street between Regent Street and Piccadilly.

The ground-floor oyster bar menu features a fine selection of Irish bivalves with oysters Rockefeller chalked up on the specials board. You can find really good smoked salmon, again from Ireland, smoked eel, pickled herrings, stuffed squid, Dover sole and a posh fish and chips with mushy peas and tartar sauce good enough to eat on its own. Sit at the marble bar and engage the shuckers, dressed in the traditional white coats, while sipping a chilled Chablis grand cru. The brown sugar meringue with strawberries and Jersey cream are celestial.

The upstairs Grill Room offers a more extensive menu, including both fish and meat, although the only non-fish or shellfish first course is foie gras. While principally a fish restaurant, the meat main-course highlights include a mixed grill that features a suckling pig sausage, fillet of beef, belly of pork and lamb chops. The grilled West Cork beef with Béarnaise and chips also sounds tempting.

Whilst Bentley's has been trading on this site since 1916, when the original Bentley's were in the oyster business with beds in West Mersea, near Colchester, its reputation seriously eroded over recent years. Richard's new energy in the kitchen has saved the restaurant for another generation and brought a calmer influence on the interior design, with an attempt to incorporate a William Morris Arts and Crafts theme. ●

Mark
Broadbent

I think Richard Corrigan is producing food in a vein of honesty, quality and intelligence. He has his finger firmly on the pulse of modern city cooking, understanding and valuing his clientele. At both Bentleys and Lindsay House, he manages to deliver all elements of the desired dining experience with verve, style and enthusiasm; he is also a great bloke to boot!

Head Chef, Bluebird

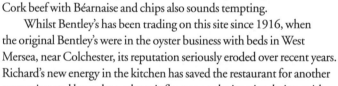

Right **The oyster bar at Bentley's.**

Gooseberry Pie

Serves 6

For the Pastry

250 g (8 oz) butter, chilled
500 g (1 lb) self-raising flour
a pinch of salt
50 ml (2 fl oz) iced water
1 egg yolk

For the Filling

1 kg (2 lb) gooseberries
225 g (8 oz) caster sugar (reserve 15–20 g (1/2–3/4 oz) to finish)
75 g (3 oz) butter, soft

1 egg, beaten
Jersey cream, unpasteurized, to serve

To make the pastry, in a large bowl, cut the butter into cubes and blend together by hand with the flour and salt until it resembles fine breadcrumbs. Next add the chilled water and the egg yolk and mix them well until combined. Cover the bowl with cling film and place it in the fridge to rest for 30–45 minutes.

Preheat the oven to 200°C (400°F) Gas Mark 6. Lightly grease a loose-bottomed pastry tin measuring 20 x 4 cm (8 x 1 3/4 in) with a little of the soft butter. Line the tin with half the pastry and allow a little to over-hang the rim. Add in layer by layer the gooseberries and sugar and fleck with the rest of the butter.

Roll out the remaining pastry and place it carefully on top of the pie. Crimp together the edges to join them. Make a couple of incisions in the top of the pastry to allow the steam to escape. Brush the top of the pastry with the beaten egg and sprinkle it all over with the reserved sugar. Place it in the oven and bake it for 20 minutes. Then lower the temperature to 160°C (325°F) Gas Mark 3 and bake the pie for another 30–40 minutes. Serve it with thick unpasteurized Jersey cream.

Le Caprice Arlington House, Arlington Street, SW1A 1RJ
020 7629 2239 www.le-caprice.co.uk

Located behind The Ritz Hotel (or would it more germane to say that it is to the rear of The Wolseley?), Le Caprice is sister restaurant of The Ivy and J. Sheekey. Legendary Maitre d' Jesus Adorno oversees the unflappable service and it is acutely difficult to secure a table during the week. However, relief can be found in the Sunday brunch menu that runs from 12 to 5 pm. ○

Cipriani 23–25 Davies Street, W1K 3DE
020 7399 0500 www.cipriani.com

Cipriani is the greatest paradox in London. The service is appalling and the food is invariably ridiculous and crudely overpriced. This isn't just our view, but a widely held belief among industry insiders and the critics. Yet, absurdly, it's one of the highest-revenue-grossing restaurants in London. The other reason we are not admirers, is that its patrons are hardly ever Londoners. They might have London homes, but also have a Fifth Avenue apartment and a yacht in St Tropez. I recently read that Nancy Dell'Olio, the ex-England manager's partner, hangs out at Cipriani and the Beckhams have recently dined there. Need I say more?

The group is now a global success and it is for this reason that we encourage you to try the London restaurant. (PP) I've visited several of the very good New York outposts. Venice is still to be experienced, but I won't be going back to the London restaurant, despite liking components of the design and the gallant white uniforms. ○

Le Gavroche 43 Upper Brook Street, W1K 7QR
020 7408 0881 www.le-gavroche.co.uk

No restaurant has won more awards than Le Gavroche and we don't just mean accreditation from the Michelin man, although it is worth mentioning that Le Gavroche was in 1982 the first restaurant in the UK to be awarded three Michelin stars. Most of the awards Le Gavroche receives are as a result of votes from industry peers, in admiration of the kitchen and front-of-house teams. More significantly, the restaurant is one of the best in London.

First established in 1967 by brothers Michel and Albert at an address on Lower Sloane Street, the restaurant moved to its current location in 1981. Despite the brothers individually establishing their own kitchens, the Roux Brothers name became formidable and well known to the nation.

Albert's son, Michel Jnr, took over the kitchen in 1991 and gradually ushered in lighter elements and subtly modernized the menus. However, the rich cheese soufflé recipe (opposite) is not one of the lighter examples.

While the kitchen has gained plaudits over the decades, Silvano Giraldin, the front-of-house maestro, should also be included as a reason for the restaurant's success. He has been with the Roux brothers since 1971 and is now a director of the company.

Another admirable feature of Le Gavroche is the attractively priced all-inclusive lunch menu. It includes a three-course menu, mineral water, wine, coffee and petits fours. Any great businessman who has entertained in London will tell you just how good this offer is. ○

Above **Inside the basement Le Gavroche restaurant.**

Bill
Baker

" I love Le Gavroche because, of its type, the food is unquestionably the best in London. It's impossible to resist the Soufflé Suissesse and, should you be there at the right time of year, there are snipe, woodcock, teal and hare. Silvano Giraldin is the best maître d' in town and knows what the customer wants, nay expects. The wine list is extensive, expensive, but there are bargains. Talking of bargains the three-course lunch (including half a bottle of good wine) is one as well. Who says it's expensive?

Wine merchant and consultant

Le Gavroche

Soufflé
Suissesse

Serves 6

140 g (5 oz) butter
65 g (2¹/₂ oz) flour
700 ml (1 pint plus 3¹/₂ oz) milk
5 egg yolks
salt and freshly ground black pepper
1 litre (1³/₄ pints) double cream
6 egg whites
200 g (7 oz) grated Gruyère or Emmental cheese

To make the soufflé mixture, first preheat oven to 200°C (400°F) Gas Mark 6. Melt 65 g (2¹/₂ oz) of the butter in a saucepan set over low heat. Using a small whisk, stir in the flour. Cook gently for 2 or 3 minutes, stirring continuously.

Take the pan off the heat and leave the roux to cool slightly. In another pan, bring the milk to the boil and then pour it over the cooled roux, whisking all the time. Set the pan over high heat and, stirring continuously, bring the mixture to the boil and cook for 3 minutes.

Take the pan off the heat and stir in the egg yolks. Season to taste with salt and pepper. Dot the surface with 1 tablespoon of the butter, cut into small pieces, to prevent a skin from forming. Set aside at room temperature.

Meanwhile, chill 12 round 8cm (3¹/₂ in) tartlet tins in the refrigerator or freezer for a few minutes. Remove and immediately grease them generously with softened butter and arrange them on a baking sheet.

To assemble the soufflé, pour the cream into a gratin or Le Creuset dish. Lightly salt the cream, then warm it gently without letting it boil. Beat the egg whites with a pinch of salt until they form stiff peaks. Pour the soufflé mixture into a wide-mouthed bowl. Using a whisk, quickly beat in about one-third of the beaten egg whites, then using a spatula carefully fold in the remainder. Using a tablespoon, heap up the mixture in the tartlet tins to form 12 moulds.

Bake the soufflés in the pre-heated oven for three minutes, until the tops begin to turn golden. Remove them from the oven and, protecting your hands with a cloth, turn out each soufflé into the dish of warm cream. Sprinkle over the Gruyère or Emmental and return to the oven for three minutes.

The soufflé must be taken to the table immediately.

The Greenhouse 27a Hay's Mews, W1X 7RJ

020 7499 3331 www.greenhouserestaurant.co.uk

Antonin Bonnet has recently been installed as the head chef and rumours are circulating of a second Michelin star. Antonin was previously cooking at Morton's and before this he was private chef to Marlon Abela, the financial clout behind Umu, Morton's and The Greenhouse.

(PP) Morton's has the most extensive wine list of any restaurant that I know with over 2,800 bins, and in 2005 won the Wine Spectators Grand Award. ◑

Ikeda 30 Brook Street, W1K 5DJ

020 7629 2730

(PP) Back in the early 1990s this was one of the first Japanese restaurants that I visited. Within six months of my first visit Mr Ikeda and I worked together on a special event for the Japanese royal family, plus another memorable wedding attended by several members of the British royal family and many other European royals. The sushi is that good.

I don't get the opportunity to visit as often as I would like, but friends tell me it remains a consistently good Japanese restaurant with intrinsically traditional virtues. For those that don't favour sushi, Ikeda still has a great deal to offer, especially when you want a substantial lunch at very reasonable prices. The tempura, rice and noodle dishes, yakitori, soups, bean curd and chefs specials such as grilled squid legs with ginger, all delight. ◑

Antonin Bonnet

"I love visiting Monmouth Coffee Shop on Saturday morning before touring Borough Market. They have the best coffee in London and the communal table is always set up with tasty butter and excellent baguettes. My favourite restaurant is Umu; the food is refined and better than any other place in London. Its relatively expensive, but in my opinion worth every penny.

Head chef, The Greenhouse

Left **Leafy St. James's Park.** Above right **On guard outside St. James's Palace.**

Inn The Park St. James's Park, SW1A 2BJ
020 7451 9999 www.innthepark.co.uk

The Royal Parks of London are among the capital's greatest assets and the arrival of a new restaurant in St. James's Park has certainly increased the overall value. What was once a dreary park café with poor-quality ice cream, bad snacks and not much else has been completely transformed. The architect Michael Hopkins has created a timber building with a turfed roof, with fittings from Habitat's Tom Dixon, and the whole operation is afforded the careful attention of seasoned restaurateur Oliver Peyton.

The food is best of British with a smart à la carte restaurant on the outer circle overlooking the lake and Duck Island. Behind the restaurant there is an informal grab-and-go area with a hot and cold buffet available during the day. If you have friends visiting from overseas, this is the place to send them on a sightseeing day out in London, with a visit to the nearby ICA after lunch. Over the summer months they operate a small bar from 6 pm until late – a great spot for an after-the-office glass of Champagne and infinitely better than standing outside some common or garden pub. ◗

Left **Outside the Michael Hopkins designed Inn The Park.**
Above **An apposite message on the staff uniforms at Inn The Park.**

Luciano 72 St. James's Street, SW1A 1PH
020 7408 1440 www.lucianorestaurant.co.uk

Rocco Forte and Marco Pierre White have combined forces to create an Italian restaurant of note. Located close to St. James's Palace and previously the Madame Prunier site in London, the restaurant design reflects the distinguished trades that neighbour the premises. Be it a prestigious wine merchant, auction house, art dealer, fine tailor, hat or cigar shop, they all have a common idiom – the Gentlemen of St. James's. The Luciano décor has many Art Deco features, employing impressive materials and fittings, but the combined result is a form that represents the area's parlance. Although the restaurant is relatively new, having only been launched in 2005, it doesn't look new, nor is it hackneyed or tired.

The dining room is at the rear of the space, with all of the walls covered in art of varying formats and disciplines, plus a few evocative black and white photographs by Bob Carlos Clarke taken and hung shortly before his untimely death. Remove the dining tables and the room could effortlessly operate as an art gallery. One of the big attractions for Luciano is the management trio in the form of Marco, the head chef, Livio, the Italian wine authority (few people know more about Italian wines than Livio), and, most importantly, the manager George Perendes. An ex-maître d' of the year, George is the omnipresent host with a unique East End meets Greece meets Italy repartee.

We recommend risotto alla Milanese ragù with osso bucco to start followed by calfs' liver. The selezione di formaggi is hard to resist. ◐

Mourad 'Momo' Mazouz

My favourite London restaurant is Sketch – although one of my own restaurants, chef Pierre Gagnaire, never ceases to amaze me and surprise with new dishes bursting with intricate flavours.

Restaurateur

Above From left Livio, the Italian wine expert, Marco, the chef, and general manager George Perendes

Momo Restaurant Familial / Mo Tearoom and Bazaar
25 Heddon Street, W1B 4BH 020 7434 4040 www.momoresto.com

Mourad 'Momo' Mazouz has recreated the Maghreb in a small cul-de-sac off Regent Street. The cuisine and culture of this atmospheric collection of North African nations have been fused with beautiful staff, electro world music and souk-like interiors. Endless artefacts, antiquities and objects collide with a lively, sometimes loud, evening ambience for an eclectic crowd. Transcending the paradigm, the menu has been energetically researched with the judicious application of a broad range of herbs and spices. While not strictly authentic, some would say it is better for not being so slavishly adherent, it also benefits from access to superior ingredients.

Next door, the Mo Tearoom and Bazaar is always busy with fashionistas sucking on a shisha or, if they feel hungry, eating kemia (Arab tapas). ◐

Morton's Club 28 Berkeley Square, W1J 6EN
020 7499 0363 www.mortonsclub.com

Unlike other cities in the world, London has a profuse panoply of private members' clubs. From the historic and, some would say, chauvinistic gentlemen's preserves of St James's to Mark Birley's Mayfair collection including Harry's Bar and Annabel's, to the younger incarnations in the form of Soho House and The Groucho in Soho. Food is generally secondary to the cocktails and company at most of these places, at Morton's however, the food quality and service are central. It is expensive to become a member, but the calibre of cooking far outstrips that of any other club. ◐

Chicken Tagine with Olives and Pickled Lemons

This traditional recipe serves 5 as a main course

1.5 kg (3 lb 5 oz) oven ready chicken
1 teaspoon of salt
1 teaspoon of ground white pepper
125 g (4½ oz) purple or green cracked olives, stoned
1½ pickled lemons
50 g (2 oz) butter
oil
1 onion, finely chopped
3 cloves of garlic, finely chopped
1 teaspoon of ground ginger
100 ml (3½ fl oz) prepared saffron
500 ml (18 fl oz) water
3 tablespoons chopped fresh coriander
3 tablespoons chopped fresh flat-leaf parsley

Sprinkle the chicken with half the salt and pepper inside and outside and keep it aside.

Blanch the olives three times by plunging them into boiling water. Leave to boil for 30 seconds, rinse under running water and repeat these two operations twice more. Change the boiling water each time. Drain the olives and keep it aside in a colander.

Remove and discard the flesh and pips from the pickled lemons. Rinse the peel and dry it with kitchen paper, then cut it into large slices. Keep it aside in a small dish.

Heat the butter and oil in a heavy saucepan, add the onion and fry gently, stirring frequently until softened and translucent. Add the garlic, ginger, saffron, the remaining salt and pepper and water and stir well to mix the spices in thoroughly. Add the chicken and turn it over to coat it with the sauce. Bring to the boil. Lower the heat, cover the pan and leave to cook slowly for one hour, turning the chicken over several times so that all sides soak up the sauce. If necessary, add a little hot water during the cooking.

Add the olives, pickled lemon, coriander and parsley, stir, cover and cook for 15 minutes. Check the seasoning. Once the chicken is cooked, if the sauce is too runny, remove the chicken and keep it aside, covered with foil to keep it warm. Raise the heat and boil the sauce for 5 minutes to reduce it. Put the chicken in a warmed tagine plate. Arrange the pickled lemon strips and olives on top. Stir the sauce and quickly pour it over the chicken. Cover the tagine dish and serve straight away, very hot.

Recipe featured in *The Momo Cookbook*, published by Simon and Schuster, 2000

Right The interior of Mo Tearoom.

How to prepare saffron

The most noble of spices, is very expensive and quite subtle to use because of its intense flavourings and colouring power that gives the dishes a special taste and a wonderful golden yellow colour.

Preparing the saffron, by turning the strands into a delicate diluted powder, allows for a more effective use. Some recipes may require you to use the strands directly, but this generally doesn't give a good distribution of the flavour, taste and colour. Once prepared, saffron can be kept in the refrigerator for three or four weeks. One teaspoon of saffron strands will give 250 ml (8 fl oz) of prepared saffron.

Heat a dry frying pan on a very low heat and toast the saffron strands very slowly, constantly checking and stirring with a wooden spoon for 2–3 minutes. When the saffron strands have reached a deep red colour (not too brown), put them straight away in a wooden mortar. Crush them very finely while still hot. The mortar can be replaced with a small bowl and wooden spoon. Pour the powder into a dry jar, making sure that you collect every precious grain, and fill the jar with 250 ml (8 fl oz) of warm water. Close tightly and shake it thoroughly to allow all the saffron powder to dilute in the water. The water immediately takes a beautiful orange colour. Leave to cool and refrigerate. Always shake the jar before use.

257

Nobu 19 Old Park Lane, W1K 1LB 020 447 4747
Nobu Berkeley 15 Berkeley Street, W1J 8DJ 020 7290 9222
www.noburestaurants.com or www.myriadrestaurantgroup.com

The original London home of Black Cod was transformed when in 1997 the illustrious Nobu Matsuhisa opened the first European branch of his now global empire on the first floor of the über-chic Metropolitan Hotel. (PP) I remember visiting in the early days when the staff were exclusively models and they dressed in fashionable designer clothes, it was revolutionary. Almost ten years on, it's still a challenge to secure a table and the paparazzi are regularly camped-out on the doorstep.

I find the interior design extremely dry, they call it minimalist, and the hype surrounding tables with views over Hyde Park is just rubbish. Firstly, it's a view over the traffic of Park Lane, especially in the evening, not the lush greenery of the Royal Park. Furthermore, it's much better to sit at the sushi bar or the chef's table at the far end of the restaurant. There is no view at this point in the restaurant, but the advantages are far superior. You are away from the noise and posturing of the main restaurant, where so many of the diners spend the evening checking-out fellow diners instead of enjoying their own company and appreciating the food. Secondly, you get an opportunity to watch the sushi masters at work, and on a recent visit we enjoyed the multi-course omakase menu where you entrust the chef to create a series of dishes that reflects the freshness of the available ingredients. (PP) On this occasion I was dining with another experienced Japanese chef with his own highly praised restaurants in New York. Due to his presence, the chef personally brought each of the amazing dishes to the table. We enjoyed at least 15 platters and each one caused constant cooing and praise. Every dish demonstrated creativity outstripping any other chef, but I must give specific mention to the sea urchin tempura.

While larger examples exist in London, the content of the sake list at Nobu is very good with many of the sake's being served in bamboo decanters and drunk from wooden cups. ●

Quaglino's 16 Bury Street, St James's, SW1Y 6AJ
020 7930 6767 www.conran.com

Most people associate Quaglino's with the 1980s, whereas it actually didn't open until Valentine's Day 1993. This new incarnation was loosely based on the earlier version opened in 1929 by Giovanni Quaglino, which ultimately became one of London's most fashionable restaurants of its day. Indubitably, the re-opening in 1993 sent shock waves across London: this was the first of a new breed of restaurant. The scale eclipsed anything London had seen before. Quaglino's was the most enviable restaurant in London when it opened and still regularly manages to thrill almost 500 people on a Saturday night. The chance to descend the staircase and hear the sound of bar jazz still draws in the crowds from far and wide.

A new chef has recently been appointed so expect the food to move up a notch in the near future. In the meantime, it's a great place for a large table of friends.

Who hasn't got a Quaglino's ashtray at home? ●

Craig James

"I love to eat at Bibendum because of the consistent food quality. You can always be assured of finding a great selection of offal and game (when in season) that is cooked to perfection in the classic style.

Head chef, Quaglino's

Above **The defining Q staircase.**
Below **Quaglino's ashtray and matches. Over 10,000 have been stolen from the restaurant since it opened in 1993.**

Gordon Ramsay at Claridge's Brook Street, W1K 4HR
020 7499 0099 www.gordonramsay.com

Of all the Gordon Ramsay restaurants, we prefer Claridge's. We also believe this to be the most beautiful hotel in London ((PP) forget the Dorchester or Lanesborough, which I happen to think are ugly).

Of the grand palace-style hotels, Claridge's is in a league of its own. (PP) Notwithstanding, my co-author has a contrary view on certain areas of the hotel. If your taste is minimalism or you enjoy the Philippe Starck creations in the form of the Sanderson or St Martin's Lane, then I respect your taste, but please don't dismiss Claridge's: it is somewhere everybody must stay at least once. Or better still, getting married here must be the ultimate. What other London wedding venue beats Claridge's? It's the definitive city hotel.

Crossing the front hall, not lobby, and the mirror-polished marble black and white chequered floor, past the grand staircase and fireplace, you immediately start to think about the social season, country house estates, ladies in hats for Ascot and aristocratic gentlemen in Savile Row suits. (PP) As a past employee of Claridge's maybe my view is romanticized: it is certainly a little rose tinted. The Hall Porters and Concierge are the very best, and can get anything the world has to offer and are regularly put to the test. Upstairs, the bedrooms and suites offer some of the most spacious hotel accommodation and the décor is just wonderful, save for one or two attempts at modern Art Deco.

Before you reach the Gordon Ramsay restaurant you could call in on the Art Deco bar or book a table for afternoon tea in the foyer under the magnificent Dale Chihuly chandelier. There is so much to experience at this hotel and the service is always of the highest order.

The Art Deco theme continues in the restaurant with eye-catching three-tier lampshades, etched glass and elements of the original Basil Ionides 1920s clean lines and columns. Thierry Despont's redesign has delivered a lavish yet respectful space. Huge comfortable armchairs, exquisite tableware and enthusiastic staff make the occasion.

(TC) I used to love the old Claridge's dining room; calm and serene, with immaculate service, the perfect place to eat a roast grouse. You could always get a table as it was very empty, which is certainly not the case now. Gordon Ramsay has certainly made it financially successful but he has, in our biased opinion, made a place for footballers and their wives or girl/boyfriends. Over decorated food, too complex and service rather unctuous too much of everything in a place where elegant simplicity once ruled. Sad, as I have already said, but the elegant classic places have almost disappeared from the London restaurant scene – the Ritz still holds its back up pretty straight.

Mark Sargeant, another member of the original Aubergine kitchen when Ramsay was master, is head chef. Whatever is said about Ramsay, he certainly appears to be supportive of his teams and encourages opportunity. Gordon retains a close connection as the chef patron, and his name is emblazoned above the door. The menus are large and not inexpensive, but you get what you pay for in terms of the overall experience. ◉

Above **Original Basil Ionides designs from the 1920s have been retained and restored at Claridge's.** Left **Claridge's doormen are the best in London.**

The Ritz 150 Piccadilly, W1J 9BR
020 7493 8181 www.theritzlondon.com

Gentlemen must wear a jacket and tie; jeans and training shoes are not permitted. This sentence succinctly elucidates everything about The Ritz.

The restaurant is a magnificently regal dining room with furnishings akin to The Palace of Versailles and guests who would readily be accepted as courtiers to Marie Antoinette. The food is grand-palace-style cooking by John Williams, a veteran of Claridge's and The Savoy Group. Service is by would-be footmen. The Palm Court is eternally popular for afternoon tea, so you need to book months in advance.

(PP) Prior to a recent fact-finding trip touring the restaurants of Russia, I would have said that The Ritz Restaurant is one of the most impressive in the world, but that was before I viewed Turandot, a £50 million restoration masterpiece in Moscow. ◉

Sketch 9 Conduit Street, W1S 2XG
0870 777 4488 www.sketch.uk.com

No other restaurant in London polarizes views like Sketch. You either love it or hate it. We fall in to the latter category, save for the cakes in the Parlour. (PP) However, I have enormous respect for the project's ambition and creativity. The place is full to bursting with ideas, idiosyncrasies and novelty, creating, in my opinion, an overload. But that isn't everybody's opinion. The brainchild of Mourad (Momo) Mazouz, also responsible for the equally admirable Momo restaurant, this project is brave and daring.

(PP) Pierre Gagnaire cooks his own style of experimental food in The Library and Lecture Room, also known as London's most expensive restaurant, but I must confess to not having dined here, although not because of the price tag. ((TC) I have, and it's terrible.) The Gallery is a projection-art space during the day and a large upscale restaurant in the evening, becoming a disco afterwards. (PP) I have dined in this area on two occasions: the first was shortly after the opening and I thought it was over priced and reflective of the other wacky elements of the project, but a second visit revealed slightly lower prices and better food, but still not to my preference.

It is definitely worth visiting Sketch because you might love it. Or you could just visit the Parlour for cakes. ◉

The Square 6–10 Bruton Street, W1J 6PU
020 7495 7100 www.squarerestaurant.com

The term 'a chef's chef' has been associated with a number of leading French chefs and, as preposterous as it sounds, a London-based chef has now also christened himself the chef's chef. You've got to admire his self-confidence. The chefs that we know universally respect Philip Howard's cooking, the Square's menu and his professional personality. In our minds, he is definitely the chef's chef.

(PP) I've been lucky enough to dine at this restaurant several times over recent years and would describe the food as modern haute cuisine. Michelin give it two stars, whatever that means.

Nigel Platts-Martin overseas the wine list, so expect a colossal choice. ◉

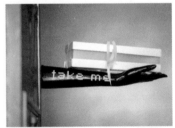

Above **Afternoon tea at Sketch.**
Left **A portrait of David Beckham seems very appropriate for the Parlour at Sketch.**

Above **Chu-toro salad with quails egg.** Left **Preparing maki rolls.**

Umu 14–16 Bruton Place, W1J 6LX
020 7499 8881 www.umurestaurant.com

London's only Kyoto restaurant, the food here is exquisite and they stock the largest sake collection in London.

When the restaurant first opened in 2004 it attracted some negative publicity connected with its £200 kaiseki menu and sadly it seemed to have an impact on the number of diners. We visited the restaurant during the initial months and found the experience to be comparatively expensive, but when you understand that the water is specially flown in from Kyoto so that the chef can use it to make tofu, the range of fish is unrivalled and many other indigenous ingredients are also imported purely for Umu, you can start to understand how the management justifies the prices and why Umu cannot be allied with any other Japanese restaurant.

Today, the same excellent standards prevail and the prices seem to be more reasonable. On three separate return visits the room was buzzing with a very pleasant crowd. The service is pure French, not Japanese. ○

Wilton's 55 Jermyn Street, SW1Y 6LX
020 7629 9955 www.wiltons.co.uk

I remember regularly dining at this restaurant shortly after Margaret Thatcher was overthrown as Conservative Party leader. On one of the occasions at least three members of her Cabinet were also present, each on a different secluded Pullman-style table or in the shady alcoves. The diners haven't changed much since those days. This book champions the new and exciting eateries in London, but also recognizes the restaurant aristocracy and perennial favourites. We have a weakness for the traditionalists and their thankless devotion to the more arduous of tasks that are purely continued in reverence to the great restaurant spirit of yester-year. Wilton's has been around for a few hundred years and retains its status as an English fine dining destination for lords, dukes, viscounts and the like.

Jérôme Ponchelle is now installed as the chef, somebody that spent nine years as sous chef to the celebrated and much missed Michel Bourdin, Maître Chef at The Connaught for 26 years, this was before the Ramsayification. (PP) I also briefly worked with M. Boudin and while he was regularly critised for his stubbornness, his food was a British accented version of Escoffier and Jérôme continues many of the same traditions at Wilton's, although using principally fish, shellfish and game in season. An ideal meal at Wilton's would include lobster cocktail to start, cold beef consommé – just because they are one of the few places that still have it on the menu, Dover sole meunière followed by Welsh rarebit or sherry trifle.

Although a Frenchman, M. Boudin was a staunch Royalist and an extreme supporter of the British royal family. Whenever a member of the British royal family visited his restaurant at the Connaught, or his kitchens, as the Queen Mother did occasionally, he would create a new dish on the menu and name it in honour of them, there it would stay for years to come. I recall the menu was littered with soups named after the Prince of Wales, desserts named after the Queen Mother and so on.

Angela Hartnett, another Gordon Ramsay protégée, is now cooking at The Connaught. Its reputed to be a good restaurant, but a few of my friends have been before and encountered bad service and others just don't want to go back out of respect to the old Connaught.

If you can't get a table at Wilton's and you want to try something similar then I suggest Green's just around the corner at 36 Duke Street. ◐

Jérôme Ponchelle

I always enjoy dining at Eric Chavot at The Capital Hotel, 22 Basil Street, SW3 020 7589 5171. Eric's cooking is classically French with creative and modern twists. Not enough people talk about his restaurant. Fortnum and Mason on Piccadilly is a great place to shop for traditional British ingredients and groceries.

Chef de Cuisine, Wiltons

Above **Gentlemen in bowler hats and Savile Row suits can still be spotted on St James's with leather briefcases and bentwood handle umbrella's.**

The Wolseley 160 Piccadilly, W1J 9EB
020 7499 6996 www.thewolseley.com

After creating and then selling The Ivy, Le Caprice and J. Sheekey, London's most respected restaurateurs Chris Corbin and Jeremy King disappeared from the scene in 2000. Much speculation circulated as to whether they would return to the floor and what would happen to their three celebrity-loved restaurants. In 2003 the rumours were put to rest and they opened The Wolseley, one of the most talked-about new restaurants to open in years.

Firstly, the building façade is deservedly listed and since opening as The Wolseley it has engendered greater credibility to one of the main thoroughfares in London, something that the neighbouring Ritz Hotel has failed to achieve for quite some time. Past the doorman, a combination of black, soft gold or brass, Japanese lacquer and large, but sparse, chandeliers (apparently modelled on the original design when the space was the short-lived Wolseley car showroom in the roaring twenties), all meet the eye.

The sound of thespian luvvies meets the ear as you progress beyond the revolving door and hopefully the management will enthusiastically welcome your arrival as all eyes turn towards the entrance, visually appraising any new arrival. Seating positions are all important. The inner horseshoe is reserved for playwrights, knights of the realm, literary agents, leading ladies and the London 'faces' one should immediately recognize. Being banished to the corners or outer sections is more obvious here than in other places, and is the restaurant equivalent of being usurped by the understudy or having your play dropped due to poor ticket sales.

Grand Café-Restaurant is the given nomenclature as it follows the tradition of the great European, although mainly Parisian and Viennese, all-day eateries of the last century. One of the key characteristics is that it is open all day every day, which has led to every other restaurateur wanting to do the same. Unlike the others, The Wolseley effusively addresses this intention with an extensive selection of menus to choose from: a chef's nightmare, but a diner's dream. Everything from Viennoisserie to hot breakfasts to an all-day menu, lunch menus, plat du jour, grills, crustacea, patisserie and cakes, afternoon tea and a dinner menu are available. The choice offered on each page of this huge carte is carefully thought through, and the pricing is fair. It should be remembered this is not gourmet food, but that doesn't mean to imply that it isn't excellent. The dish options range from French coq au vin or bouillabaisse to British summer pudding or Teutonic Wiener (Wien refers to Vienna) schnitzel. A hamburger, or Jewish chopped liver or chicken soup with dumplings, a hint of Italian, and not forgetting the Austrian connection, all combine to create a summary of the best dishes from across Europe, based on what people want to eat, not what the chef wants to serve.

Of particular interest is the tableware, which you can now purchase from The Wolseley's online shop. While the vast majority of equipment has been sagely selected, we won't be the first person to comment on the diminutive wine glasses and small tabletops.

Watch out for St. Alban, a new restaurant shortly to be launched by Chris and Jeremy. ○

Above **The Wolseley façade on Piccadilly.**

Notting Hill

Over the last forty years Notting Hill has gone from virtual slum and almost no-go territory to one of the most affluent areas in London. In 1965 the annual Carnival came to the area, initially set up to help quell the race riots that had started in the late 1950s and early 1960s. It is now one of the most colourful events in London. The Afro-Caribbean community embraced Carnival and Notting Hill hasn't looked back since. While most Notting Hill residents usually leave the neighbourhood during the last weekend in August when the Carnival takes place, the streets experience the influx of over one million people.

Outside Carnival, the area has achieved global appeal thanks to Richard Curtis's romantic comedy *Notting Hill*, with Hugh Grant and Julia Roberts. Property values rocketed after this film and the already busy Portobello Market hit every tourist's to-do list.

The area still retains a slightly bohemian edge and a counter-culture element, but that is certainly in the minority. Today, it is the value of the large white stucco and Victorian terraced houses that draws most people's attention. Commercial property rents have witnessed an equally stratospheric increase and the number of independent traders is rapidly reducing. Therefore, we can only assume that the restaurateurs and food retailers struggle to make any sort of profit. So, please support the independents and avoid the big groups.

A further measure of Notting Hill's wealth has been signalled by the recent arrival of The Ledbury, a serious fine-dining restaurant with food and a wine list that wouldn't be out of place in Mayfair.

Assaggi 39 Chepstow Place, W2 4TS
020 7792 5501

When we asked Nino, along with Pietro, one of the owners and chef, if the restaurant still had a Michelin star his honest answer was 'I don't know.' Of course, we are personally aware of the Michelin guides but usually use the merits as a negative influence – although not exclusively. We had heard a rumour that Assaggi had once been awarded a star so that prompted the question. But all Nino could say is that the restaurant had been virtually full for the last eight years and it genuinely doesn't matter to him if they have a star or not. Nino cooks for his customers and the joy of a busy dining room, and certainly not for the Michelin inspector.

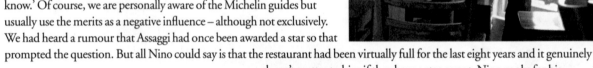

Although Nino is from Sardinia, the food at Assaggi is more general Italian. The portions are generous and the flavours full on. The menu is printed only in Italian, but when you ask for a translation the staff don't just provide the words in another language they explain how the dish is prepared, the component ingredients and how wonderful the taste sensation will be. Having both visited thousands of restaurants over the years, we can say with confidence that the staff at Assaggi are certainly in the top five for well-trained employees. However, somehow we think they haven't actually received any specific training, instead they just watch the chefs, day in, day out. They have tasted the dishes first hand, and that enables them to speak from the heart, not the training manual.

We particularly recommend the Pecorino con Carpegna e Rucola as a first course, followed by carre' d'agnello con fave. And the veal chop is pretty damn good. The taglionlini al granchio, made with nine different herbs and crushed walnuts, is a lovely pasta dish. On rare occasions they also have a main course of milk-fed lamb where a tiny lamb is used and you get the whole leg. They don't have a dessert menu; the staff simply visit your table and tell you what Nino has available that night. (PP) The bavarese with espresso coffee is a particular favourite.

Above **Nino Sassu in his kitchen at Assaggi.**

Don't expect an over-designed dining room. Part of the charm of this place is that it is simply a room above a half-decent pub. ●

Oliver Peyton

"I love Assaggi – it is without a doubt the best Italian restaurant in London. Totally unpretentious, it serves truly genuine imaginative Italian food. The owners, Nino Sassu and Pietro Fraccari, are always in the restaurant and it's obvious they care passionately about food.

Oliver Peyton, restaurateur for Mash, Inn The Park and the National Dining Rooms

Far right **Sardinian bread.** Right **Broad beans being prepared to accompany to roast rack of lamb.**

Books for Cooks 4 Blenheim Crescent, W11 1NN

020 7221 1992 www.booksforcooks.com

Janet Street-Porter recently said that cookery books are the new porn. If that is the case then Books for Cooks is a hard-core sex shop. At the rear of the shop they have a small test kitchen and café where you can get a simple lunch or cake while you enjoy a cursory read of your new purchase. ○

The Cow 89 Westbourne Park Road, W2 5QH

020 7221 0021 www.thecowlondon.co.uk

An institution in Notting Hill and Tom Conran is the local champion. At the genesis of the gastropub movement in London, The Cow helped fashion the original and best format, something that has little connection with latter versions that have started to miss the point and ultimately degrade the term gastropub.

Downstairs is a great boozer, or saloon bar as it is called, with proper ales, Guinness that tastes better than at most other places, bottled British and Continental beers, and much more. The short-order kitchen on the ground floor is perfect for lunch. The menu includes fish stew, and sausages braised in beer and onions. Or maybe a pint of prawns or a plate of oysters will hit the spot. Good grub at reasonable prices served by sexy girls and boys.

(PP) Upstairs, the small dining room serves, in my opinion, the best food in Notting Hill. That doesn't mean that it is striving to be a full-on restaurant or chase stars. It just has an attentively planned menu and first-rate cooks in the kitchen. The ingredients are intensely seasonal and come from the finest sources. Tom is passionate about provenance, good animal husbandry, artisan producers and regional farmers. Unlike many others in the trade, Tom also respects the symbiotic existence between restaurateur and supplier. In essence, the menu is intrinsically and proudly British, but they also have few detours to the Continent.

Tom has curated a fascinating collection of posters, tasteful pub memorabilia and Paul Slater art. All combine to form to an urban idyll where you can contentedly while away hours with friends. ○

Roast Best End of Elwy Valley Lamb with Pea Shoots and Mint Pesto

Serves 2

For the Marinade

1 best end rack of lamb, trimmed
(We like to use the organic Welsh lamb from the Elwy Valley, but English is as good.)

4 cloves of garlic, sliced

sprig of rosemary

sprig of thyme

olive oil

For the Mint Pesto

2 big bunches of fresh mint (picked)

1 handful of pine nuts

1 clove of garlic

pinch of sea salt

juice of $\frac{1}{2}$ lemon

200 ml (7 fl oz) extra-virgin olive oil

To serve

2 handfuls of fresh new pea shoots, available locally from May to June, washed and drained

Drizzle the lamb with olive oil and sprinkle the garlic and leaves of the rosemary and thyme over the top. Leave to marinate for 12 hours.

Put all ingredients for the mint pesto together into a blender. Purée for 2 minutes or until you have a smooth consistency. Set aside.

Remove the lamb from the marinade and place it on a chopping board. Cut the lamb in half to make two portions and discard any leftover marinade.

Preheat the oven to 240°C (475°F) Gas Mark 9. Place an ovenproof frying pan over a medium to high heat, and add a tablespoon of oil. Place the lamb in the frying pan with the bones pointing up. Fry the meat until the bottom has browned to a rich mahogany colour. Then turn the meat skin-side down in the frying pan and place it into the hot oven. After 20 minutes, the lamb will be medium rare. (Alternatively, leave for 30 minutes for well done.) Take it out of the oven and set it skin-side up on a plate, loosely covered with foil, to rest for 10 minutes.

Put a handful of pea shoots on to each four plates. With a sharp knife, slice the lamb between the bones into cutlets. Arrange the cutlets on the shoots. Drizzle the mint pesto and any resting juices over the lamb. Finish with a pea shoot sprig on top and serve.

Left **Chefs and amateur cooks flock to Books for Cooks.** Opposite **The Cow dining room where some of the best food in Notting Hill can be enjoyed.**

Crazy Homies   125 Westbourne Park Road, W2 5QL
020 7727 6771   www.crazyhomieslondon.co.uk

Inspired by the street vendors and taquerias of Mexico, Tom, Cynthia (Tom's wife) and Sage (Tom's sister-in-law) have created a neighbourhood hangout where you can really let your hair down.

Previously the shebeen that Christine Keeler (infamy from the Profumo affair) and Stephen Ward visited with Lucky Gordon, the space has been sensitively reshaped to Tom's idiosyncratic style with plenty of help from Dutch artist Mr Wim. A small tequila bar is located on the ground floor with cosy corners to enjoy your totopos corn chips with salsa or a taquitos-rolled tortilla. The menu in the subterranean dining space extends to burros, enchiladas, light salads and shrimp cocktails. Every meal ends with churros (doughnuts) with chocolate. The beer and tequila list is the best in town. ○

E&O   14 Blenheim Crescent, W11 1NN
020 7229 5454   www.eando.co.uk

This is another celebrity hotspot by Will Ricker. They serve great Eastern and Orient (E&O) pan-Asian food and cocktails in glamorous and sometimes noisy surroundings. ○

Electric   191 Portobello Road, W11 2ED
020 7908 9696   www.the-electric.co.uk

The Electric is an essential part of modern Notting Hill life. The landmark building includes an ornate cinema that is operated in a thoroughly up-to-date manner with large comfortable armchairs, footstools and side tables, where you can also get proper food and drinks before the movie. The ground-floor Anglo-French brasserie forms the epicentre of cool Notting Hill. Open for breakfast, lunch and dinner seven days a week, the menu addresses every taste. The breakfast and brunch menus are particularly good and during the day they have a carving trolley where you can get beef Wellington or Suffolk pork. Upstairs they have a private members' club similar to the other Soho House outposts, with a bar, restaurant, The Study and The Playroom. ○

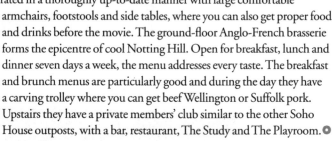

Above **Inside Crazy Homies with Mexican beers and cocktails.**

The Grain Shop   269a Portobello Road, W11 1LR
020 7229 5571

Here you can buy inexpensive organic vegetarian take away food from a buffet – ideal for eating as you stroll through the market on a Saturday. ○

The Grocer on Elgin   6 Elgin Crescent, W11 2HX
020 7221 3844   www.thegroceron.com

Ready-meals from supermarkets and corner shops are full of preservatives and E numbers, and are devoid of any discernible flavour. For the time-pressed workaholic there is, thankfully, a healthy and tasty alternative in the form of The Grocer on Elgin. They prepare restaurant-standard meals that are presented in sophisticated vacuum-sealed packaging, or sealed in parfait jars. You can get a Thai vegetable curry, a confit duck leg or guinea fowl tagine that can be quickly reheated and will prove ideal for a late midweek sofa supper after a long and busy day. ○

Hummingbird Bakery 133 Portobello Road, W11 2DY
020 7229 6446 www.hummingbirdbakery.com

A high-quality American home-baking shop, the Hummingbird
Bakery specializes in cupcakes, New York-style cheesecake, apple
pie, pecan pie, Key lime pie, Mississippi mud pie, banana bread,
sweet and savoury muffins and great cookies. Stop in and try the
cupcake of the day on your way to Portobello Road Market.
Closed on Mondays. ○

Above **Cupcakes
on display in the
Hummingbird
Bakery.**

The Ledbury 127 Ledbury Road, W11 2AQ

020 7792 9090 www.theledbury.com

Notting Hill was once a relatively rundown London enclave known for its West Indian residents and the annual Carnival. It is now more closely aligned as the home to City bankers, high-flying lawyers and successful entrepreneurs, plus a certain political party leader who likes to cycle to work. Oh, and a small film with a floppy-haired actor has also influenced its metamorphosis. The habitués of The Ledbury are representative of the new Notting Hill.

Having trained under Philip Howard at The Square in Mayfair, Brett Graham opened the Ledbury kitchens in 2005 and has already scooped a string of awards, not least the Michelin man's approval. The menu is modern haute cuisine, probably a little too architectural and precise for our liking, but certainly favoured by others. They also have a nine-course tasting menu that in itself sends a message of intent. You can also expect a comprehensive wine list. ◗

Brett Graham

" I love Ottolenghi at 63 Ledbury Road. They sell great pastries and their croissants are some of the best you can find in London. My favourite London restaurant is Pied á Terre on Charlotte Street. It serves great food, really good flavours, is always consistent and a pleasant intimate space.

Head Chef, The Ledbury

Above **Upholstered and embroidered chair backs at The Ledbury and a very smart dining room.**

Des Hallett

"

Turnham Green Terrace in Chiswick is a great foodie enclave in London. I enjoy visiting Macken Brothers (see page 39) for my meat and Covent Garden fishmongers (see page 39). The deli, Mortimer and Bennett (see page 39), is excellent, plus the local bakery and a few other food shops along this pleasant street all work up my appetite.

Head Chef, The Cow

Above **Kalifornian burger (Aberdeen Angus pattie, plus bacon, cheese, guacamole, roast tomatoes and sour cream), fries and a chocolate shake at Lucky 7.**

Lucky 7 127 Westbourne Park Road, W2 5QL
020 7727 6771 www.lucky7london.co.uk

The classic hamburger is at the heart of Lucky 7, but it also delivers so much more. The pattie is 100% aged organic Aberdeen Angus, the bun is baked locally to a special recipe, the red onion, tomato and pickle are chosen for flavour and are sliced by hand. It seems simple, but so many 'hamburger joints' don't offer these essential basics.

Tom Conran has sensitively created this bijou, authentic but modern East Coast-style diner. Booth seating, an open kitchen, genuine eclectic 1950s-style fittings and diner tableware have all been fused with irreverent artwork to create a snug informal environment. Fast service and cool music make this a favourite among locals. Lucky 7 bridges the gap between café and restaurant, making the perfect all-day all-people destination.

Jumbo Wally (pickled dill cucumbers), 'homeslaw', spicy black beans, beer-battered onion rings and tasty French fries complement the extensive choice of burgers. The milk shakes are the best – try the five-dollar shake. ●

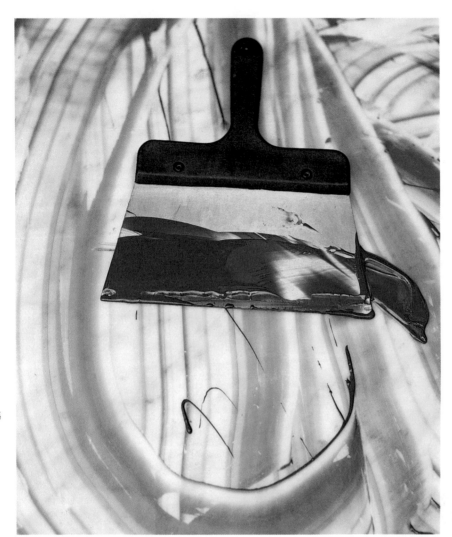

Melt 59 Ledbury Road, W11 2AA

020 7727 5030 www.meltchocolates.com

Chocolate contains phenyl ethylamine, a chemical related to amphetamines, and raises blood pressure and blood glucose levels. The result is that we feel more alert and experience a sense of well-being and contentment. Eating chocolate is believed to make the brain release b-endorphin, an opioid peptide, which is the driving force behind the pleasurable effects. Phenyl ethylamine is known as the 'love drug' and is thought to be the reason why chocolate is said to be an aphrodisiac. The chemical mimics the brain chemistry of a person in love, so when levels of phenyl ethylamine are high in the body it relieves the depression of unrequited love. *Go to Melt to get your phenyl ethylamine high!*

The all-white minimalist open-plan kitchen allows the team to pour large quantities of chocolate on to the counter in front of shoppers while the air fills with a strong chocolate hit. ●

Louise Nason

I always make a delicious meal when I buy fish from this great fish shop attached to Kensington Place Restaurant. Park outside on the double yellow – but watch out for a ticket! They deliver, which is very useful when preparing for a party.

Founder, Melt

Above
The chocolatier's marble work surface is at the heart of the Melt shop.

Warm Chocolate Sauce

By Louise Nason

Serves at least 4 children and 2 adults

180 g (6 oz) dark chocolate (at least
61% cocoa solids), such as Valrhona
Caraibe, 66%

227 ml (8 fl oz) organic double cream

Break the chocolate into pieces and set aside.
Pour the cream into a saucepan and place it
over a medium heat. Heat the cream until it
is just starting to come to the boil. Remove it
from the heat and add the chocolate pieces.
Using a wooden spoon, stir with energy to
amalgamate the chocolate and the cream.
You will end up with a rich, glossy sauce.
Pour on to ice cream.

Negozio Classica 283 Westbourne Grove, W11 2QA
020 7034 0005 www.negozioclassica.co.uk
This is a small store, bar and lounge devoted to Italian high-end style
selling a range of exclusive products such as knives from Tuscany,
balsamico from Modena, buffalo cheese, pesto and wildflower honey.
Or you can just call in for a cappuccino, a glass of wine or a grappa. ○

The Spice Shop 1 Blenheim Crescent, W11 2EE
020 7221 4448 www.thespiceshop.co.uk
Whilst studying for an international business degree in 1990, Birgit
Erath started a small weekend stall on the Portobello Road market. The
weekend project soon became a serious business and in 1995 the shop
on Blenheim Crescent, a stone's throw from the original stall, opened
and is now one of the most unique spice stores in the UK. Spice shops
and market stalls are often ubiquitous in other corners of the world, but
a store purely devoted to herbs, spices, salts, peppers, chillies, nuts and
a few fresh herbs or beans is quite novel in London.

Birgit now travels the world finding new spices and creating blends
and mixes often based on ancient family traditions. If you want to get
serious about cooking dishes from the subcontinent or Asia, this is the
starting point. Or you can simply call in for seasonings, as they have a
huge range of salts from Maldon or fleur de sel to a naturally forming
and mined Diamant de Sel from Kashmir in Pakistan. ○

Tapas Garcia 246 Portobello Road W11 1LL 020 7221 6119 and
R. Garcia and Sons 248 Portobello Road, W11 1LL
A piece of everyday Spain in the heart of Notting Hill, the deli and food
store has been established for some time, while the tapas bar and café
next door has recently opened. They only operate a menu on Friday
and Saturday evenings, when you can enjoy authentic paella, tortilla,
calamaris, Boquerónes, huevos a la Flamenco eggs with chorizo and
paprika from staff with a pure Española pedigree. ○

Above **Notting Hill
graffiti outside
The Spice Shop
is of a slightly more
refined nature
than most other
areas of London.**
Opposite **R. Garcia
and Sons Spanish
supplies.**

Tavola 155 Westbourne Grove, W11 2RS

020 7229 0571

(PP) Whenever I'm interviewing for a head-chef position I usually find myself looking for candidates who have worked in seminal kitchens and with inspirational talents. Alistair Little's name usually appears on my lists. Certainly anybody who worked at his eponymous restaurant in Soho in its heyday is bound to be a prime candidate. And now Alistair is the driving force behind this exceptionally good delicatessen.

Everything that makes it into the store is of the highest quality and the prepared foods made on site are simply superb. I recently collected a pork, foie gras and bacon pie. Wow! It was good! ○

This page **Beautifully displayed deli items for sale inside Tavola.**

Left **Classic three-tier afternoon tea stands.**
Above **Over 150 teas and infusions from around the world at Tea Palace.**

Tea Palace 175 Westbourne Grove, W11 2SB
020 7727 2600 www.teapalace.co.uk
Tea in all its guises, and there are many, is available to sup or to take home at this modern, elegant and ladylike establishment. Afternoon teacakes and a fine cuppa go together, well, like tea and scones, or strawberries and cream. In addition to the finger sandwiches, crumpets, shortbread and tarts, they also have a creative breakfast and lunch menu. The tea range is truly international and you can also buy teapots, strainers and caddies. ○

Des Hallett

After The Cow, the Angelsea Arms (see page 224) is my favourite gastropub in London. I'm a local and have also worked there. They serve great terrines and simple, tasty food.

Head Chef, The Cow

Tom's Deli 226 Westbourne Grove, W11 2RH

020 7221 8818

Notting Hill is overloaded with delis, but Tom's was the first, and still retains a prime position, not to mention the cool factor that most of those in the new crop don't even understand. The adjoining café serves the best breakfast and eggs Florentine in London and the ready-to-eat meals and prepared foods are also first rate. A perfect place to begin the trudge through Portobello Market. ●

Above **Food for adults and youngsters at Tom's Deli.** Opposite **Tom's perfect eggs Florentine.**

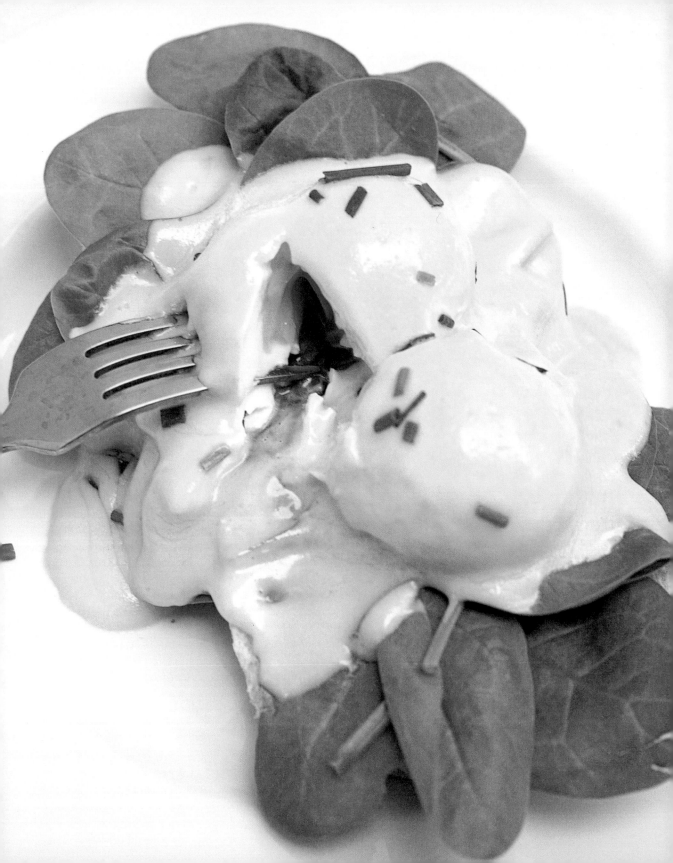

Southwark

The Southwark that is referred to in this chapter consists of three separate areas all on the south side of the Thames.

Firstly, Shad Thames, the area east of Tower Bridge, was until the early 1990s a collection of derelict warehouses that were once used to store tea and spices that had arrived by ship into the Port of London. The largest and most dominant of these is Butlers Wharf. This building formed the centrepiece of Terence Conran's redevelopment of the area. At the time, people thought he was mad to consider opening restaurants, cafés and bars here. Many, many people ate their words. Other warehouses that are named after the goods that were previously stored within have now all been converted to residential developments. We both have homes in the area and we are easily able to call on the many restaurants and, until its move to larger premises, the Design Museum. The area is regularly used for photo shoots or by filmmakers attracted by the cobblestone streets.

Secondly is the Borough. This area has been known by this name since 1550 to contrast it with the City. The centrepiece of the area is undoubtedly, Borough Market. Now with deserved global recognition, this is the country's leading fine-foods market and somewhere everybody, not just foodies, *must* visit.

The third area is Bankside, which is inextricably linked with Sir Giles Gilbert Scott's power station, which, since 2000, has the housed Tate Modern. Near the Tate you can also find Shakespeare's Globe Theatre, the Hayward Gallery, the IMAX cinema, Oxo Tower and the Royal Festival Hall, to mention just a few of the great arts and cultural attractions.

Roast Saddle of Pork with Fennel

Serves 8

At the Anchor & Hope we buy rare-breed pork, that is, traditional, slow-growing breeds such as the Middle White, Tamworth and English Lop. After slaughter, the meat should be matured for ten days to allow the skin to dry out and the flesh to tenderize. Farmers' markets or very good butchers are the places to look for meat like this.

Get your butcher to cut a rack of six chops with the belly still attached. The meat needs to be boned next, and a section of rind over the loin removed, so that when the saddle is rolled the loin is completely encircled by the belly. This will protect it from the fierce heat while cooking. Enough rind needs to be removed so that none is rolled into the middle.

rack of 6 pork chops, belly attached, boned and rolled
sea salt and freshly ground pepper
125 ml (4 fl oz) olive oil
1 onion, sliced
3 heads of fennel, sliced, fronds reserved
1 bulb of garlic
1 sprig of rosemary, chopped
pinch of nutmeg (optional)
1 teaspoon of fennel seeds

Preheat the oven to its highest setting. Score the skin of the pork with a sharp knife and season generously, pushing salt into the cuts. Place a roasting tin on a low to medium heat on the stove. Add most of the oil and the sliced onion and fennel, (reserving the fronds). Add seasoning and let them sweat gently.

Chop 3 cloves of garlic, the fennel fronds and the rosemary and place them in a bowl. Season them with salt, pepper and perhaps a little nutmeg. Moisten the mixture with a little oil and pack it around the loin.

Now you must tie the saddle up so the belly completely encircles the loin.

Remove the vegetables from the tray and put them to one side. Place the rolled saddle on the tray, sprinkle the fennel seeds over the skin and put it into the hot oven to crackle the joint. After about 30 minutes when the skin is really starting to crackle and the fat is starting to run, add the vegetables with the rest of the garlic cloves to the tray. Turn the oven right down to about 120°C (250°F) Gas Mark ½. Depending on the size of the joint, it will probably take about 3–4 hours to cook. Test it at 30-minutes intervals by inserting a skewer into the middle of the joint and then touching it against your lips. When the skewer feels warm but not hot, turn the oven off, leaving the door ajar slightly. Allow the pork to rest for at least 30 minutes. The belly should be meltingly tender and the loin just cooked.

Anchor & Hope 36 The Cut, SE1 8LP
020 7928 9898

Unprepossessing portals lead to some of the best-tasting food in London, but don't expect comfortable surroundings or fawning service. The no-reservations policy here, usually results in long delays before you are seated and it is often necessary to share a table with other diners in this rather poky dining room. Service is relaxed, but once you get to know the staff a foodie rapport and perspicacious recommendations are sure to follow.

The menu focuses on flavours and ingredients of an excellent quality cooked with skill, but without any fuss or unnecessary garniture. Although the dish descriptions are laconically written, you can be assured of first-class provenance. Expect hearty British favourites alongside a plate of Spanish ham or pork rillettes, which are better than those in Lyons, and vitello tonnato to challenge the best of Italy. You can enjoy duck hearts on toast; garlic soup; tripe and chips; cassoulet; roast teal and faggot; game birds in season; Bath chap and pickled onion; smoked herrings and lentils; rhubarb fool; chocolate and hazelnut cake; and perfectly conditioned cheese. These great dishes formulate an enviable menu, but the real character is revealed in the sharing dishes, which include salt piglet with choucroute for four or grilled whole sea bass with spring vegetables and aioli or baked stuffed duck or slow-cooked spring lamb with white beans and wild garlic for five.

Much procurement time and an excellent palate has produced a concise wine list that perfectly mirrors the proprietor's desire to deliver pronounced tastes from small, mainly Old World, producers.

Above **Rolled loin and belly of pork awaiting the Anchor & Hope ovens.**

Above **Interesting art on a backdrop of simple white walls and the original brickwork at Baltic.**

Baltic 74 Blackfriars Road, SE1 8HA
020 7928 1111 wwwbalticrestaurant.co.uk

An impressive selection of Eastern European cuisines is offered on the menu at Baltic.

As you pass the busy bar, which serves one of the largest vodka selections in London, you enter a larger dining room with a high-vaulted glass atrium, exposed beams and a wooden truss ceiling. The simple white painted walls and interesting art seem to be the trademark of most stylish restaurants serving well-researched foods.

The menu includes a tour across Siberia, Poland, the Ukraine and Russia and progresses well beyond the excellent beetroot soup and cabbage. Beef stroganoff, Wiener schnitzel, spiced beef and sausage paprika goulash have all been given a modern touch and lightness. You can also go decadent with blinis and caviar.

Sunday evening, always a difficult night for restaurants, are jolly affairs with professional jazz musicians playing in the background. ◉

Blueprint Café 28d Shad Thames, SE1 2YD
020 7378 7031   www.conran.com

From an elevated position atop the Design Museum, the panoramic views bestow Tower Bridge, The Gherkin and Tower 42 to the west and the vertiginous towers of Canary Wharf to the east. River traffic also provides further curiosity at probably one of the busiest stretches of the Thames. Sebastian Conran has thoughtfully designed miniature Blueprint binoculars for each of the tables so that the diners can inspect the topography in more focused detail.

While the views are attention-grabbing, most people visit for the food and to enjoy the company of charismatic Jeremy Lee. Blueprint has been open for over 15 years and Dundonian Jeremy has been the *cook* – not the *chef*, for more than a decade. As a graduate of the Simon Hopkinson school of gastronomy and having worked with Alistair Little, Jeremy's food is intensely seasonal and the embodiment of modern classical cuisine. Drawing influence from Elizabeth David, Jane Grigson and Claudia Roden, the twice-daily changing menu captures the best of European regional cooking.

Jeremy is passionate in his support for artisans, farmers and fishermen who produce the best-quality ingredients. Often, to the consternation of the company accountants, the kitchen will receive lamb carcasses, whole rare-breed pigs or other beasts on Monday but will ensure everything is used by the weekend. Intelligent menu planning, unusual cuts, the use of the entrails, combined with an extensive range of cooking styles – from simple grills to slow braises – all feature.

With such a great view and imaginative cooking, the room is purposely simple. White walls, a blond-wood floor, Thonet bentwood bistro chairs, linen-free tables, David Mellor cutlery and a few Philip Sayer black and white photographs of influential designers provide all that it needs.

(PP) Fortunately, Blueprint Café is close to my home in Shad Thames and Jeremy is a great friend. Sadly, the constraints of a working life prevent me from visiting as often as I would like. ◉

Chris Wood

My favourite restaurant in London? Difficult one. That's like asking me what is my favourite Beatles track… probably harder. I'd have to opt for Blueprint Café at Butlers Wharf. Yes, my last supper would be eating a meal at Blueprint… beautiful 'sod the food margin' ingredients… talented kitchen… simple clean design… and those views. Jeremy Lee is a genius – and so is 'She Said She Said'.

Managing Director,
www.toptable.co.uk

Left **Jeremy Lee (third from right) lunching with his team.**

Plaice, Peas and Bacon

This dish is a lovely way to pair fish and peas, a great treat when the first peas come into season and are small and succulent. At the restaurant we buy crates of the ones we see and love, pod like crazy for a day, then cook them all, cool them quickly and have them in the fridge to litter the menu liberally in soups, broths and salads, and to accompany meat and fish alike. Lightly buttered with much mint they never fail to delight. The addition of a soft buttery lettuce cut up small is excellent.

Serves 2

2 handsomely sized whole plaice
150 g (5 oz) unsalted butter
2 onions, chopped very small
small piece of excellent smoked streaky bacon, weighing about 200 g (7 oz) or so
great clutched handful of peas per person
sea salt
pinch of sugar
big handful of picked mint leaves, chopped
a fully charged pepper mill

An obliging fishmonger will fillet the fish for you (fishmongers are generally most affable), and dare to suggest that he does it there and then for you, from fish you have agreed on with the man himself.
All fish should be spanking fresh but the slightly less-ranked fish such as plaice tend to survive less well than their more noble kindred.

Once in the kitchen, gently heat a heavy-bottomed pot. Melt the butter therein. Add the onions and let cook slowly and gently for 30 minutes or so until they become uncoloured, softened and sweet. Slice away any skin and nodules in the bacon and roll it up very tightly, securing it with a proper knot. Cut the bacon into small pieces and add to the onions, stirring it occasionally, letting it cook gently.

Set to with the peas and have the troops rally round should there be spare hands in the vicinity. Place a big pan of water to boil upon a fierce heat. When the water is boiling with great wrath then drop in the peas with a big pinch of salt and a wee pinch of sugar.

Now depending on your pea, 4 or 5 minutes to 20 minutes may be required to cook the vegetables depending on their age and size. Boiling is vital and only once cooked should they be removed from the heat, but absolutely not from the water in which they are cooked. Let the pan sit, settle and cool.

The peas will remain brilliant and quite perfect. Only by eating will the degree of cooking be known, so test a few to ensure the peas are soft and yielding.

Preheat the oven to 220°C (425°F) Gas Mark 7. Take a lovely big baking dish and tip in the cooked onion and bacon. Keeping back 150 ml (5 fl oz) of the water, drain the peas and scatter in the dish. Strew with the chopped mint and mix lightly, adding a little salt and pepper.

Take the fish from the fridge and lay the fillets out, with the side of the fish that was attached to the bone uppermost. Grind pepper evenly and lightly over the fillets. Lay, peppered-side down, side by side over the peas and until both are comfortably settled and not overlapping. Add in the water from the pea pot and then cover the dish well with tin foil. Place in the oven and let cook for 15–20 minutes until the fish is completely white and firm to the touch. Serve up at once, hopefully with some peeled, boiled little new potatoes.

Ox Tongue and Green Sauce

Needless to say, already cooked tongues can be acquired and many butchers still steep their own tongues in brine. However, great pleasure and satisfaction are to be had from making a brine that fills a kitchen with marvellous smells and gives the tongue an assured texture and flavour.

You can steep a few tongues at a time as they don't go off, and should they prove to need a little longer in the brine, then nothing could be easier than to leave a few extra days. They do keep very well in a sealed container, submerged in the cooking liquor. Another small thought is that we prefer to use rain water in our brine but bottled still mineral water is very good. A modicum of patience is required for this recipe as the tongues must steep for 4 or 5 weeks.

Serves 6 dainty appetites, or 4–5 trenchermen

Southwark

289

1 or 2 ox tongues

For the Brine

6 fresh bay leaves

a wee bushel of thyme

4 carrots, peeled

3 onions, peeled

4 celery sticks, chopped into large pieces

2 leeks, chopped into large pieces

12 black peppercorns

a great handful of flat leaf parsley, picked and washed

12 plump anchovy fillets

a heaped tablespoonful of capers, rinsed and drained

3 cloves of garlic, chopped

10 tablespoonfuls of very good extra-virgin olive oil

Put all the ingredients for the briine into a great pot and set over a high heat to come through a lively boil. Let the brine cool. Scrupulously clean a plastic container, which has a very close-fitting lid. Sit the tongues in the container. Strain the brine through a fine sieve and pour the liquid over the tongues, covering them completely. Place a plate on top to ensure that the tongues are wholly submerged. Put the container in to the fridge and let sit undisturbed for the next 4 or 5 weeks.

After the passing of the requisite amount of time, drain the tongues and let them rinse a while under running cold water. Tie the bay leaves and thyme into a small bundle. Place the tongues, chopped vegetables and bundle of herbs into a large pot and sit it over a gentle heat. Fill the pot with enough cold water to cover the tongues.

Bring the pan to a simmer and spoon away any foamy substance that has risen to the surface. Lower the heat and let the pan simmer for 3 or 4 hours until the tongues are quite tender. The tongues should offer no resistance to a small knife inserted to the thickest part. Should there be even the slightest resilience then let the tongues continue cooking for a further 30 minutes or however long is required.

When the tongues have cooked, remove them from the heat and lift them from the water. Let them sit for a minute before removing the coating surrounding the tongue. This will peel away quite effortlessly whilst still hot, with a little aid here and there from a small knife applied to loosen any part that may stick. Once peeled, return the tongues to the pot. Let cool. Remove the tongues to a container. Strain the stock and pour over the tongues. Seal the container and store until required.

To make the green sauce, place the parsley, capers and garlic in a food processor along with the anchovies. Render them small, adding the olive oil in small amounts until a paste of sorts is achieved. Remove to a small bowl and cover until required.

When readying to eat, cut the tongue into slices about 3 mm (1/8 in) thick. Place them in a pan and cover them with the some of the stock. Sit the pan over a gentle heat and bring slowly to a simmer. Leave thus for a few minutes until thoroughly heated.

Now, it is usual to serve the green sauce in a bowl or some such but generally speaking folks err towards the timid so it is preferable to stir the sauce into the pot alongside the slices of tongue and release the fresh and invigorating fragrance of the sauce in the pan, along with its brilliant colour.

Borough Market 8 Southwark Street, SE1 1TL
020 7407 1002 www.boroughmarket.org.uk

Over 10,000 Londoners flock to Borough Market every weekend
and enjoy one of the best food experiences in the country, if not
globally. Ask any foodie in London and they will inevitably list a
Saturday morning visit to Borough as a *must do*. Not only is the
food and drink selection excellent, the feel-good factor is palpable.
All 10,000 visitors revel in the artisan products in such atmospheric
surrounding, but probably more prominent is the enjoyment derived
from buying one's household provisions direct from the small artisan
producers, growers, fishermen, farmers and butchers and being able to
eschew the big supermarkets.

Historically focused around a wholesale fruit and vegetable market,
the weekend fine-foods market has over 70 stalls. From regional British
dairy products to olive oils, herbs, spices and dried fruits, cereals,
patisserie, the best fish, shellfish, aged beef, rare-breed pork, game birds, all manner of lovingly prepared foods are here. Many of
the stalls sell single items such as the Isle of Wight tomatoes or single
cheeses. The Cool Chile Company, Scandelicious, Turnips, Booths,
Northfield Farm, Furness Fish, The Ginger Pig and Elsey and Bent are
particularly good stalls to seek out.

The market is teeming with people at the weekend and as you stroll
along the cramped walkways you might find yourself bumping in to a
whole roe or buck deer straight from the fields and hanging on a railing
awaiting the knife. Still feathered pheasants or a huge monkfish, mounds
of oysters and truckles of cheese are all at Borough Market in a very raw
and tempting state.

If you are not planning to visit the market for your weekly shop it
is also a great brunch or lunch destination. There are plenty of excellent
stalls offering real meat burgers, lamb koftas and proper pizza slices or
you can simply gorge on the many free tasters offered by the stalls.

A few traders operate on Thursdays with the main market open
from midday until 6 pm on Friday and 9 am–4 pm on Saturdays. ○

Top left **Vegetables displayed on the Elsey and Bent stall.**
Top right **The market flourishes under the Victorian railway arches.**
Left **Playful displays from Furness Fish, one the of the best.**
Right **The market is moderately busy on Fridays and completely overwhelmed on Saturdays.**

Craig James

I love to shop for food in Harrods, it's a complete joy. The selection of quality produce is always overwhelming and the atmosphere is amazing.

Head Chef, Quaglino's and Butlers Wharf Chop House

Brew Wharf Brew Wharf Yard, Stoney Street, SE1 9AD
020 7940 8333 www.brewwharf.com

Brew Wharf takes its inspiration from Alsatian bistro cooking, prepared with all British ingredients sourced exclusively from Borough Market across the street.

As the name implies, Brew Wharf boasts its own micro-brewery producing the bar's two real ales; one made entirely with Fuggles hops and the other with Goldings, a nod towards the nearby Hop Exchange, which made Borough synonymous with Kentish hops. The highly rated Greenwich-based Meantime Brewery provides an extensive bottled and draught-beer range; the wheat beers are particularly good.

Vinopolis, the adjoining wine museum, is also worth a visit.◗

Butlers Wharf Chop House The Butlers Wharf Building,
36e Shad Thames, SE1 2YE 020 7403 3403 www.conran.com

Redolent of a cricket pavilion or boat shed, the Chop House has English oak walls, ceiling slats and floorboards. With heavy timber furniture, zinc and marble tops in the bar and smart linen in the restaurant the Chop House looks the same today as when it opened over ten years ago. Hopefully it will still look the same in ten more years.

The cooking is true best of British with many regional specialities and a few recipes otherwise only seen in the history books. Rook pie, potted haugh, Lop chop and roast squirrel have recently been seen on the menu. Steak, kidney and oyster pudding is a signature dish alongside fish and chips with mushy peas and roast rib of beef with proper Yorkshire puddings. Celebrate the seasons with asparagus, gulls eggs and game – they normally have a specific game menu offering at least three or four different birds, summer fruit pudding and much more. Follow your meal with a large plate of British cheeses and oatcakes.

You'd think this gutsy masculine menu was the preserve of city chaps, but no. Very often young 'ladies who lunch' can be seen tucking in to ox liver or chargrilled t-bone steaks.

A good selection of English still and sparkling wines are available, with the remainder of the list focusing on terrific claret and burgundy. If the the eccentrically named English ales catch your attention, try Black Sheep, Spitfire or Pendles Witches Brew.

In the shadow of the late nineteenth-century Horace Jones and John Wolfe Barry Tower Bridge, the outside tables are particularly romantic on a summer's evening or when the bridge bascules (French for seesaw) are raised to allow a Thames barge with terracotta sails to pass underneath.◗

Above **Craig James, head chef enjoying his labour in the shadow of Tower Bridge.**
Left **Craig's smoked mackerel and leek terrine with horseradish dressing.**

Steak and Kidney Pudding

Serves 8 healthy portions – the way it should be served.

3 lb Dexter chuck steak, diced into 5-cm (2-in) pieces

100 g (3¹/2 oz) flour

75 ml (3 fl oz) oil

1 large onion, finely sliced

30 ml (1 fl oz) Worcestershire sauce

100 ml (3¹/2 fl oz) Guinness

¹/2 bunch thyme

500 ml (17 fl oz) beef stock

1 bay leaf

700 g (1 lb 8 oz) ox kidney, core removed and diced

For the Suet Pastry

500 g (1 lb) plain flour

250 g (8 oz) beef suet (Atora brand is best)

1 teaspoon baking powder

pinch salt

2 eggs, beaten

cold water

To make the filling: Roll the chuck steak in the flour. Shake off any excess to leave a fine coating of flour. Heat the oil in a frying pan. Place a few pieces of the steak into the oil at a time and sear it until it is deep brown on all sides making sure the pan always has about a 2 mm (¹/8 in) covering of oil so the steak does not stick. Remove the steak from the pan and place in a deep baking dish and set aside.

Preheat the oven to 150°C (300°F) Gas Mark 2. Place the onion in a pan with the Worcestershire sauce and the Guinness over a medium heat. Allow it to boil until the liquid has reduced by two-thirds. Pour the liquid over the chuck steak, and add the thyme, beef stock and bay leaf. Place a piece of baking parchment on top of the meat and then cover the dish with foil. Place it in the oven. It is important not to cook the meat too aggressively. The liquid should bubble gently, otherwise the meat will become tough and dry.

Put the diced kidney in a pan and cover it with water. Place over a medium heat and bring to the boil. Then pour off the hot water, place the pan in the sink and run cold water over the kidneys until chilled then set aside. When the meat mixture has been in

the oven for 1 hour 30 minutes, add the kidneys. Mix them in thoroughly, reseal the dish and place the meat back in the oven. Cook for a further 1 hour 30 minutes or until the meat is tender. Remove the meat from the oven, allow it to cool then place it in the refrigerator to chill.

To make the suet pastry: Place the flour, suet, baking powder and salt in a mixing bowl. Add the eggs and begin to work the ingredients together. Add cold water as required to form a dough, but do not allow it to become too wet. Be careful not to overwork the dough as it will become tough and difficult to handle.

Grease and flour a pudding bowl. Divide the dough into two balls, with one twice the size of the other. Roll out the larger ball, adding more flour as required, until it is round in shape and about 6 mm (¹/4 in) thick. Line the pudding bowl with the pastry, leaving the pastry overlapping slightly.

Remove the steak from the liquor. Remove and discard the bay leaf and place the steak back into the baking dish, and check and adjust the seasoning. The gravy should be quite thick by now. If not, you can remove the meat, then reduce it in a pan until a suitable consistency is reached.

Place the steak and kidney mixture into the dough-lined pudding bowl. Roll out the other ball of dough to the same thickness as the lining, and lay it over the top of the pudding bowl. Make sure there is not too much air trapped in the top by pressing down on the lid with your fingers. Seal the pastry lid on to the lining by working your way around the edge of the bowl, pushing hard on the outer rim. Cut off any excess pastry. Cover the pudding bowl with baking parchment and tie it securely using kitchen string. Steam the pudding by placing an old plate in the bottom of a pan, and putting the pudding on top of the plate. Fill the pan half way up the side of the bowl with water, cover and boil for 2 hours, taking care not to let the pan become dry. Alternatively, you could use a pressure cooker and reduce the cooking time to 1 hour 30 minutes. Once cooked, turn out and serve.

Above top **Mutton legs from Farmer Sharp's stall at Borough Market.**
Middle **Mrs Kings Pork Pies.**
Left **Chalking-up the daily specials at The Garrison.**
Right **Breads from de Gustibus.**

Farmer Sharp at Borough Market

Fridays 12 pm–6 pm, Saturdays 9 am–4 pm

Mutton has enjoyed a resurgence over recent years, not least due to the vigorous efforts of HRH The Prince of Wales *and Farmer Sharp*. The Herdwick breed is at the core of the new movement. Originally introduced to the UK by the Vikings and farmed by the Cistercian monks, the sheep now thrive on Cumbria's hilly terrain. Farmer Sharp hangs the mutton for three weeks before it appears at the now world-renowned, thanks to American *Gourmet* magazine, Borough Market stall.

Under the green Victorian railway arches and amongst a few loosely scattered pelts, Farmer Sharp and his skilled team are on hand to advise and entertain. Whole beasts are flung to the well-worn wooden butchers block to prepare every cut imaginable while you watch in awe. In this cellophane-free zone, devoid of any supermarket-style packaging, everything from French trimmed best ends to the now-popular entrails, such as the hearts, liver and kidneys are portioned and prepared.

Glorious crimson-coloured Galloway beef hung for a minimum of five weeks, together with responsibly reared pink veal is also available from this excellent farmer-meets-butcher-meets-retailer. Moreover, bespoke Herdwick wool jumpers can also be ordered whilst you collect your supper. ○

The Garrison 99–101 Bermondsey Street, SE1 3XB

020 7089 9355 www.thegarrison.co.uk

Here is a lovely neighbourhood pub with a menu that exceeds most other attempts at gastropub grub. The prices are competitive and the French-bistro-meets-American-diner dishes are prepared with some skill. The space is decorated in an eclectic fashion with mostly reclaimed furniture sensitively juxtaposed with a few modern pieces. The slightly raised seating booth overlooks the kitchen and provides a cosy spot for a weekend brunch.

The basement includes a mini cinema available for private hire and ideal for birthdays. ○

de Gustibus 4 Southwark Street, SE1 1TQ

020 7407 3625 www.degustibus.co.uk

An excellent artisan bakery on the edge of Borough Market, it is open all week and also has a stall within the market. They sell home-made breads, from Mediterranean ciabatta to San Francisco sourdough. ○

Mrs King's Pork Pies Borough Market

Fridays 12 pm–6 pm, Saturdays 9 am–4 pm

Don't expect a smart website or even an email address. This is simply a team of two brothers and their wives making and selling the best classic-recipe Melton Mowbray pies the country has to offer. Originally formed as a family business in 1853 in the village of Cotgrave, at the heart of Melton Mowbray country, the current owners champion the original recipes. The meat comes only from the shoulder of pigs fed on whey from nearby Stilton dairies, the pastry is formed without the assistance of a tin and the jelly, added after the pies have been baked and cooled, is a derivative of boiled-down trotters. To the disappointment of Ian Hartland, who mans the market stall each week, the heads and spleen are no longer used for the jelly since the dreaded BSE crisis of the late 1990s.

M. Manze Pie and Mash 87 Tower Bridge Road, SE1 4TW

020 7407 2985 www.manze.co.uk

Only a few examples remain in London and this provides one of the better experiences.

Monmouth Coffee Shop 2 Park Street, SE1 9AB

020 7645 3585 www.monmouthcoffee.co.uk

A small, ethically operated coffee shop offering an impressive range of coffees made with filter-paper cones, this is an ideal spot to repair before or after touring the market.

Jamie Oliver

"I really love going to Borough Market – it's one of my favourite places to go to on a Saturday morning, as well as being one of the best food markets around. The stalls sell the most amazing fresh produce to some of the great restaurateurs and greengrocers in London. I always make sure I get there as early as possible so I can have a chat with the producers and really get into the vibe!

Chef and restaurateur

Above
The communal table at Monmouth Coffee Shop.

Randolph Hodgson

"

The resurgence of British farmhouse cheeses that has occurred over the past twenty years has been mirrored by a similar resurgence of British restaurants. As a result of the near-extinction of our cheese-making tradition, we have embraced this resurgence with the zeal reserved for things we almost lose and the success of so many new restaurants is no doubt due to a similar phenomenon.

This break with tradition has produced a fresh approach to both restaurants and cheese.

Whereas continental cheeses populated the typical cheeseboards in pre-1990 London restaurants, the situation has reversed so that British cheeses are now prevalent and this has been made possible by the ever-increasing numbers of new cheeses.

This air of freshness and reinvention of tradition was behind the redevelopment of Borough Market. A little-known ancient market down on its luck, Borough now stands as a symbol of new British food retail. Unlike its continental counterparts, which have a strong regional focus, Borough sells food from all over the world, reflecting the British tradition of import.

My favourite restaurants include Clarke's (Sally Clarke was one of my first restaurant customers) and I like Anchor & Hope and St. John for their no-nonsense approach and gutsy cooking.

Owner, Neal's Yard Dairy

Right The un-wrapped cheese on the service counter inside the shop.

Neal's Yard Dairy 6 Park Street, Borough Market, SE1 9AB
020 7645 3554 www.nealsyarddairy.co.uk

Quite simply the best place in London to buy British cheese. This shop is a retail experience of note and you can be assured of nonpareil cheese in perfect condition. The original branch was opened in the 1980s in Covent Garden and when the Borough warehouse shop opened in 1996 the company was catapulted to pre-eminence in the world of cheese. Randolph Hodgson has principally been responsible for the development and his name is now synonymous with making and maturing British cheese.

Keen's, Montgomery's, Isle of Mull, Westcombe and Daylesford seem to be the most popular Cheddar styles available. Then you have the Welsh goat's cheese, the blues, the creamy and many more. They have a burgeoning wholesale arm and operate a global mail-order system. They also sells a few other dairy and creamery offerings, like good butter, cream, crème fraîche, eggs and milk. During the winter they sometimes have a raclette stand outside the shop for an Alpine-style cheese indulgence. ●

farm cheese from

RET
WHOL
EXP

estd. 1979 in

Above **Large cheeses maturing at Neal's Yard Dairy.**
Right **The Dayleford Organic Cheddar-style cheese made by Joe Schneider on Sir Anthony and Lady Bamford's estate in Gloucestershire.**
Left **Outside Neal's Yard on a quiet mid-week day. The area is mobbed on Saturdays.**

DAYLESFORD

MADE BY JOE SCHNEIDER,
ON THE DAYLESFORD ESTATE,
GLOUCESTERSHIRE.
UNPASTEURISED COWS MILK.
TRADITIONAL ANIMAL RENNET.

£ 17.00 /kg

Oxo Tower Restaurant and Brasserie
Oxo Tower Wharf, Barge House Street, South Bank, SE1 9PH 020 7803 3888 www.harveynichols.com

Reputed to be one of the top three most profitable restaurants in London, the Oxo Tower is bound to attract occasional criticism for its sky-high prices. Here restaurant dining is all about occasions, special dates and the odd honourable proposal while the brasserie offers simpler fare. One thing there is no doubting about the Oxo Tower is the amazing views across the river towards the modern and classical architecture of the capital.

Last Valentine's Day the restaurant was offering one lavish couple the opportunity to hire the entire top floor for private use at a staggering £80,000. **○**

Le Pont de la Tour
The Butlers Wharf Building, 36d Shad Thames, London SE1 2YE 020 7403 8403 www.conran.com

The South Bank is blessed with many excellent restaurants. The original, and almost certainly still one of the best, is Le Pont de la Tour. In the 1980s when Terence Conran was masterminding the Shad Thames redevelopment and transforming derelict warehouses into cool riverside apartments it was Le Pont de la Tour with its bar, grill, deli, bakery, wine shop and 'posh' French brasserie that was at the centre: the first Conran gastrodrome.

Today the urbane Giuseppe de Wilde oversees the whole operation. If you are lucky enough to meet Giuseppe you will soon recognize why some say that God designed him to be a restaurant manager. With slick-backed black hair, Saville Row suits, presence in abundance and an anglicized French accent, he's the perfect host and passionate about his business.

The bar and grill serves the best plateaux de fruits de mer in London. Set on a three-tier stand the dustbin-lid sized trays with oysters, lobster, cherrystone clams, Dorset crab, langoustine, mussels, cockles, winkles and whelks are all set on ice and served with shallot vinegar, a large lemon and mayonnaise. They also offer simple grills and salads and a pianist adds to the mood in the evenings.

The main dining room is all about understated luxury and James Walker styles his menus in a similar manner. Lobster salads, daube of beef, whole Dover sole, roast foie gras, calves' liver and whole Barbary duck á l'orange are typical. The desserts are simple in description with intense innate flavour and integrity, and include tarte Tatin, petit pot au chocolat and poached pears with bay leaf custard.

Most people know Le Pont because of its outside dining terrace – one of the best al fresco dining spots in London. Open for almost six months per year, the prime location underneath the extensive awnings and heat lamps affords great views of Tower Bridge and the river traffic, plus the endless stream of people strolling along the Mediterranean-like promenade.

To the local resident or visitor just passing, the adjoining wine shop offers a vast collection of the finest and rare grand crus. The shop also includes a small tasting table where private events can be arranged. The Salon Privé features a large map of Burgundy etched on to the window, with poster-sized framed labels from the legendary châteaux of the area. **○**

James Walker

" It's a real treat eating food that I can't cook myself, and I love the feeling of institutions, so Mr Chow and Royal China in Queensway (especially for dim sum on Sunday) are always top of the list. When we feel like a fish feast we head for J. Sheekey.

Head Chef, Le Pont de la Tour

Above **Dining on the terrace at Le Pont de la Tour is one of the best al fresco locations in London.** Right **The staff briefing before a busy lunch service.**

298 **Roast** The Floral Hall, Borough Market, Stoney Street, SE1 1TL
020 7940 1300 www.roast-restaurant.com

Probably the most perfect location for a restaurant dedicated to the best of British cooking, Roast is housed in a cast-iron and glass structure above the Borough Market stalls. The salvaged and restored portico, previously forming the entrance to the Floral Hall at the Royal Opera House, Covent Garden, crowns the market entrance on Stoney Street. With Borough Market drawing thousands of people every weekend, the new portico is sure to be an enduring commercial and architectural success.

Iqbal Wahhab, previously the founder of the Cinnamon Club in Westminster is on a mission to elevate the profile and quality of British ingredients at his restaurant. He has assembled a team of equally passionate individuals, including a forager to search out wild herbs, leaves and vegetables, all committed to championing provenance, rare breeds and all things British. The centrepieces of the menu are the spit-roasts and dishes such as Tamworth pork chop with red onion and caper salad.

In addition to the enticing lunch and dinner menus, the Roast breakfast selection includes oysters Kilpatrick, lobster omelette, Inverawe Smoked Loch Etive trout with scrambled eggs, kedgeree with smoked haddock and a poached egg, plus the considerable Full Borough, which consists of Ayrshire bacon, Cumberland sausage, fried bread, black pudding, grilled tomatoes and field mushrooms, plus your choice of eggs. ○

Above **The Borough breakfast at Roast.** Right **Roast restaurant is perched on the first floor behind the glass and iron structure that previously formed the entrance to the Royal Opera House's Floral Hall in Covent Garden.**

Gourmet Tour

Southwark

Take a light supper on Thursday and build up an appetite for a full day on Friday.

– Start with breakfast at Roast.
– Buy some cheese at Neal's Yard Dairy.
– Tour Vinopolis Wine Museum.
– Walk along the river past Tate Modern, Shakespeare's Globe Theatre and the Millennium Bridge until you reach The Cut and lunch at Anchor & Hope.
– After lunch head to the Oxo Tower viewing platform and take a strong coffee or Earl Grey tea as you gaze across the river towards the city skyline. A similarly great view is also available from the café on level two and the restaurant on level seven at the Tate Modern.
– Walk back to Borough Market and revel in the foodie atmosphere, talk to the many stallholders and find out more about the provenance of the fine foods. Possibly buy a few treats for Saturday.
– Half a dozen oysters and a glass of Champagne at Wright Brothers.

Or

– A glass of manzanilla and a plate of Joselito jamon at Tapas Brindisa.
– Walk along the river towards Tower Bridge and Butlers Wharf, then enjoy a small British ale at the Chop House.
– Saving the best for last, it has to be a tour round the Design Museum, followed by a great supper at Blueprint Café in the company of food genius Jeremy Lee.

Tapas Brindisa 18-20 Southwark Street, SE1 1TJ
020 7357 8880 www.brindisa.com

A converted potato warehouse on the edge of Borough Market this small bar and dining room delivers a true tapas experience. The name Brindisa is derived from the Spanish word 'brindis' meaning to 'raise your glass' or 'make a toast'. We suggest you raise a small glass of fino, manzanilla or olorosso in celebration of all things Spanish over a simple plate of hand-carved Joselito. You can stand in the bar and jamoneria (traditional ham-carving corner) and enjoy grilled anchovies, salt cod or croquettes, or take a seat under the shelves of specially imported products and order a range of small individual plates of montadito tapas, although we find the coffee rather astringent.

Underneath Roast restaurant along Stoney Street, Brindisa also has a small shop open Tuesday to Saturday selling an extensive range of Spanish tinned fish, olive oils, vinegars, cured hams and innumerable other Iberian comestibles. ○

Tate Modern Bankside, SE1 9TG
020 7887 8888 www.tate.org.uk

In the 1990s the Victoria and Albert Museum press office announced that it had an ace café with a good museum attached. Since this point, museum and gallery dining has been as good as that in the high street, and in many cases significantly better. Certainly all of the Tate cafés and restaurants are professionally managed and the menus demonstrate creativity on a par with many of the galleries esteemed artists. The restaurant on level seven of Tate Modern has an eclectic modern European menu and innovative wine list. The café on level two is a simpler refuelling point before taking on Dali Surrealism or Lichtenstein and Warhol Pop Art.

The dining room has spectacular north- and south-facing views across London, plus a brightly coloured wall-art commission called Guanabara created by Brazilian artist Beatriz Milhazes. The two previous commissions have been by Fiona Rae in 2002 and Hamish Fulton in 2000. ○

Right **Strolling through Borough Market on a Friday afternoon.**

Roasted Monkfish Tail with Puy Lentils and Basil Sauce

Serves 4

For the Sauce

4 bunches basil
500 ml (17 fl oz) vegetable stock
a drop of olive oil

For the Lentils

250 g (8 oz) Puy lentils
1 carrot
1 leek
1 celery stick
1 onion
40 g (1½ oz) thyme
1 bay leaf
parsley stalks
sea salt
1 tablespoon red wine vinegar
half bunch of parsley, chopped

For the Monkfish

4 monkfish tails
1 bunch chives, finely chopped
150 g (5 oz) finely chopped ginger

Make the sauce by placing a small saucepan of salted water over a high heat and bringing it to the boil. Put some ice and water into a bowl and set aside. Pick the basil leaves and discard the stems. Drop the leaves into the boiling salted water until they start to purée when rubbed between your finger and thumb. Remove them from the heat and drain them. Refresh them in iced water and then squeeze them dry. Put the basil leaves into a blender with the vegetable stock and olive oil and blend everything until it is smooth. Set aside until you are ready to serve.

Now prepare the lentils by putting them into a saucepan of cold water and placing them over a high heat. Bring the lentils to the boil. Drain and cover them with clean cold water. Add the carrot, leek, celery, onion, thyme, bay leaf and parsley stalks. Season with Maldon sea salt and cook slowly until the vegetables and lentils are slightly soft. Remove the saucepan from stove and let the vegetables and lentils cool down in their own stock.

Once cooled, lift out the carrot, celery and onion dice them finely and add them back to the lentils. Discard the leek and herbs.

To finish, preheat the oven to 220°C (425°F) Gas Mark 7. Sear the monkfish in an oven-proof frying pan until golden, then place in the oven and roast for 6–8 minutes. When they are cooked, top them with the chives and ginger. Reheat the lentils, adding a drop of red wine vinegar and chopped parsley.

Divide the lentils on to four plates, place the monkfish on top of the lentils and spoon the warm sauce around.

Village East 171–173 Bermondsey Street, SE1 3UW
020 7357 6082 www.villageeast.co.uk

Is it gentrification, a village in the city or just a pleasant environment? Only a short walk from London Bridge or Butlers Wharf and the river, Bermondsey Street is a feel-good area. Like nearby Shad Thames, the vicinity has an historic food-warehousing link – Shad Thames dealt mainly in spices and tea and Bermondsey has inextricable links with chocolate. Many of the original warehouses are now trendy apartments or hip creative-design offices. Add a little green, a florist, some quirky retailers – The Cockfighter of Bermondsey, and Zhandra Rhodes's Fashion, Textile and Design Museum – and it suddenly attracts serious urbanites.

When Village East opened in early 2006 it certainly put Bermondsey Street on the map, if it wasn't there already. The owners of this upscale style-led multi-faceted operation also run the nearby Garrison gastropub. They've seriously pushed the envelope with Village East. Dover sole, chateaubriand, lobster salad and a chef who has gained his stripes in Michelin-style restaurants all tally to make something of an outing far above your usual neighbourhood eating place. Chi-chi cocktails, Scandinavian furniture, oversized lampshades and a 100-plus wine list all make a statement.

The artistic graphics on the menu and the table literature demonstrate the owner's creative flair. And Village East serves a great roast leg of lamb on Sunday until 4 pm. ●

Above **The Village East bar.**

Ben Wright and Robin Hancock

"
We love Racine, it encompasses all the flavours of a Parisian bistro de luxe in its honestly prepared and delicious food, its atmosphere and its impeccable service!

Owners, Wright Brothers Oyster and Porter House

Wright Brothers Oyster and Porter House 11 Stoney Street, SE1 9AD
020 7403 9554

A relative newcomer to the Borough Market scene, this small home to the best bivalves and crustaceans seems absolutely compatible with the excellence that surrounds it. Ben Wright and Robin Hancock, the two family friends passionate about oysters, are behind the business and have previously been growing, importing and supplying oysters to London's top chefs. Their restaurant has achieved famed status by being nominated as number one on *Wallpaper* magazine's list of the top ten things to do in London.

The dining space consists essentially of an L-shaped counter overlooking the oyster display and shucking activities, a few raised long tables with stools, and a tiny open kitchen for preparing the few cooked dishes on the menu. The exposed brick walls and electrics offer a hint of Manhattan fused with the classic sign writing of a Parisian zinc bar.

French Pousse en Claires, rocks from Cornwall and natives from the Isle of Mersea on the Thames Essex estuary are specialities – oysters, that is. The menu is written on the blackboard above the counter and includes plateaux fruits de mer, whelks, prawns, lobster, crab and much more. They also have a delicious oyster rarebit, and a steak, oyster and Guinness pie where the oysters are served on the side, ready for dunking in the pie sauce. ●

This page **Dining at the bar whilst watching the chefs shucking oysters at Wright Brothers Oyster Bar.**

Index

Staff, Service Charge and Tipping

Throughout this book we have extensively discussed the people aspects to our business and how quirky personalities, world-class chefs, distinguished maitre d's and influential proprietors can make or break a business. The other essential ingredient is, of course, great staff. We cannot forget the pivotal role staff play in the attainment of their leader's crusade to provide the best service.

It would be easy to wax lyrical, extolling unreserved praise on all staff, but that would be inappropriate, naïve and a false reflection of the real situation. Who hasn't experienced an evening of delicious food in pleasant surroundings, but felt short-changed because the waiters attitude and ineptness has spoiled an otherwise perfect dinner? Equally, we usually engage friendly rapport with our local butcher's, fishmonger's and shopkeeper's in the hope of receiving sagacious recommendations leading to a tasty supper. Good staff can make or break a business, irrespective of who sits at the top of the tree or wears the toque.

The best staff gravitate to the most professional employers and it is down to the management to hold-on to these star performers. Ultimately, the retention question can only be answered with fair pay, good conditions, clear policies, the opportunity to learn and civility amongst colleagues, not to mention the odd laugh and an off-duty beer.

Service charge and tips are invariably a component of the waiters pay, and in some situations, the chefs remuneration can also include a direct contribution from their patrons. Eternally a vexed question, the majority of London restaurateurs have sought to overcome awkward situations by introducing a discretionary service charge that will allow reasonable funds to be raised so that the staff can receive a relevant wage commensurate with the experience provided at the table. It also helps visitors from overseas to understand the local practises and customs.

However, this system has also presented its own problems. Over recent years the government's Treasury department endeavoured to reclaim retrospective taxes on what they thought was a huge loophole, falsely believing that restaurateurs were universally pocketing the extra revenue for themselves and staff were not paying sufficient taxes or other statutory contributions. The bureaucrats employed bully-boy tactics in their attempts to both create policy and then apply the new regime to prior years. Sadly, a few small restaurateurs yielded and others fought the case to eventually prove how ridiculous the proposals had become.

As a consequence of the costly legal battle, transparent policies to control the collection, administration and allocation of the tronc (the name given to the combined tips and service charge) have been introduced. Other restaurateurs have dropped the service charge approach and now suggest that diners should simply give what they deem appropriate. In these situations the monies are habitually pooled and then become subject to the same tronc rules and regulations.

Excepting a few, the standard service charge percentage added to the customer bill is 12.5%. A sum that, even at the most successful restaurants, only covers a small percentage of the total labour payroll cost. Therefore, you can be quite sure that in most circumstances all of the money ultimately makes its way to the staff if in a sometimes convoluted fashion.

It is worth mentioning the service charge is discretionary and optional, if you don't believe the service warrants that amount, then simply speak with the manager and remove or reduce the amount. Don't be afraid or embarrassed. This is something that every manager is legally obliged to do without any qualms or hesitation. Hopefully, the message will proficiently permeate to the staff and they will realise that the service at the table directly impacts their pay.

Its still a potential mind-field for the diner and discomfiture often prevails, especially when the service has been below the perceived par. These words only scratch the surface of a huge subject area, however, one thing is for certain, if the employers pay a decent wage and provide an enjoyable environment, it will hopefully become manifest at the table.

Published in 2007 by
Conran Octopus Limited
a part of Octopus Publishing Group
2–4 Heron Quays, London E14 4JP
www.conran-octopus.co.uk

Text copyright ©
Conran Octopus Limited 2007
Recipes copyright ©
individual copyright holders
Photography copyright © Lisa Linder 2007

The right of Terence Conran and Peter Prescott to be identified as the Authors of this Work has been asserted by them in accordance with the Copyright, Designs and Patents Act 1988.

British Library Cataloguing-in-Publication Data. A catalogue record for this book is available from the British Library.

Publishing Director Lorraine Dickey
Editor Sybella Marlow
Art Director Jonathan Christie
Book Design Untitled
Photography Lisa Linder
Production Manager Angela Young

ISBN-13: 978-1-84091-486-3
Printed in Spain

Authors' note: The majority of the research for this book was completed in the summer of 2006. Forgive us if some of the facts have changed by the time you read the book.